HOW TO GET A JOB ABROAD

In this Series

GET A JOB
ABROAD

Roger Jones
BA DipTESL DipEd MInstAM DPA

Second Edition

How To Books

© Copyright 1989 and 1991 by Roger Jones

First published in 1989. Second edition published in 1991 by How To Books Ltd,
Plymbridge House, Estover Road, Plymouth PL6 7PZ, United Kingdom. Tel:
Plymouth (0752) 705251. Telex: 45635. Fax: (0752) 695699.

British Library Cataloguing in Publication Data

Jones, Roger
   How to get a job abroad.—(How to books)
   I. Title   II. Series
   331.12

ISBN 1–85703–003–6

Text Design & Typesetting by
Nuprint Limited, 30b Station Road, Harpenden, Herts AL5 4SE.

Reproduced, Printed and Bound by
Dotesios Ltd. Trowbridge, Wiltshire.

Contents

Preface

to the Second Edition

Following the success of the first edition *How to Get a Job Abroad* I am grateful to have the opportunity to update the information included in this new edition, and also to incorporate some additions, notably to the bibliography, the 'useful addresses' section and the list of recruitment consultants.

There have been a number of significant developments on the world stage since 1989, not least in Eastern Europe, in southern Africa and the Gulf region, and these could well bring in their wake new opportunities for expatriate employment. At present the picture is far from clear, and it is not always possible to discern precisely where these opportunities will lie.

However, one can predict that in countries, like Britain, where unemployment is unfortunately once more on the increase more and more people will be considering the overseas option. It is an option that has its perils as well as its perks, as expatriates in Kuwait and Iraq have found in recent months, and the survivors will be those who prepare themselves thoroughly for the challenges ahead.

I hope this new edition will assist you to anticipate and survive the rigours of the expatriate life. Good luck!

Roger Jones

Introduction

This book has three objectives: to look at the range of opportunities for employment abroad, to create awareness of what working abroad involves and to offer guidance on how to prepare for the challenge.

To cover the whole spectrum of opportunities would demand a book of encyclopaedic proportions. A volume of this size cannot presume to answer every question that crosses the mind of a would-be expatriate. However, I trust that it will at least provide food for thought and help point individuals in the right direction.

I am most grateful to those people who have pointed *me* in the right direction since I embarked on this work. They include Clare Hogg, Editor of *The Multinational Employer,* Keith Edmonds of Expats International, Bernard Dixon of the International Committee of the IPM, David Harrison of Godwins Ltd, David Whitehead and Jennifer Choudhuri of Employment Conditions Abroad, Claire Stewart of the Centre for International Briefing at Farnham Castle, Robert Brown of Moran, Stahl and Boyer, Charlotte Swift of Towers, Perrin, Forster and Crosby, Michael Berger, Rosemary Thomas and others.

None of these are to be held responsible for any shortcomings within the book. Some of the information, alas, will be out of date before the work appears in bookshops, as is the fate of any volume of reference. Moreover the advice given is of a general nature and does not take into account individual circumstances.

'Taking up a job abroad is a traumatic experience, and not only for the breadwinner,' observed the late Harry Brown. If this handbook helps to ease some of the trauma and enables individuals and their families to cope successfully with the challenges of a foreign environment, then the time and effort involved in writing it can be considered well spent.

1
Working Abroad: Is it an Option for You?

'There's one thing I admire about you British. You're so adaptable.'

The speaker, a Turk, was explaining his reasons for choosing British staff to work in his organisation rather than any other nationality. A flattering comment maybe, but how true is it?

Certainly, we do have a reputation for being inveterate globetrotters. Since the days of Sir Francis Drake we have been venturing far from our shores, and this trend has accelerated with the development of modern air transport.

Most people go abroad on vacation—to sun themselves on the beaches of the Mediterranean, to visit relations in Australasia, Canada or the United States, to view the monuments of the past, to find new and unusual experiences.

But a sizeable minority—in the region of 200,000—leave Britain every year to work in another country. Their reasons for doing so can be remarkably diverse:

- a lack of opportunities at home
- a desire to travel or live abroad
- a wish to extend their professional experience
- a better salary or promotion
- they have to—it is a requirement of the job
- family reasons (e.g. marriage to a national of another country)
- a sense of vocation (e.g. to help the Third World or spread the Gospel)

200,000 may seem an enormous number, but it must be remembered that relatively few of these will be taking up permanent appointments abroad. Many of the posts in foreign countries tend to be on contract terms—so a similar number of expatriates will be returning at the same time.

This contrasts with the situation in the past when a posting to another country usually represented a lifelong commitment. You joined the colonial service, the Indian Army or a firm with extensive overseas involvement, and stayed overseas—apart from intermittent leave—until retirement. Nowadays it is virtually impossible for people to spend the whole of their careers in one location. Moreover, the need is for people with particular skills—IT specialists, engineers and teachers—rather than generalists who learn the job as they go along.

Another difference is that the age range of people taking up posts abroad has widened. The jobs market is more fluid than it used to be, and people are more prepared to change direction these days, either by choice or from necessity.

The age spectrum
What kind of people want to work abroad?

- At one end of the scale there are young people who are keen to see the world before they settle down to a fixed career. They may decide to take a year or two off between school and college or between college and the world of work, and want a job—or a succession of jobs—that will help them support themselves in this venture.

- Further up the scale there are people who decide from the outset on a career that will enable them to spend much of their life in foreign countries, in the diplomatic service or in the services, for instance. A fair proportion of these will have already had experience of living abroad and know more or less what to expect.

- There are also young professionals who are not interested in long-term careers abroad, but see a spell overseas as an important part of their career development. Their concern is to broaden their experience. If it is a way to improve their finances as well, so much the better.

- Older people are less likely to regard working abroad as a means to an end. They will already have progressed in their careers, but may feel the urge to try something different—even if only for a short spell. Age no longer seems to be a barrier to overseas employment, provided that a person is adaptable and resilient.

- A final category consists of people who have never thought of working abroad but find themselves sent off to a foreign posting. This is very much a sign of the times. Companies—particularly large ones—are no longer confined within national boundaries, and are keen to create an international cadre of key staff.

Dream and reality

People in Britain who have never worked abroad are often envious of those who have. They are persuaded by glossy holiday brochures into believing that every foreign location is highly desirable. They think of the sunshine and the sights but not of the mosquitoes or the business hassles.

But working in a foreign country is very different from a brief holiday visit where your sole aim is enjoyment. On vacation you are so entranced by the novelty of a particular place that you do not stop to consider that the heat, the traffic jams or the quaintness of the locals could begin to get you down after a while.

An overseas posting is not a holiday from your normal humdrum life. Indeed, anyone who is merely looking for escape from the challenges and traumas of life at home, would do well to forget the idea of a posting abroad altogether. A job in Java

is no haven for escapists, but requires realists who are able to meet challenges on all sides, not just one.

Even moving to another job in your own country can be something of an upheaval. You have to learn new methods and become acquainted with a new set of people. But moving from Guildford to Guinea involves a good deal more readjustment than a relocation to Grimsby. You will need to come to terms with a different living environment:

- different food
- different customs
- a different language
- a different climate

'Variety,' notes Cowper, 'is the very spice of life that gives it all its flavour.' A successful expatriate is someone who is able to appreciate life's infinite variety—the good and the bad. This involves accepting unfamiliar vistas, values and traditions, and also giving something in return. You cannot stand aloof from what is happening around you. Instead, you will need to modify your behaviour and attitudes to blend in with your new surroundings.

Coping with a strange environment

Environment is a factor that should not be overlooked. Your skill and that of your nearest and dearest in adapting to it could be just as crucial to your success as your ability to do the job.

This is particularly true if your family is with you. So long as they are content, you will have a stable home base where you can retire and relax after the traumas of the day. If they find the place a drag, their feelings will in turn begin to sap your morale.

In some jobs you are protected to some extent from your environment, particularly if you live within an expatriate community. A British military base in West Germany or Hong Kong bears many similarities to its counterparts in Britain. If you are posted to a major capital, the chances are you will find a substantial British community there who can help you acclimatise.

On the other hand, you might find yourself out on a limb both at work and away from the workplace. You could be the only British employee in a particular organisation, and opportunities to socialise with other Anglo-Saxons might prove few and far between. In such cases your qualities of resourcefulness and adaptability will be tested to the full.

How would you cope in such a situation? This is the kind of

question that you need to ask yourself before you make any binding commitment. Don't assume that conditions in Tuvalu are the same as they are in Tunbridge Wells. If you do, you could be in for an enormous shock when you get there. The stories you hear of people arriving at post and taking the next flight home because they can't cope are, unhappily, very often true.

Such disasters benefit no-one. And so one of the aims of this book is to persuade people to look before they leap. There are plenty of work opportunities in foreign countries for the right person. Finding them is in many respects the easy part of the business; convincing an employer that you can make a success of the job and your period abroad is harder; coming to terms with your new environment can be hardest of all.

What makes working abroad so different?

The days have gone when you could go out to some distant clime and recreate your own little England around you and expect the local populace to adjust to your whims and fancies. Nowadays, the adjustment needs to come from *your* side. Here are a few of the major differences you will need to contend with:

- **Minority status.** For the first time in your life perhaps you will find yourself in a minority. Even if you do not manifest different racial features from the bulk of the populace (as you would in the Far East and Africa) your behaviour, attitudes and accent will make you stand out.

- **Climate.** In the UK we are used to a climate which avoids extremes. Other climates can be much harsher. Would you be able to withstand temperatures in excess of 90°F or below -25°F?

- **Communication.** There is always plenty of scope for misunder-standing, particularly if you have an imperfect grasp of the language of the locals, whether it is the spoken language or body language.

- **Working practices.** Working hours and vacation entitlements may differ from UK practice, and the whole company culture may seem strange. Your responsibilities could turn out to be more all-embracing than you expect.

- **Social customs.** What is acceptable in one culture (e.g. con-sumption of alcohol, backslapping or kissing in public) may not be so in another. You will need to learn the traditions of the country in order to avoid causing offence.

- **Different values.** You might find yourself in a country where the values are different from your own. For instance, loyalty to one's company may take second place to family loyalties.

DO YOU FIT THE PART?

You may be quite certain you would like to work abroad. The question is: Will any employer be prepared to send you abroad on an assignment or offer you an overseas contract? This section is designed to help *you* decide.

First, forget the idea that the only qualities needed for an overseas posting are youth and a willingness to learn. Clare Hogg of *The Multinational Employer* sums up the current trend in this way:

> 'The profile of the expatriate is changing. He is becoming more senior and more qualified. *He* may sometimes be a *she*. Employers are expecting better value for money—they are selecting more carefully, spending more money on training and putting less into the pay packet. The exercise of sending an employee overseas is becoming much more finely tuned.'

Mrs Hogg is talking principally about permanent employees, but her remarks apply with equal validity to contract personnel. Employers are becoming more selective, and the days of boundless opportunities for everyone are now over.

To put it in a nutshell, a recruiter is looking for **competence** and **value for money.** If he can find someone who can do the job as well as you for half or a quarter of the salary, he will do so. The main reason, for example, that the demand for British craftsmen in the Middle East has declined is that Filipinos, Koreans, Pakistanis and Indians cost less to employ.

However, the law of the jungle can also work to your advantage in the international labour market. In recent years, for instance, British managers have been more popular with multinational employers than people from other countries—partly because British salaries are often lower compared with those in North America and on the European Continent.

For any job abroad—apart from work experience schemes for young people and casual work—employers require:

- good qualifications
- professional experience
- the right personal qualities

Qualifications

The days when a school leaving certificate was sufficient to find you a job in an overseas location are now past. Most other countries have enough people with secondary education of their own these days, and so they no longer require the services of a semi-skilled expat.

This applies not only to the well paid jobs. British voluntary service organisations that would take people straight from school 30 years ago are now much more demanding. A **degree** or **equivalent qualification** is generally the minimum requirement for this kind of work these days.

In my survey of agencies recruiting for abroad, the importance of a degree-level qualification was frequently stressed. While some recruited for vacancies at the supervisory level—for which a City & Guilds qualification was sufficient—generally speaking, this particular qualification was regarded as the absolute minimum.

Foreign employers tend to place more importance on degrees and certificates than experience, and often recruit the person with the best qualifications—even if there are others who can acquit themselves more ably.

There is usually a particular reason for this—namely, government restrictions on expatriate labour. In order to be able to employ an expatriate they may well have to prove to their Ministry of Labour that they cannot recruit a sufficiently qualified local national. This applies as much to Australia and Canada as it does to the Third World countries.

So if you are keen to work abroad, have a look at your qualifications first of all. Are they really likely to impress? If not, see if you can improve them by attendance at night courses, doing correspondence courses or taking a year or so off for full-time study.

Experience

Experience is important. A glance at the recruitment literature of several large multinationals will confirm that they are unwilling to send any of their permanent staff abroad until they have spent a few years gaining experience at home.

The importance of experience also applies to contract work.

Employers are not interested in raw recruits. They want people who:

- have proved themselves in their chosen vocation
- are familiar with the world of work and its responsibilities
- are able to discharge their duties without the need for supervision.

Experience of working abroad is regarded as a plus.

Most recruitment firms will tell you that three years' work experience is generally regarded as an absolute minimum, and many more years for senior posts.

Similarly, voluntary service organisations require people who are not only qualified, but have plenty of practical experience to their name. That is obviously why the average age of today's volunteers is around 30.

Personal qualities

Sending a person abroad is an expensive business, but nothing is more expensive than an assignment that has to be aborted. As Clare Hogg observes:

> 'The financial losses extend beyond the obvious relocation recruitment expenses to the effects of low performance, project delay, and so on.' *Management Today*, April 1982.

It is not just leaving the job early that can be a problem. Some employees manage to stick it out till the end, yet operate at a much lower level of efficiency because they or their families have not adjusted to the environment properly. And once more their company or organisation is losing out. 'Non-technical considerations are just as essential to the success of an overseas posting as any amount of professional skill,' insists Mrs Hogg.

Organisations that have had their fingers burned in this way now take greater care in choosing personnel. They no longer choose expatriate employees on the strength of their technical expertise alone, but realise that professional competence and suitability for an overseas assignment are by no means the same thing.

Assessing your personal qualities

What makes a successful expatriate? There are plenty of different opinions on this issue, and very often selectors rely on their own intuition rather than proven selection criteria. This is perhaps not surprising in view of the absence of any accurate assessment tool.

However, necessity being the mother of invention, such an assessment tool has now been developed to aid recruitment personnel. The **Overseas Assignment Inventory (OAI)**, as it is called, was originally devised in the mid-seventies by Dr Michael Tucker for the screening and selection of Peace Corps volunteers. Its objective is to assess an individual's capacity for adjustment to living overseas.

The OAI is not a psychometric test but rather a list of attitudes and attributes that provides a profile of an individual's ability to adjust to a foreign environment. It takes the form of a questionnaire followed by a behavioural interview.

The main users of the OAI to date have been major companies in the United States. However, the assessment technique has been refined and adapted for use in Europe, and now European firms too are starting to use it for candidate selection.

Don't be put off if you are asked to submit to such a test, since it appears to be as fair a form of assessment as you are likely to encounter. While the OAI cannot guarantee to select the perfect expatriate each time, it can certainly help to reduce the possibility of failure in selecting expatriates.

The OAI Profile measures the following attitudes and attributes:

- expectations
- openmindedness
- respect for other beliefs
- trust in people
- tolerance
- personal control
- flexibility
- patience
- adaptability
- self-confidence/initiative
- sense of humour
- interpersonal interest
- spouse/family/communication

Full details of the Overseas Assignment Inventory are available from Moran Stahl and Boyer Ltd, Merrill Lynch Relocation, 136 New Bond Street, London W1. Tel: 071-629 8222.

In Britain the use of tools such as the Overseas Assignment

Inventory in deciding whether to offer a candidate a job abroad is still not very common. Nevertheless, experienced selectors do pay attention to personality traits when assessing a person's suitability for overseas employment—and so should you when thinking of applying.

Assessing your own suitability

> 'The most underrated, though the most effective, method of selection is self-selection. Really thorough briefing will give unsuitable candidates a chance to see their unsuitability for themselves, thus saving all concerned much pain and grief.' Clare Hogg.

Ask yourself the following questions and invite other members of your family to do the same.

- Do you have very firm convictions/prejudices?
- Is your health indifferent?
- Do people sometimes find you brusque and tactless?
- Do you distrust foreigners?
- Do you tend to be very set in your ways?
- Are you easily upset—by delays, the inadequacies of others, and so on?
- Do you have difficulty in seeing the funny side of situations?
- Are you intolerant of methods that conflict with your own?
- Are you reluctant to abandon home comforts?
- Are you ever moody?

If you find you have answered 'yes' to the majority of these questions, you need to resign yourself to the fact that you are probably not cut out for a foreign lifestyle. You will feel much happier staying in Britain, and the rest of the world will heave a sigh of relief if you do!

To be a success in a foreign location, this is the sort of person you need to be:

- openminded—prepared to accept alternative points of view
- adaptable—able to fit in to your new surroundings
- balanced—possessing a stable outlook on life
- resourceful—able to respond appropriately to new situations
- healthy—able to cope physically and mentally with stress and strain
- diplomatic—careful not to offend foreign sensibilities
- patient—a particular virtue in many Third World countries

- tolerant—of others' methods, religions, life styles, and so on.
- communicative—able to put your ideas across clearly and effectively
- empathetic—able to understand and respect foreign cultures

Of course, how important these qualities are will depend very much on your prospective environment. You could form part of an extensive expatriate community and have little contact with local people, as might be the case in the services, a large metropolis or a construction camp. But in more out-of-the-way locations you could be very much on your own, and your qualities could be tested to the utmost.

OTHER CONSIDERATIONS

Age

Mature people, who find that British employers prefer young recruits, may find that this is less of a problem with posts abroad. Foreign employers do not discriminate so much against older candidates. Indeed, in some countries age is regarded as synonymous with wisdom, and the older you are the more the employer likes it.

Indeed, the only potential problem is your physical health. But provided you are fit, mentally alert and adaptable, there should be few obstacles to your securing and taking up a foreign posting.

Your spouse

It is becoming common for accompanying wives and husbands to be invited to participate in an interview, particularly in the case of senior appointments, and this is a practice to be welcomed.

Spouses may have to play a much more significant role in their partners' careers than they do at home. There may be visitors to be entertained, company wives to be looked after, and possibly even responsibility for some of their partners' duties to be shared. Indeed, the personality of the spouse could be crucial for the success of the overseas assignment.

The working woman

While the status of women has improved enormously as far as employment is concerned in Western Europe, North America and Australasia in recent decades, this is not really true in most of the rest of the world. Male-dominated societies still see the woman's place as being in the home, and have difficulty in accepting them on equal terms in the work place.

For this reason many organisations operating in these areas prefer to recruit male candidates rather than female ones; so while there are certainly opportunities abroad for women, they are by no means as numerous as postings for men.

2
The Search for a Job

First of all, forget the idea of becoming a Dick Whittington who books a flight to a distant land in the belief that he will find a job soon after landing—such a plan is likely to land you in deep water with the immigration officials! Even if it doesn't, it can prove an expensive lesson if your plans don't work out—as they probably won't.

If at all possible, get yourself fixed up with a position before you board the plane or ferry. There are several good reasons for doing this:

- There is a well developed international job recruitment market in the UK offering a wide range of opportunities that are open to everyone.
- If you are recruited in the UK you will probably be provided with your airfare to your job and other perks.
- The organisation that recruits you will be used to dealing with British applicants which means there should be little, if any, misunderstanding.
- With luck you will be offered a briefing on the job and the country, which will enable you to get off to a good start. If not, there are plenty of other sources of information and advice to prepare you for life in the country or region in question.
- Most governments nowadays impose restrictions on foreigners who wish to work in their countries, so you will need to obtain an appropriate visa before you arrive there (EC countries are an exception to this rule).

This last consideration is the most crucial of all. In many cases you need to have your paperwork in order before you leave this country, otherwise you might find you are regarded as an illegal immigrant.

As for the process of finding a job, there are basically two approaches, no matter when you are looking:

- You see one advertised and apply for it.
- You use a speculative approach.

Both methods can work when it comes to getting a job abroad, but you must know where to begin.

ANSWERING AN ADVERTISEMENT

This is the most common way of getting a job, either here or abroad. But first you have to find the vacancy.

Looking through the overseas job advertisements is a good starting point, since you get some idea of the range and locations of jobs on offer. Here are some suggestions as to where you might look:

- **UK Newspapers.** Some of these have specialist appointment sections on certain days of the week e.g. banking and accountancy; public appointments; educational appointments, and so on (see table). Generally speaking, Thursday is the best day for job advertisements.

    The Daily Telegraph   *Financial Times*
    The Sunday Telegraph   *Daily Mail*
    The Guardian   *Daily Express*
    The Times   *The Independent on Sunday*
    The Sunday Times   *The European*

- **Specialist journals.** These are particularly numerous, and periodicals that appear weekly tend to be more likely to carry extensive job advertising than monthlies and quarterlies. Examples are:

    Accountancy   *Construction News*
    British Medical Journal   *The Economist*
    Caterer and Hotelkeeper   *Nursing Times*
    Computer Weekly   *Times Educational Supplement*

- **Vacancy bulletins** such as:
    Careers International, PS Publishing, Speer House, 40-44 The Parade, Claygate, Surrey KT10 9QE. Tel: 0372-68833.
    Graduate Post (Newpoint Publishing, St James's Lane, London N10 3DF).
    Opportunities Abroad (published by Christians Abroad). This

Specialist recruitment advertising calendar

	Guardian	Independent	Times
Monday	Creative Media Secretarial	Engineering Technology IT	Education Secretarial
Tuesday	Education	Financial Secretarial	Public sector Technology Legal
Wednesday	Public sector	Media Marketing	Media Marketing Secretarial General
Thursday	Financial Business	Education Public sector General	Financial Secretarial General Banking
Friday	Legal Environment Technology Leisure	Legal	

deals mainly with vacancies in voluntary, missionary and aid organisations.

Jobfinder (Overseas Consultants, PO Box 152, Douglas, IOM).

Nexus (Expat Network, 520 Fulham Rd, London SW6 5NJ. Tel: 071-384 1878). Monthly.

Overseas Employment Newsletter (Overseas Employment Services, PO Box 460, Town of Mount Royal, Quebec, Canada H3P 3C7. Tel: 514 739 1108).

Vacancy supplement to *Home and Away*, (Expats International, 62 Tritton Road, London SE21 8DE).

Vacancy supplement to *The Expatriate* (First Market Intelligence Ltd, 56A Rochester Row, London SW1P 1JU. Tel: 081-761 2575.)

Intel Jobs Abstract (Intel, Duke House, 33 Waterloo St, Hove BN3 1AN).

- **Foreign newspapers**. Although you can always take out a subscription to foreign journals this can be expensive; one alternative is the reading rooms of some larger embassies and high commissions which often have them. Some large public libraries have a selection of these newspapers too—e.g. London's City Business Library, 106 Fenchurch Street, London EC3M 5JB. Tel: 071-638 8215. One final possibility is to ask any friends or relations abroad to send you any promising job ads in the local papers.

- **Other publications**, which might include house journals or job annuals such as *Graduate Opportunities, DOG—Directory of Opportunities for Graduates*, or *Job File*.

> **Health warning:** There have been instances in the past of rogue businesses advertising non-existent jobs abroad and asking would-be applicants to send money for air fares. Such advertisements should be treated with scepticism. If the job is genuine you should normally expect an interview and the fare paid to your posting by the employer.

THE SPECULATIVE APPROACH (IN THE UK)

If you wait around for the right vacancy to crop up in the advertisement columns, you could be waiting in vain. Not all vacancies abroad are advertised, simply because employers already know of people they can call on to take up the post. After all, why should they spend money on expensive advertising when they already have a bevy of suitable candidates?

Rather than merely responding to events, it often pays to take the initiative and let prospective employers know that you are ready and willing to work in a foreign location. You are, in fact, advertising yourself, though in a way which may seem less obvious.

Some people imagine that the speculative approach means sending off a round robin indiscriminately to all and sundry. This method has been known to work, but more often than not the results are disappointing.

The key to success is **targeting.** You need to identify the companies and organisations that may well have a need for people like you, and the agencies that specialise in recruitment for your particular area of work. You also need to make use of your network of personal contacts. Let's look at these ideas in greater detail.

Opportunities within your own organisation

If you are in the employ of an organisation, what better place to start your quest?

- Many larger firms have subsidiaries and associate companies in foreign locations, and personnel transfers between countries are increasingly common.
- Smaller outfits could offer opportunities in foreign parts as a representative or on secondment to a client.
- In the public sector there will also be opportunities—most notably in the Foreign and Commonwealth Office, the Department of Trade and Industry, the Overseas Development Administration, the British Standards Institute, but also in other branches of the service.

The fact that your staff notice board contains no foreign vacancies does not mean that they do not exist. Mention to one of your superiors that you are keen to work abroad and ask for suggestions. Experience abroad is increasingly regarded as an essential component in executive career development by a number of internationally-minded companies, so you would certainly be doing yourself no harm by asking.

Do not expect quick results. To attain your goal you might need to transfer to a different department within your organisation—export sales, for instance. You might also need to undergo a course of preparation, such as language training.

Personal contacts

Do you know anyone who works abroad or has done so in the past? If so, you could ask him how he set about getting the job and if he knows of other vacancies in his particular organisation.

Don't be afraid of mentioning your overseas aspirations to others who may not be such obvious leads, such as your companions down at the 'Red Lion', colleagues at your aerobics class or even your Uncle Donald; they may have connections with organisations abroad, or be able to suggest useful contacts.

Other contacts you might consider approaching are business colleagues—past and present, tutors—past and present, pen friends, former classmates, former employers and so on.

Official contacts

Your professional association or trade union may have suggestions or even be able to arrange a placement. The Royal College of

Nursing, for instance, operates a scheme to enable nurses to gain experience abroad, and the National Federation of Young Farmers Clubs also operates an exchange scheme for its members.

Foreign Embassies and High Commissions in the UK are *not* usually equipped to advise on job opportunities in their respective countries, and the same is true of most British diplomatic missions abroad. However, they may well have reference material you can consult and several have reading rooms where you can peruse the newspapers for job advertisements.

Chambers of Commerce are likely to be more helpful, whether they are foreign chambers in Britain or British chambers in other countries. British Council offices abroad can be a useful source of information, too, particularly for anyone looking for a job in education. (Useful addresses like these are included in the relevant country section.)

Approaching employers direct

This is becoming more and more common as an approach, but your chances of success will be greater if you set about your task systematically.

1. Keep an eye on overseas news items in the trade and professional press. If you read that a British company has been awarded a contract in Madagascar, that the Government has decided to step up development assistance to Vanuatu, or that a leading consultancy plans to extend its activities to Mongolia, it may pay you to approach these organisations immediately, if you have the appropriate qualifications and experience— before they get round to advertising for additional staff.

2. If possible, find out before applying whether the international company relies solely on local expertise abroad, or whether you will have to spend some years in the UK with a company before being sent overseas. If either of these is the case, perhaps you are wasting your time applying.

3. On the other hand, there are organisations with significant overseas interests where a high proportion of the British recruited staff will be expected to work in foreign countries as a matter of course, such as British and American Tobacco, the Standard Chartered Bank, the British Council and Oxfam. If in doubt, look at their recruitment literature or under their entries in directories such as *DOG (Directory of Opportunities for Graduates)*.

4. Once you've chosen a company, send off your CV along with a covering letter explaining why you are keen to work for that particular outfit and what skills you have to offer.

5. Don't be disappointed if you hear nothing. Some organisations are inundated with speculative applications and are just not equipped to handle them. If you send a stamped addressed envelope with your application, however, they might at least acknowledge your letter.

Some people submit speculative applications to foreign employers or subsidiaries of multinational firms. Names and addresses can be found from national trade directories or telephone directories. At least two organisations—Overseas Consultants and Overseas Employment Services—publish directories of American and Canadian firms operating overseas and of firms operating on the Arabian peninsula and in Australasia.

Agencies/recruitment consultancies

An increasing number of jobs are handled by intermediaries on behalf of both foreign and British based employers. They have various names—**employment agencies, recruitment consultants** and **executive search consultants** being the most usual descriptions. Normally the first category handles general appointments while the latter two are involved in the recruitment of top or middle management either through advertisement, candidate register or by a process known by the alarming title of 'headhunting'. However, a considerable number of employment agencies handle executive recruitment as well, sometimes through a subsidiary. Many, although by no means all, of these agencies specialise in particular employment sectors—nursing, computer staff, accountancy staff, and so on—so find out who specialises in what before you make an approach. Otherwise you might unwittingly approach a catering agency when your area of expertise is heavy engineering!

Looking at the classified advertisements in specialist journals is a good way to discover which agencies are active in your field. (Elsewhere in this book you will find a select list of agencies that were involved in overseas recruitment when this book was being compiled.)

There are certain advantages in using agencies, provided they are reputable organisations with plenty of experience of recruiting for jobs abroad:

- They generally recruit for a number of employers rather than just one.
- They can sometimes indicate the type and level of jobs open to you.
- They may be able to give you an idea of trends in the overseas jobs market.
- They can often give you a frank assessment of both job and employer.
- Many operate a candidate register—which you should try to join.
- They should know precisely how to present your credentials to a foreign company.

Although recruitment agencies are often helpful to applicants, remember that their clients—the people who pay for their services—are the employers rather than you the applicant, so don't expect them to move heaven and earth to place you in a job. Ringing them up every day demanding to know how your application is progressing will probably be a waste of time. On the other hand, you could get a phone call right out of the blue to see if you are still interested in a position.

Many of the large recruitment organisations have branches overseas, though they are often run as separate organisations. Overseas Consultants and Overseas Employment Services both publish directories of employment agencies abroad, and *The Executive Grapevine* includes a large number of recruitment consultancies operating abroad.

Jobcentre facilities

Many Jobcentres hold details of vacancies open to British nationals in other European Community countries under the SEDOC scheme, or in Austria, Norway and Sweden under the International Clearing of Vacancies (ICV) scheme, and elsewhere—often for skilled and qualified people.

If you cannot find a suitable vacancy, you can send details of your experience and requirements to the EC or ICV Employment Services of your choice. This generally involves completing an application form and supplying copies of work references, certificates or diplomas. The information will then be sent on to prospective employers.

Placing a 'Situation Wanted' advertisement

This is a similar approach to a speculative letter except that you are using the advertisement columns of a newspaper or journal to publicise your availability for employment. If you are keen to work in a particular country, you could try such an advertisement in a suitable publication. Dealing direct with a foreign newspaper is possible, but you might have problems with language and the transfer of money. Unless you happen to be in the country or have a contact there who can place an advert for you, it may prove more convenient to go through their agent in the UK. Among the largest media agencies are:

Publicitas Ltd, 525 Fulham Road, London SW6 1HF

Joshua Powers Ltd, 46 Keyes House, Dolphin Square, London SW1V 3NA

Frank L Crane Ltd, 5–15 Cromer Street, Grays Inn Road, London WC1H 8LS

Overseas Media Ltd, 289 Green Lane, Palmers Green, London N13 4XX

Overseas Publicity Ltd, 91–101 Oxford Street, London W1R 1RA
Colin Turner Group, 122 Shaftesbury Avenue, London W1V 8HA
International Graphic Press, 6 Welbeck Street, London W1M 7PB

For more precise information as to who is represented by whom, consult *Willing's Press Guide* or *Benn's International Media Directory*. A number of British publications have an extensive overseas readership and you might consider advertising in one of these. Such advertisements occur from time to time in *The Economist*, for example.

Miscellaneous

If you are a client of an outplacement or careers counselling agency, they may operate a system whereby your details are circulated to prospective employers. The expatriate service organisation, Expats International, runs a similar service for its members.

VISITS 'ON SPEC'

Much of this chapter has been devoted to finding a job abroad before you leave Britain. Why not go to a foreign country and conduct your job search on the ground?

This may seem the obvious way to go about things, but in practice there are snags. One major problem is that governments impose restrictions on foreigners who want to work in their countries, so as not to put at risk the employment opportunities of their own nationals.

While it is possible to visit many countries as a tourist or in order to transact business, in the majority of places you will not be allowed to take up paid employment without the correct visa. If you do find a job, you may well have to leave the country, apply for a work visa (or similar document) and wait for your application to be approved. In the case of the United States this process can take up to a year, by which time the job you found may have gone.

There are exceptions. Within the European Community there is free movement of labour between most member countries which means that a UK or Irish passport holder may enter these countries both to look for a job and take up employment without restriction. But in other parts of Europe and the rest of the world—including Commonwealth countries—you have to go through the proper formalities if you want to work.

On the other hand, if you happen to be visiting a country for other reasons—on a business trip or on holiday, for example—

there is no harm in enquiring whether there are work opportunities available. An offer might come right out of the blue, as happened to a friend of mine who went for a holiday on a Pacific island and was asked if he would like to take up the post of Deputy Attorney!

There are certainly advantages in visiting a country before you decide to apply for a job there:

- You will be able to see what conditions are like there at first hand rather than relying on second or third hand information.
- You will be able to meet prospective employers and decide whether you are likely to get on well with them.
- You will have an opportunity to assess whether you would be able to adapt to the way of life of the country.
- You may be able to start making domestic arrangements such as finding accommodation for yourself or schooling for your children.

To find a job in the country itself, look through the advertisement columns, approach recruitment agencies, write off speculative letters—just as you would do in the UK. However, do not expect the same kind of terms you would be entitled to if you applied for a job from the UK, such as travel and luggage allowances. You are more likely to be offered a contract on local terms, i.e. on the same conditions as a local person. As this might mean no housing allowance and liability to local income tax, the implications of the contract would need to be looked into carefully.

LOCATING JOBS ABROAD—THE PROS AND CONS

Method	
Through advertisements	*pro* The commonest method. You know a vacancy exists. *con* You may be up against stiff competition.
Job with current employer	*pro* You do not need to transfer to another employer. *con* Relatively few employers offer jobs abroad.

Use of personal contacts	*pro* You may be able to circumvent recruitment procedures. *con* They will tend to offer suggestions, not firm leads.
Use of official contacts	*pro* They may be able to offer information or foreign contacts. *con* They are unlikely to offer a recruitment service.
Speculative approach to individual employers	*pro* A well targeted approach can sometimes open doors. *con* Success usually depends more on luck than judgement.
Speculative approach to recruitment agencies	*pro* Agencies usually have a wider range of vacancies on offer. *con* Not all operate candidate registers or recruit for abroad.
Using Jobcentres	*pro* A service that circulates jobs and candidates' details. *con* Somewhat bureaucratic with no certainty of a match.
Situation wanted advert	*pro* Your details will be read by a wide selection of people. *con* It may not be seen or acted on by recruiters.
Foreign visits on spec	*pro* You can find out about the country and job prospects. *con* It is a costly exercise if you don't land a job.

3
The Recruitment Rigmarole

Hopefully, by now you will have unearthed an interesting vacancy or identified an organisation that could use your skills. The next step is to convince the recruiters that you are the man (or woman) for the job.

It sounds simple, but it isn't—particularly in these days of increased competition. It's not really enough to rely on your native wit to win the day. You have to impress the selectors right from the word go. This means:

- A well written letter of application on unlined A4 notepaper
- A clear and well thought out curriculum vitae/personal history/ resumé
- A neatly filled-in application form supplying all the required information
- A recent photograph (or photographs) of yourself and photocopies of your qualifications (although this is not usually needed for jobs in Britain it seems almost standard for overseas recruitment).

If you can type all your documentation (or have it typed), **do so**—even if it seems a chore (especially if, like mine, your handwriting is a sight for sore eyes!). Remember too that word processors can often produce a more impressive document than a manual typewriter, since you can remove all the mistakes before printing it out.

If your application is good enough, you will hopefully be invited for an interview. Sometimes you may just have to take some tests (in recruitment competitions for the European Commission, for instance). The interview could be just an exploratory interview with a recruitment consultant—the first of a succession of interviews—or it could be the real thing.

Eventually, on the basis of your documentation, your performance at the interview, and your references, the organisation will decide whether or not to offer you the post.

This sounds simple enough, yet recruitment for positions abroad can be a lengthy process lasting months rather than weeks. This can prove irritating for anyone not well-endowed with patience, so in order to understand what you are letting yourself in for, let us consider a hypothetical case.

How the recruitment process works

1. Richard Wagner, manager of the Sierra Madre copper mine decides he needs a training manager. He asks Giuseppe Verdi, personnel manager at the HQ of the El Dorado Mining Group to recruit someone.

2. Verdi decides he will have to recruit from abroad so he contacts the London based recruitment consultancy Gilbert & Sullivan. Edward Elgar, a consultant at Gilbert & Sullivan, says he will be quite happy to help, and asks Verdi to send a detailed job description together with terms and conditions of service.

3. Verdi does so and Elgar looks through his register of candidates to see if he can find a suitable person. As he can't, he drafts an advertisement and places it with *Mining Monthly, Training Officers' Gazette* and *The Sunday Times*.

4. The advertisement appears in the latter two journals, Elgar receives 60 enquiries and sends off job details to each of the enquirers. He cannot begin selection yet as he is still waiting for the advert to appear in *Mining Monthly*. Eventually the next issue of *Mining Monthly* is published and the Sierra Madre advertisement attracts another 100 enquiries. Elgar sends off more job details.

5. Elgar sits down and sifts through the final applications—some 130 in all—and decides to interview a dozen or so of the candidates. He sends off invitations to the twelve most promising and informs the others that he does not propose to take their applications any further.

6. In the end he interviews just ten candidates—two fail to turn up for interview—and decides to recommend four of them to Verdi. He sends off their papers to Verdi for him to make the final choice.

7. Verdi announces that the company's managing director Hector Berlioz is coming to Europe the following month for an international mining conference and would like to drop in to

interview the four shortlisted candidates. Elgar arranges for
the four to meet him, contacts their referees, and informs the
other six on the shortlist that they are not included on the final
shortlist.

8. Berlioz interviews the four and provisionally accepts one John
   Constable provided his medical proves satisfactory and the El
   Dorado Government grants him a work permit. Elgar
   arranges for Constable to have a medical, while Berlioz
   instructs Verdi to send Constable's details to the Ministry of
   Labour. (Verdi warns Elgar that the Government vetting pro-
   cess may take time since none of the civil servants in the El
   Dorado Ministry of Labour speaks English).

9. Eventually the permission is granted, Constable is pronounced fit, and he is given a contract to sign. However...

10. There are certain clauses in the contract which are extremely
    hazy, so Constable asks for some clarification before he signs.
    Elgar contacts Verdi; Verdi has a word with Wagner; and
    Constable receives a reply which satisfies him. He signs.

11. Constable now has to go to the El Dorado Embassy in
    London, present his passport, the work permit, his contract of
    employment, birth certificate, marriage certificate and six pas-
    sport size photos in order to gain an entry visa. He completes a
    detailed visa application form and is asked to return to collect
    the documents in seven days.

12. Once Constable's documentation is in order he boards the
    plane for El Dorado.

When I say that recruitment for an overseas posting can seem
an endless rigmarole, I really mean it. In fact, the hypothetical
case I have described has been fairly straightforward. What would
have happened if some hitch had occurred in the process?

Dealing direct with foreign employers

In a sense Constable is fortunate in being able to use a British
intermediary who is familiar with recruitment practices both in
Britain and El Dorado. Elgar is therefore able to explain Constable's qualifications and experience to his client Verdi and advise
on the appropriate conditions of service for a person of his calibre.
Thus there should be little scope for misunderstanding.

Misunderstandings *can* occur, however, if you are dealing direct
with a foreign employer.

- **Language difficulties.** Try to be as precise as possible in expressing yourself and be prepared to explain unfamiliar terminology. The problem can be both one of language and of culture. Mention that you were the President of the Oxford Union to an Italian, for instance, and he might assume you are a leading trade unionist. Reference to your treasureship of the Duckington-in-the-Mud Bowling Club is more likely to confuse than enlighten.

- **Unfamiliarity with British qualifications.** While a Texan employer will understand what a BSc stands for, he might be bewildered by such acronyms such as MIEE, MIMM or MICE. The more so a German.

- **Differences in recruitment practice.** A continental employer will be more interested in your certificates than in your achievements outside the world of work, and, like many American employers, may ask for transcripts of your grades or open testimonials.

The way to overcome such difficulties is to spell out your experience and qualifications in detail, relating them if possible to the equivalents in the country in question. Translate your CV and letters if you can.

Don't use unfamiliar acronyms. If you are a Member of the Institute of Electrical Engineers, say so and explain what you had to do to get this title. Did it involve passing an examination? If so, how many years' study led to the award? What level is it equivalent to in the educational system of the foreign country?

Some professionals avoid recruitment consultancies, regarding them as an extra and unnecessary link in the recruitment chain. In fact, a good recruitment consultant can often speed up the process if they understand exactly what the foreign client wants and has experience of finding the type of person who would best fit into the organisation. Let's look more closely at the recruitment process.

REPLYING TO AN ADVERTISEMENT

When you see a job advertised, read the instructions carefully.

- Do you have to telephone or write for an application form?
- Do the recruiters just want you to send along a CV?
- Who should you contact?

It is important to get it right. If the employer mentions an application form, there is no point in preparing an elaborate application of your own. At the early stage a short note asking for a form and further details is all that is needed.

If, on the other hand, they want a CV, send a good one...accompanied by an effective letter of application.

A speculative letter
The important thing about a speculative letter is that it has to arouse interest. A letter opening with the words 'My name is Aloysius Merryweather and I am looking for a job' is likely to be consigned to the waste-paper basket before you can say 'Jack Robinson'; so you need something that is short and snappy and draws attention to your strengths as far as this particular vacancy is concerned. Emphasise any of the following if they apply to you:

- A successful track record abroad
- An ability to motivate people of other nationalities
- Technical skills
- Achievements—particularly in a foreign environment
- Adaptability and resilience
- Specialised knowledge of the area in question
- Language ability

Should you send a CV as well? There are two schools of thought. One is that at this stage you are only trying to interest the prospective employer and therefore don't want to give too much away. The other is that to present a detailed CV will save time in the long run. The decision is yours.

If you are dealing with someone in a non-English speaking country you may make an impression if you can send a letter in the language of that particular country, but make sure it's accurate. However, if you are after a job in Abu Dhabi or China and cannot write Arabic or Chinese, don't panic! Just pen some good, clear English prose.

Remember to express yourself in a courteous rather than a matter-of-fact way. In Latin countries especially people use extremely elegant formulae in letter writing.

The letter of application
If you are applying for a particular job, don't assume that a completed application form or CV should stand alone or be accompanied by only a cursory note. The accompanying letter is the first contact the selector has with you, so it needs to look good.

Tel: ...   Blackberry Cottage
                                            Sloe
                                            Brambleshire BR1 2YZ

                                            5th April 19--

Jack Mulberry
Consultant
Damson International
Strawberry Hill
London SW30 1AB

Dear Mr Mulberry

I am writing in response to your advertisement in this week's
Horticultural Express for a Horticultural Adviser to the Guava
Soft Fruit Project in Papua New Guinea.

The post sounds an exciting one to which I could undoubtedly
make a substantial contribution. I would therefore be grateful if
you could send me further details on the position, together with
an application form, if required.

Yours sincerely

Josiah Plumb

Specimen Request for Job Details

Tel:...   13 Tanner Court
                                           Crown Hamlet
                                           Stirling ST5 8MT

                                           31st September 19--

Managing Director
Mark Dinar Bank (Overseas Division)
50 Dollar Square
London EC1 9ZZ

Dear Sir

The recent report in the Financial Times about your ambitious
expansion plans prompts me to enquire whether you have any
vacancies in your international operations.

I am very keen to become involved in overseas banking as I
believe it offers intellectual stimulation as well as the opportunity
to work with people from other countries. I have lived abroad for
extended periods—in Zambia, Guatemala and Austria—and
developed close relationships with people of other nationalities.

I am proficient in three foreign languages and have recently been
awarded a degree in economics by the University of Lirapool. As
for practical experience, during my time in Austria I helped
organise an international seminar entitled 'Banking 2000', and
was consulted on a number of occasions by a leading bank in
Innsbruck.

If you feel it would be useful, I would be very happy to drop by
for an exploratory chat—with no obligation, of course.

Yours faithfully

Ivor Catchpenny

Model Speculative Letter of Application

A letter can answer a lot of questions about you:

Can you spell?
Are you prepared to make an effort?
Can you communicate well?
Do you know how to write a business letter?
Are you keen on the job?
Do you understand what the job entails?

Most important of all it gives you an opportunity to make a statement about yourself to the selector before he starts wading through your CV or your application form. It should:

- explain why you want the job
- give three or four factors which mark you out as the ideal candidate
- finish on a positive note.

The curriculum vitae

Like the letter of application, a CV has to look impressive, but don't try to impress the recipient with a document of inordinate length. Recruiters are not usually interested in people's memoirs! Instead, keep it concise and to the point (ideally, just one side of A4 paper; two sides at the most). Have it typed if you can't type it yourself. Preparation of a CV can be a lengthy process, but if you get it right first time it is well worth the time and effort. There are basically two types:

- **The chronological CV.** This is the most familiar type which details your experience in chronological order. Examples are given in this book.

- **The functional CV.** This type of CV is sometimes used by candidates with many years of experience behind them. Instead of using a chronological approach for the work experience it focusses on particular areas of expertise.

While this can be a powerful tool, some recruiters may find it confusing. I therefore suggest that, when applying for jobs abroad, you use the chronological method and highlight your expertise in the letter of application. Your CV should contain:

- **Personal details.** Your name, address, telephone numbers (work and home), date of birth, nationality. Place of birth, marital status, religion are optional.

- **Education.** Educational institutions attended with dates and examinations passed. If you left school decades ago there is no need to go into detail about your GCE results. Include any courses you have attended in recent years and any diplomas/ certificates you are currently studying for.

- **Summary of work experience.** An optional section in which you outline your main areas of expertise.

- **Employment Record.** List the jobs you have held, the organisations you have worked for with addresses and dates. Give a concise description of your responsibilities in each post, particularly in the case of those you have held during the past five or ten years. If you have had a long and distinguished career, be brief about the jobs you held twenty years ago. On the other hand, if you are right at the beginning of your career include details of holiday jobs and traineeships.

- **Interests and activities.** Foreign employers are unlikely to pay much heed to this section. British recruiters will, because they like evidence that the applicant has a well-rounded personality. List the sports you play, the clubs and societies you belong to, particularly those in which you hold office.

- **Other Information.** Possession of a valid driving licence or passport, language abilities, membership of professional associations, awards you have received, time spent abroad— these are just a few of the items you might mention.

Don't assume that the length of your CV should be commensurate with your age. The CV of a young applicant could well take up as much space as that of an older person. The difference lies in the approach.

Younger applicants at the beginning of their careers will need to *elaborate* on their achievements so far; go into some detail about your attainments at school and college, including social interests and positions of responsibility you have held. Vacation employment should also be mentioned to indicate familiarity with the world of work.

Mature applicants, by contrast, need to *condense* their career details. Employers are more interested in your recent achievements than in your attainments of 20 years back. Only brief details of your educational attainments need be provided, though courses taken in recent years should certainly be mentioned to show that

Tel: . . .

Shelley Cottage
Coleridge Walk
Tennyson Wells TE4 2TZ
United Kingdom

31st December 1989

Mr Bruce Forster
Personnel Manager
Maugham IT Services
O'Casey Close
Sydney, NSW
Australia

Dear Sir

I am most interested in your vacancy for a Senior Programmer advertised in this week's edition of 'Computer Weekly', and wish to be considered for this key post.

Although very happy with my present employers, I believe the time has come for me to try something new. Australia's IT sector seems to offer plenty of challenges these days, and I am sure I would feel at home in a progressive firm such as yours.

I have many years' experience in computers, as you will see from the enclosed CV, and have worked on IBM, ICL and Nixdorf machines. Apart from successfully completing assignments for both British and foreign firms, I have also been involved with public sector installations in a number of different countries.

In this particular field you need someone who can keep his cool, communicate effectively with people who are not computer-literate, and work to the most exacting standards. Look no further, for I am your man.

I look forward to meeting you to discuss the contribution I can make to the continued success of your organisation.

Your sincerely

W A Wordsworth

Specimen Accompanying Letter for CV

Personal History
WILLIAM ALAN WORDSWORTH

Address: Shelley Cottage, Coleridge Walk, Tennyson Wells TE4 2IZ
Telephone: 0123 87654 extension 5 (daytime); 0123 98765 (home)
Date of Birth: 29th February 1950
Marital Status: Widower
Place of Birth: Dundee

EDUCATION
1961-1966   Robert Burns High School, Land's End, Cornwall
GCE 'O' Levels in English Language, Greek, Mathematics, Physics and Swahili.
1966-1968   The Byron College of Further Education, Truro, Cornwall
City and Guilds Certificate in Electronics
1975-1978   Yeats University, Sligo, Eire
BSc in Computer Science

SUMMARY OF WORK EXPERIENCE
Electronics: Assembly and design of printed circuit boards
Information Technology: Computer programming and systems analysis
Management & Training: Supervision of IT projects and induction of clients' staff

EMPLOYMENT RECORD
1968-1975   Eliot's Electricals, Browning Way, Cowperville:
Apprentice, later Assistant Designer
1978-1979   Hardy Computer Services, Auden Square, Spenderbury:
Computer Programmer
1979-1985   Milton Computers Ltd, Pope Street, Great Donne:
Computer Programmer, later Systems Analyst
During my time with Milton I was in charge of introducing and implementing major computer systems for foreign clients such as Hugo Chemicals in Paris, Dante Data Services in Turin, and Mörike Motor Works in Stuttgart.
1985-   Shakespeare Computer Consultants, Johnson Row, Rochester:
present   Senior Consultant
I have designed and supervised a number of major projects, notably the installation of a computerised accounting system at Rochester District Council Headquarters and a computerised traffic control system for the Ras Al Khaimah Police Force.

INTERESTS
Ice Hockey, Judo and Ballroom Dancing
Treasurer of the Rochester and District Operatic Society
Member of Rochester District Countil (1986-1989)

OTHER INFORMATION
Member of the British Institute of Management
Fluent in Swedish, Swahili and Urdu
Holder of a full and unendorsed British driving licence
Available to take up new position at three months' notice.

Specimen CV for a Mature Applicant

you are up-to-date in your field and still intellectually active. Similarly, employment in the early part of your career can be treated cursorily (unless it has direct relevance to the job currently being applied for), while the last two or three jobs held should be described in some detail, especially if the scope of the job is not apparent from the title.

The application form

Most people find the completion of application forms a terrible bore. However, many organisations prefer to have candidates' details in some standardised format to make comparison easier, and they may not be prepared to consider you if you don't return their form fully completed. So you have to make the best of a bad job. But beware; filling in a form is not a job that can be rushed.

1. Read it through carefully, making notes (alternatively make a photocopy of it and do a rough first version on the copy).
2. Take a black pen and begin to fill it in with a copy of your CV at your side for reference (if you are a good typist, you might consider typing in the information, but not if the result will be messy; neatness is vital).

Particular points to note are:

- **Address** for correspondence. Make certain that this is likely to remain valid for the next six months. If not, choose one that will.

- **Contact telephone number.** Organisations are most likely to want to contact you during office hours. If you are difficult to get hold of, give the number of a relation or neighbour who can relay messages to you.

- **Education.** If you are dealing with a foreign organisation that may not be familiar with the British educational system you may have to offer some explanation. e.g. 'GCSE—General Certificate of Secondary Education (an examination taken by 16 year olds)'; 'HND—Higher National Diploma (equivalent to ...in your country).'

- **Work experience.** Fill in the details as required even though you may be duplicating the information on your CV. If there are any lengthy interruptions to your employment, you may have to account for them. If there is any information that you do not wish to disclose at this juncture (e.g. reasons for leaving a particular job), leave the space blank. Make sure that you have listed the jobs in the correct order. Some forms ask for chronological order, others reverse chronological order where your current or most recent job comes first.

- **Referees.** These need to be people who can vouch for your good character, your prowess at work, or your academic attainments. Make sure that they are willing and available to do this. If you know that one of your referees is about to go off on an expedition up the Amazon, find a substitute.

- **Salary requirement.** If the form asks you to state the level of salary you want, be careful. If you ask for too much, you are possibly eliminating yourself from the contest. One alternative might be to insert the words 'To be discussed at interview'.

- **Declaration.** At the end of many application forms you have to sign a declaration that the information you have provided is true. Check that this is so, since misleading information can lead to disqualification.

When you have completed the form look back over your handiwork, correcting any small errors that may have crept in and asking yourself what kind of impression it gives of you. Check if there are any vital details that have been left out, such as membership of a professional body or courses you have recently attended. If there are, try and include them somewhere on the form.

Sending your documents

Send your application as quickly as possible—to demonstrate your keenness for the job and to be ahead of the rest of the pack. Make sure you send off all the documentation required—the application form, your CV (whether requested or not), photocopies of your qualifications (if specified), passport size photographs (if specified) and a good covering letter (essential).

Before you finally send it off, stand back and ask yourself what effect all this information is likely to have on the recipient. If he receives a few dozen applications for the same post, is there anything that will make yours stand out?

If not, then something is wrong. Perhaps you need to redo the application, or at least make a mental note to try better next time. Perhaps the use of different paper—thicker or pastel-coloured— would make the difference between success and failure.

Always use first class post. If you are sending it abroad you

Tel:

14 Epstein Close
Gainsborough
North Yorkshire

31st December 1989

The Manager
Overseas Services
Rembrandt Recruitment
Rossetti Row
London SW51 8DD

Dear Sir

With reference to your advertisement in 'The Guardian' for an English speaking secretary in South Germany, I have pleasure in submitting an application.

You will note from my curriculum vitae that I have worked as a secretary for a firm of solicitors and an estate agency. More recently, in order to broaden my experience, I have worked on a temporary basis for an English travel company and a French bank. These recent appointments have proved very enjoyable and have prompted me to look for a suitable position abroad.

I know South Germany well, having participated in the European Ice Skating Championships in Garmisch Partenkirchen on two occasions, and spent a holiday with my pen friend in Munich. I get on well with people of all nationalities, and having acquired a knowledge of German through attendance at evening classes I shall have no problems in communicating with your clients and their employees.

I do hope you will see fit to recommend me to your clients. I am, of course, willing to attend for an interview at any mutually convenient time.

Yours faithfully

Angela Sutherland

Specimen Accompanying Letter

Curriculum Vitae

ANGELA SUTHERLAND
14 Epstein Close
Gainsborough
North Yorkshire
Tel: 0999-121212

Born 16th May 1967 at Gainsborough. Unmarried. British nationality.

EDUCATION
1978-1983 Landseer High School for Girls, Gainsborough
GCE 'O' Level: History (C); French (C); English (C)
CSE: Maths (2); Art (2)
1983-1985 Sickert Commercial College, Leeds.
RSA Diploma in Secretarial Studies

EXPERIENCE
1985-1987 Lowry and Lowry, Solicitors, 24 High Street, Gainsborough
Secretary
1987-1988 Whistler Estate Agency, 25 High Street, Gainsborough
Secretary and PA to Manager
Since June 1988
Turner-Constable Temps Agency, 26 High Street, Gainsborough
Secretary

INTERESTS
Ice Skating
Embroidery
Bridge

OTHER INFORMATION
I hold a full driving licence and a First Aid certificate
I have visited France, Germany and Switzerland
I am currently attending an evening course in German at Gainsborough College of Further Education

Specimen CV for a Younger Applicant

might look into more secure ways of despatching it—by express
post or recorded delivery, for example.

The wait

This is a period when your patience will be sorely tried—but don't
keep telephoning to find out if your application has arrived or to
persuade the organisation to get on with the recruitment process.
Such impatience is understandable, especially if the job is one that
you really want, but try and find something else to do in the
meantime!

A wise applicant has plenty of irons in the fire. Do not assume
that you'll get the post you have set your heart on. Instead, look
round for other opportunities and fire off a volley of applications
in other directions as well.

If the post is being advertised internationally, the wait will be
even longer. A quick decision is a rarity in the case of recruitment
for overseas jobs. Even if an advertisement includes the words
REQUIRED URGENTLY you will be lucky to be bound for your
foreign posting even two months after the date of its appearance.

The test

Some organisations—governmental and intergovernmental ones
in particular—subject candidates to a test as a preliminary to the
interview. The test might be designed to measure intelligence,
aptitude, or personality, or to measure certain skills, such as
drafting ability, linguistic ability, and so on. Normally you will be
given some indication as to the form the test(s) will take in
advance.

Don't regard the test as yet another obstacle along the path to
finding a job; a good test might be better at measuring a candidate's competence than a badly conducted interview.

Preparing for interview

Sooner or later you will receive a letter through the post either
declining your services or inviting you for interview. If it is the
latter, congratulations, but don't assume that it is downhill all the
way from now on. After confirming that you are able to attend at
the time and place specified, you need to embark on some intensive preparation:

- Read up about the job, the country and the organisation for
  which you will be working.

- Think hard about the qualities needed for the job and how you would measure up to it.
- See if you can get in some interview practice.
- Think of a few questions you would like to ask about the job.
- Try to envisage the type of questions the selectors are likely to ask and how you might answer them.

Possible interview questions

Why do you want a job outside the UK?

What attracts you to Ruritania (this job)?

How well do you get on with foreigners?

How do you feel about the current political situation in Ruritania?

What experience do you have of working abroad?

What adjustments do you expect to have to make?

Why should we offer you this job?

What changes would you want to make to the organisation, if appointed?

Where do you see yourself in 5 years' time?

What are your strengths (weaknesses)?

What problems do you envisage having to overcome?

'...and how do you react to unusual wildlife, Miss Jones?'

What sort of salary do you require?
What other jobs have you applied for?

The interview itself

A lot of people dread interviews—not least some interviewers. Alas, the interview is by no means the most scientifically foolproof way of deciding whether a person is suitable for a particular job. If you are not offered a job after the interview, remember that this setback might not be a reflection on your ability, but rather lack of discernment on the part of the selector(s)!

This is particularly true in the case of recruitment for posts abroad. If the selectors' expertise lies in recruiting people for jobs in the UK, there is a risk that candidates will be judged by inappropriate criteria. The person who fits in well at head office might not be in the right type for a challenging post in Namibia.

While it helps if you can display knowledge of, and an interest in, the country concerned, remember that this may only be of minor interest to the recruiters, whose main concern is to fill a particular post. Your aim during the interview is to convey a good impression and convince the selector(s) that you are capable of performing all the duties connected with the job.

Dos and don'ts at the interview

- Dress smartly
- Arrive in good time
- Try to establish some rapport with the interviewer(s)
- Be polite
- Be as natural as you can
- Look at the interviewer(s)
- Keep calm

On the other hand:

- Don't sit down until invited to
- Don't argue
- Don't interrupt
- Don't make jokes
- Don't run down your present or previous employer
- Don't get on your hobby horse
- Don't lie or make exaggerated claims.

Aftermath

After the interview there may well be another considerable wait, followed by either a telephone call or a letter. It may contain an invitation to a further interview. This is not a mistake or evilmindedness on the part of the organisation; obviously the first interview you attended was by way of an initial selection. Rejoice that you have been included in the final shortlist and carry out the same procedures as you did before the original interview.

However the letter may convey bad news: that you have not been selected. While this will obviously be a disappointment, *don't* lose your cool. What you need to do is write back to the organisation that interviewed you to:

- thank them for meeting you, and
- express the hope that they will bear you in mind if a suitable vacancy arises in the future

Who knows, the appointee may decide not to take up the position, in which case you are once more a strong contender for it.

Tel. Morrisford 12345   5 Vauxhall Drive
                                                         Morrisford
                                                         Austinshire AB1 2CD

                                                         14 July 19--

Roger Rover Esq
Personnel Director
Automotive International
Talbot Road
Morgantown

Dear Mr Rover

I am writing to say how much I enjoyed meeting you and other
members of your firm when I came along for an interview
yesterday.

I look forward to hearing the results of your deliberations.

Yours sincerely

George Riley

A Follow-up Letter After an Interview

Tel. Morrisford 12345   5 Vauxhall Drive
                                               Morrisford
                                               Austinshire AB1 2CD

                                               16th July 19--

Roger Rover Esq
Personnel Director
Automotive International
Talbot Road
Morgantown MG20 1PQ

Dear Mr Rover

Many thanks for your courteous letter of the 15th regarding my
application for the post of Regional Representative, Tahiti.

While I am naturally disappointed that I did not get the job, I
would like to take this opportunity to thank you for giving my
application such careful consideration.

I wonder if you are likely to have any similar vacancies in the
future. If so, I would be very interested to hear from you.

My very best wishes for the continued success of your company.

Yours sincerely

George Riley

A Reply to a Rejection Letter

4
Coming to a Decision

You have now had the interview in which you should have learned more about the job, you have succeeded in landing the post, and you have been offered a contract. The ball is in your court, and you have to decide whether to take up the offer or not.

THE EMPLOYER

If the job is with an organisation that is well known for dealing with its employees fairly, you need have few qualms about taking up the posting. However, not all jobs are with the likes of Shell or the Foreign and Commonwealth Office. You could be working for an overseas firm or government about which you know practically nothing except for some sketchy information with your job description. If you have any doubts about the credentials of the organisation, you would be wise to check:

- Try to meet a former expatriate employee of the organisation
- Consult a business directory dealing with the country concerned, such as *Kompass*
- Ask your professional association or trade union if they have any details on the organisation
- Check with the British Embassy or Chamber of Commerce in the country of operation
- Check with an expatriate service organisation, such as Expats International
- If you are being recruited by an intermediary, ask if they can supply comprehensive details.

Although a good many employers of expatriates are reputable, there are, alas, some instances of employers who fail to honour their commitments to employees, and people have returned home considerably out of pocket as a result.

To take legal proceedings against them, particularly in a foreign court, can be complicated and costly, and there is no guarantee you will win; so look before you leap.

THE SALARY PACKAGE

Many people are enticed into taking up positions overseas by the prospect of a higher salary. Even if you are not, as is the case with missionaries or volunteers, you need to be sure that the package on offer will be adequate to support you and your family, if you have one.

To think solely in terms of the salary figure on offer can be misleading. Usually you will be offered a **package** of benefits both in cash and in kind. This will consist of at least some of the following items. The more items on offer, the better the package:

- Basic salary
- Allowances:
  Overseas cost of living allowance
  Hardship allowance
  Accompanied spouse allowance
  Education allowance for children
- Benefits:
  Pension
  Life insurance
  Medical cover
- Free or subsidised housing
- Termination bonus
- Paid leave at regular intervals
- Fares and baggage allowance to and from the posting

On this basis, for example, a job paying £20,000 with free housing and a pension contribution could well prove more attractive than one paying £25,000 with no extras.

There are also other points to remember. The total package may look fine, but is it all yours? Don't overlook the following which could affect your prosperity:

- Tax liability (Is the package tax-free or do you have to pay income tax either at home or in the country to which you are posted?)
- Social security payments (What deductions are made to cover these?)

- Extra expenses you are likely to incur by reason of living away from home (for example, maintaining two households).

Currency problems

For some postings, you might need to think about the currency you are to be paid in. If the company has suggested paying you in local currency, you need to find out:

- Is the currency convertible?
- How much of my salary can I repatriate?
- Is the salary tied to an international currency (e.g. the dollar, sterling)? If not, you could lose out if any devaluation takes place against other currencies.

Even if you are paid in an international currency, be prepared for shocks. In the eighties a number of British people whose salaries were paid in dollars found that in sterling terms they lost out when the dollar weakened against the pound.

Cost of living

Don't forget that there are likely to be differences in the cost of living between your home base and your foreign posting. Some capital cities—Tokyo, for instance—can be very expensive indeed. On the other hand, there are places where you can live like a lord on a relatively modest salary.

If you can, check that your pay level will be at least comparable to the rates offered to nationals of the country concerned, particularly if you are heading for high salary level countries such as the USA, West Germany, Sweden, Switzerland or Japan. Is the organisation concerned after your skills and expertise, or merely cheap labour?

Salary differentials

International salary differentials can cause considerable bitterness. In overseas oil operations, for instance, where there is a mix of nationalities, the pay for executives and technicians from different countries often reflects their country of origin rather than their abilities.

A British employee may therefore find he is earning less than his counterparts from other parts of Europe and the US. On the other hand, he could be earning several times as much as a highly qualified technician from India or the Philippines.

Many multinational employers are aware that this can be a very thorny subject and are starting to use remuneration and cost of living comparisons prepared by organisations such as Towers, Perrin, Forster and Crosby (TPF&C), Runzheimer, Business International, and Employment Conditions Abroad. Most of these reports are quite expensive for an individual to buy, but if you have a chance to see one, you can judge for yourself whether you are being fairly remunerated (see Bibliography).

Dual income families
Finally, dual income families could face a problem if one partner takes up a job abroad and the other who accompanies him/her is unable to take up salaried employment there. It is therefore vital to find out whether the earning partner's enhanced salary package will compensate for the other's loss of income.

THE JOB ITSELF

If the job is with an American or British organisation you can usually count on getting a detailed description of your responsibilities; however, organisations in other countries may regard such details as irrelevant. They may assume that if you are competent at your job then there is no need to spell out exactly what you have to do. You will be required to do what is necessary, no more and no less.

What can you expect?
People who have worked abroad before will have a pretty shrewd idea of what to expect, but a newcomer to the world of international employment really does need a proper job description; even if the job appears to be the same as the work you are used to in the UK, it will probably be different.

For example, if you are posted to a Third World country, you may well be expected to spend part of your time training up your subordinates. You might also find that a significant part of your work is taken up with personnel matters.

The differences you will encounter will force you to look again at your methods and attitudes. According to David Wheatley of Employment Conditions Abroad:

> '...the expatriate has to recognise, understand and adjust himself to unfamiliar styles of management and concepts of organisation.... What would be considered a dynamic and effective management style at home may

now be perceived as quite unacceptable in the new
environment.'

Your long-term future

Whether you are off on a short-term assignment or taking up a
contract which will last several years, think about what will happen
after this job before you leave. Do you see your future life as a
series of overseas contracts—which can be a precarious existence
at times of world recession—or can you look forward to a long-
term future with your employer?

If your assignment is a short one—6 months or less—you
ideally need to make sure that you have already secured your next
job before you go. If you are off on a longer contract, make
contact with organisations which could be useful when the time
comes for you to move on—recruitment agencies, potential
employers, and so on.

If you have landed a job which looks fairly permanent, don't
assume that your future will take care of itself. In your distant
outpost you might become the victim of the 'out of sight, out of
mind' syndrome, which means that when promotions are discussed
back at headquarters, you are not in the running.

Nobody wants to become forgotten, so you should look into
ways of keeping your career pattern active while you are away. If
you work for a large organisation, find out if they operate a mentor
system whereby there is someone in head office looking after your
career while you are out of the country.

FAMILY MATTERS

If you are single, you really only need to worry about whether you
yourself are well suited to an overseas posting. But if you're
married, and perhaps have a family, it's a different story...

At one time it was more or less taken for granted that a wife
would follow her husband to his posting abroad, and this still tends
to be the norm. But today other patterns are emerging; wife and
husband may decide to go different ways for the duration of one
partner's foreign posting, or it may be the wife who lands the job
abroad and the husband who is the accompanying spouse.

In this chapter I am assuming that it is the husband who is
posted to a foreign country and the wife and children who accompany him or not, as the case may be, for the simple reason that this
is still the most common pattern. If you are the rare exception,

please make allowances, and for 'wife' read 'husband' and vice versa.

Your wife

Although the pattern of family life in this country has changed considerably over the past decades, with an increasing number of wives following careers of their own, very few postings abroad are able to cater for this interest, and a wife generally has to resign herself to being a non-working dependant. This is because many countries are keen to keep job opportunities for their own nationals, and are therefore unwilling to issue work permits for wives as well as husbands.

Many organisations prefer wives to accompany husbands and offer generous allowances for this. Their motives are not completely altruistic, however. The wife may be required to help her husband in his job—in entertaining visitors, for example. This is particularly true of the wives of diplomats and senior businessmen. It is also generally true that a wife's presence boosts the morale of an employee, acts as a stabilising influence, and thus enables him to work more effectively.

Unfortunately, less attention tends to be paid to the morale of the wife, who may have more to adjust to than the husband. While the latter has a job which is probably not fundamentally very different from what he is used to, the wife has to get used to a completely new routine in a totally unfamiliar environment. And if she is used to a busy professional career, she may have difficulty adapting to her new life. Among the chief complaints of expatriate wives are:

- Boredom—with having nothing to do
- Frustration—at not being able to pursue their chosen profession or engage in useful work
- Loneliness—particularly in places where the expatriate community is minimal or the husband spends a lot of his time away on trips.

She may also have problems adapting to the expatriate society where she is expected to socialise with women she would not normally get on with back home, or accept the 'pecking order' that sometimes exists in expatriate communities where the ambassador's or company boss's wife takes the lead and the others are expected to follow.

On the other hand, she may relish the life; in some countries, households employ servants who take over many of the household chores, and wives are able to use their time to develop new interests, to study, to meet new people, to travel, or to spend more time with the children.

An accompanying spouse ideally needs to be briefed on the country in question in as much detail as her husband, so that she can prepare herself accordingly, or—if the situation sounds very grim—opt to stay at home. Try finding answers to the following questions:

- What restrictions will there be on your movements? (In Saudi Arabia, for instance, women are not allowed to drive cars.)
- Will there be any expatriates in the area you will be able to turn to for advice? (In most capitals there is a well organised British community; elsewhere you could be on your own.)
- How secure is the area where you'll be living?
- What is the attitude of the locals to European women?
- What sort of duties will you be expected to perform in connection with your husband's work?
- What kind of household assistance will be available, if any? And what do you need to know about handling servants?
- Is there any possibility of your taking up paid employment? (Probably not, except in Europe.)
- Are there any voluntary groups you might join?
- What type of leisure and study facilities are there?

The key to survival is to keep yourself occupied, and if you are going to accompany your husband, start planning your life at post *now*. Remember that you are going to have to give up a lot when you leave these shores; you will no longer be able to pop round for a chat with your friends, watch your favourite TV programmes, or attend club meetings. Your life may seem empty and meaningless unless you find ways of filling it.

Even worse, you will end up feeling morose and disconsolate, and start bombarding your husband with complaints. If a married employee terminates his contract prematurely, it is often because of his wife's failure to adjust rather than his own.

The Career Development Centre for Women offers specialist careers and planning advice for wives who have a mobile lifestyle due to the nature of their husband's occupation. The Centre's 'Portable Careers Portfolio for Women' scheme covers such matters as transferring skills, coping with change and strategies for keeping in touch. The address is 97 Mallard Place, Twickenham, Middlesex TW1 4SW. Tel: 081-892 3806.

The pros and cons of separation

Not all wives accompany spouses to their overseas postings. They may have pressing reasons for remaining in the UK or they have no choice in the matter. A number of jobs, particularly in the Middle East, are bachelor status postings for any one of a number of reasons:

- There is no married accommodation available
- Living conditions are difficult or hazardous
- Lower ranking employees do not qualify for accompanied status
- The employer or host country prefers unattached people.

To compensate for the periods of separation, employees are often given frequent and generous leave entitlement—say, three months at post, one month off.

Although the majority of wives who have the option *do* accompany their husbands there are some who do not, for a variety of reasons, such as:

- The wife needs to stay at home to look after the children
- The wife wishes to pursue her own career
- The wife suffers from poor health or cannot stand harsh climates
- There are elderly relatives to be cared for.

While a short period of separation is generally quite acceptable, prolonged periods away from home can cause problems for a marriage. Partners can become estranged or start to seek other emotional outlets, and from then on it is only a small step to marital breakdown. This may be less of a problem in well established marriages or where a wife has a supportive family around her.

Remember that a foreign posting can put pressure on a marriage whether the post is accompanied or not. If your marriage is already in a fragile state, a job abroad—whether accompanied or otherwise—could prove the final nail in the coffin.

Your children

One of the joys of being a parent is watching your offspring grow up. Usually, younger children can live with their parents at a foreign posting, and this is the most popular option.

As they grow older, however, their education becomes a major factor and you may have to decide whether to rely on the local educational facilities or to put them into a boarding school in the UK or a third country. When coming to a decision, you need to bear in mind the character of the child as much as what is established practice in the country concerned. There are a number of options once children reach school age:

Children accompany parents to posting
This has always been popular with Americans and as a consequence there are American international schools or community schools in virtually every capital of the world. In Europe, the Gulf States and most Commonwealth countries, there are usually schools—both primary and secondary—for expatriate children which follow the British curriculum or prepare their pupils for the increasingly popular International Baccalaureate. British military bases have schools run by the Service Children's Educational Authority, which functions like any local education authority in the UK.

As soon as you receive news of your posting abroad, the onus is on *you* to make enquiries as to what educational provision there is for expatriate children in your particular locality. Dean Associates is one organisation that provides educational information on day schooling for the children of families likely to be abroad for a limited period. 'We give parents the implications of choosing international, national or local state schools bearing in mind that their children will have to return to their "home" education system,' says consultant Margret Price. (Address: 51 High Street, Emsworth, Hants P010 7AN. Tel: 0243-378022.) The *ECIS Directory* is a useful handbook in this regard if you cannot find details from other sources. (The European Council for International Schools, 21B Lavant Street, Petersfield, Hants GU32 3EL.)

Once you have ascertained that a suitable school is available, make contact with the principal immediately to find out more details and then to secure a place for your child. Virtually all these schools are independent organisations with only a limited number of vacancies, and they may not be in a position to accommodate last-minute applications.

If you find that there are no suitable schools locally, that does not rule out the idea of children accompanying you to your posting abroad. They could, for instance, study by correspondence or you—or your wife—could teach them yourself under the World-wide Educational Service Home School System. This is a complete educational programme for the under-13s whereby parents with no teaching experience can educate their children under the guidance of a WES tutor. (WES, Strode House, 44-50 Osnaburgh Street, London NW1 3NN. Tel: 071-387 9228.)

Mercers College provides a complete tuition service by correspondence for children living abroad with their parents from the pre-school stage up to the age of 18. It prepares them for such examinations as GCE 'A' Level, GCE Overseas 'O' level, GCSE and the Public Schools Common Entrance Examination. (Address: Ware, Hertfordshire SG12 9BU. Tel: 0920-465926.)

Children are sent off to boarding school
Boarding education is still a popular choice for families who move around from country to country at regular intervals, and has the merit of avoiding disruption to a child's educational career. Many employers offer allowances which will partly offset the fees.

Some local authorities run their own boarding school and if your children are in the state system, find out what provision they make. Most boarding education, however, is provided by the independent sector and you would be wise to consult an advisory service such as Gabbitas, Truman & Thring or ISIS (the Independent Schools' Information Service) as well: Gabbitas, Truman & Thring, 6-8 Sackville Street, London W1X 2BR; Independent Schools Information Service, 26 Caxton Street, London SW1H 0RG. See also *The Parents Guide to Independent Schools* (SFIA Educational Trust, 15 Forlease Road, Maidenhead, Berks SL6 1JA. Tel: 0628-34291).

If your child attends a day school, and is either reluctant to leave it or at a crucial stage of his or her education, you could look into alternatives. Perhaps he or she could be boarded out with relations or family friends who live close to the school. Or, if your offspring are exceptionally mature and responsible, you could leave them in charge of the house. Generally speaking, however, parents are reluctant to leave their children unsupervised to this extent!

Some parents may have qualms about breaking up the family in this way, but it has to be said that a number of children—particularly older ones—enjoy living away from their parents. In any case, families are usually together for the school holidays.

The boarding school you choose need not necessarily be located in the UK. There may well be excellent schools within the country or region where you are posted, and greater proximity will offer the possibility of more frequent contact.

Wife remains in UK to look after children
Sometimes this decision is made for you, as in the case of bachelor status posts abroad. But there may be other strong reasons for choosing this particular option—for example, if a child has crucial examinations in the near future, you may be anxious that his or her studies should be disrupted as little as possible. It is not a sensible policy to switch schools when a child is in the middle of a GCSE or 'A' Level course, and there is a lot to be said in favour of one parent remaining behind to maintain a stable home background and offer advice and encouragement.

Such a decision is not an irrevocable one. In some cases it may mean the wife remaining in Britain for only a matter of months before joining her husband at post. However, if the children are still a long way short of their teens, there is probably little point in following such a course for the children's sake alone. Indeed, living abroad can be more enriching educationally for them than staying in suburbia.

Elderly relatives

An increasingly important factor is the plight of elderly relatives—usually mothers or fathers—especially if they form part of your household and are dependent on you. Even if they do not live with you, those who are single or widowed may well depend on regular visits from you to keep their morale up, and for shopping or other services.

In some cases they represent a problem, particularly if they are disabled; you may be faced with the prospect of having to put them in a rest home or of one of you staying behind to keep an eye on them. In others they represent a solution to a problem; able-bodied ones may be able to provide a home base for your children, enabling them to continue their education at schools with which they are familiar; or they may be keen to move off to foreign climes with you.

Obviously, every situation is different and has to be judged on its merits. But if you have elderly dependants, their welfare during your absence is certainly one matter that needs to be gone into. Organisations such as Help the Aged or Age Concern may be able to offer advice.

Age Concern, Bernard Sunley House, 60 Pitcairn Road, Mitcham, Surrey. Tel: 081-640 5431.

Help the Aged, 8-10 Denman Street, London W1A 2AP. Tel: 071-437 2554.

YOUR NEW ENVIRONMENT

Will you fit in? This is the final—and perhaps the most important—consideration. Your qualifications may be impeccable and you may be regarded as an expert in your field, but this will not necessarily be enough.

An alien environment is bound to affect you in one way or another. Some people flourish in it, while others find living abroad a stressful experience. If you are going to be posted to a place for some time, it needs to be a place where you can feel at home. You cannot divorce your job from the context in which you will be performing it.

The physical environment

This is an important consideration, particularly for people who are not in the best of health.

- **Climate and altitude.** Most people are able to adapt to different climates without difficulty. However, hot climates can be trying for some—particularly if accompanied by high humidity. Of course, if you have access to modern comforts such as air conditioning, life will be eminently bearable.

  If possible you will need to adjust your lifestyle to suit the climate—perhaps by doing as much work as you can in the morning and taking an afternoon siesta. Also, remember that high altitudes can be hazardous for people who are not physically fit.
- **Health considerations.** Medical science has made tremendous strides in the past century and places which were once regarded as 'the white man's grave' need no longer be approached with fear and trembling. Provided you take simple precautions—like boiling drinking water, cooking food, having the prescribed vaccinations—there is no reason why you should not live as healthily as at home; in any case, you may well be required to take a medical before you take up your posting.

The socio-cultural environment

'No man is an Island, entire of itself; every man is a piece of the continent, a part of the main.' Donne's words also have relevance to the expatriate. When you are posted abroad you cannot cut yourself off from your social environment, however strange. In the past, the British expatriate often found himself in a powerful position where he could impose his own customs and norms. This

was true whether you were a colonial administrator or a missionary. The locals were expected to conform to your standards,
whether they liked it or not.

The world, however, has moved on since then. Independent
nations no longer have a foreign élite who dictate to them how to
manage their affairs. They like to do things their own way, and
they expect foreigners to respect and adjust to their customs and
values rather than try to replace them. As the International Committee of the Institute of Personnel Management notes:

> 'Cultural awareness, role flexibility and the ability to
> communicate effectively across cultures have become
> pre-requisites for successful expatriation.'

Today's expatriate manager has to be more sophisticated these
days if he is to succeed, and this applies to his employer as well.
Bob Garrett, in the *Handbook of Management Development* (edited by A. Mumford, published by Gower), points out:

> 'Valuing differences while seeking common ground on
> which to build is the province of the statesman/diplo-
> mat. Neither are commonly found on executive boards,
> and yet the future of business through the exchange of
> learning, knowhow and technology would seem to
> involve more and more the crossing of national cultural
> boundaries in a sympathetic manner to those bound-
> aries.'

This awareness is needed even if you are posted to a country which
is part of the Western world. If you go to work in the US, for
instance, it is a mistake to assume that the locals share precisely
the same attitudes as you. The US—like Australia, Canada and
New Zealand—has its own distinctive culture, which you need to
understand properly in order to be 100% effective in your job.

If you go to a European country, the differences are likely to be
much more striking than in English-speaking countries. As well as
the people speaking a different language, their laws are different,
and so are their institutions, their food, their etiquette, their way
of conducting business and their family life.

Identifying cultural values

How can you prepare for these differences? The key is to begin by
understanding one's own system of values and perceptions, and
then set those of other cultures against this. Geert Hofstede's

study of national differences among large numbers of employees in more than 40 different countries might be a useful starting point (*Culture's Consequences*, Sage, abridged edition 1984). Hofstede identifies four key dimensions that provide maximum differentiation between national cultures:

- **Individualism**—favouring independent rather than collective action. The USA, Australia, Britain and the Netherlands, for example, clearly favour the individual. Pakistan, Guatemala, Taiwan and Indonesia, by contrast, tend to be extremely collectivist in their attitudes.

- **Masculinity**—How dominated is society by male values? In Japan, Germany, Mexico, and Italy Hofstede found that traditional male values were very well entrenched. In the Netherlands, Chile, France and Sweden male dominance was much less pronounced.

- **Power Distance**—The extent to which inequality is accepted. Countries such as Nigeria, Malaysia, Panama and India showed high rates of acceptance of inequality. Israel, Denmark, New Zealand and Britain, on the other hand, were more strongly egalitarian.

- **Uncertainty Avoidance**—concern for order and security. People from Portugal, Uruguay, Belgium and Japan were very concerned that order and security be maintained. In Singapore, Denmark, Hong Kong and Britain people were found to have more relaxed attitudes to law and order.

Another piece of research from André Laurent ('Once a Frenchman, Always a Frenchman': *International Management*, June 1980) found that North Americans and Northern Europeans took an instrumental view of business, where relationships between a boss and his subordinate are impersonal and authority is associated with role or function in the organisation. However, in Latin countries the opposite was true. Here the manager's role is defined by social status and his authority comes from his personal and functional attributes.

The woman in a man's world

A woman planning to take up a position abroad needs to pay particular attention to cultural attitudes, because while men in the Western world are prepared to see women as professional equals (however grudgingly), this is not true elsewhere. In the Third

World, for instance, you will have to accept that you will not be as free to act as you are at home, and you will probably need to seek social diversions within the expatriate community rather than outside it.

Life for an expatriate woman overseas can be frustrating at times. You may be expected to adopt Victorian modes of dress and behaviour, and your response to male colleagues and acquaintances will probably have to be cool and guarded in order to prevent misunderstandings. As Ludmilla Tütung puts it in *The Traveller's Handbook*:

> 'Western women are regarded in most of the underdeveloped countries, and even in Southern Europe, as nothing better than loose women. If you want to avoid trouble you must listen to some unwritten rules.'

In order to assess your 'survivability ratio' it makes sense to find out from other women expatriates how they have fared in these situations, and ask them if they have any tips for you. Then ask yourself if you will be able to tolerate the restrictions you may be placed under.

SOURCES OF INFORMATION

Decisions on whether or not to take up a position abroad are often made on the basis of insufficient information. Ideally, a comprehensive **briefing** should form part of the decision-making process, but in practice this rarely happens until after the contract has been signed—if at all. It may therefore be up to you, the employee, to take the initiative. You could begin by:

- reading up about the location of your posting
- contacting people who have experience of the place.

Even if you have a good idea of what to expect, your landing at a foreign posting will feel much softer if you and your family are properly briefed before you arrive; and it is certainly in your employer's interest to ensure that you make the transition to your new environment as smoothly as possible. The Employment Conditions Abroad brochure points out:

> 'Insufficient briefing is one of the most significant causes of failure in expatriate personnel. Lack of adequate briefing for the spouses and other members of

the family also indirectly affects the performance of the organisation that employs them.'

Premature repatriation can prove an expensive business, but even so only a few employers brief their staff adequately before despatching them to another part of the world. Of course, if you have travelled the world before, any form of briefing may seem superfluous. However, if you have not lived in the country of your forthcoming posting, take nothing for granted. Indonesia is not the same as Singapore; Zaire is quite different from Zambia.

If no mention is made of a briefing session, it is a good idea to ask for one. A number of organisations have staff who are knowledgeable about the country to which you are to be posted, and it should be easy enough to arrange a meeting between you and them.

Some companies and organisations arrange their own briefings. Others will arrange for you to make a preliminary visit to the country before you commit yourself irrevocably. If the posting is to a European country this is an easy matter to arrange. If you are heading to Vanuatu, however, your employer might balk at the added expense.

Briefing Centres

Not all organisations have facilities to conduct proper briefings, and may offer you the chance of attendance at a **professional briefing centre**. Among the best known in the UK are:

The Centre for International Briefing, The Castle, Farnham, Surrey GU9 0AG. Tel: 0252-721194. This is the Rolls Royce of Briefing Centres—an independent, non profit-making organisation, which has been in existence for more than 35 years. It has an ongoing programme of residential briefing and communications skills courses, each of which covers one of five regions:

- The Middle East
- Asia
- Africa
- Latin America, the Caribbean and the Pacific
- North America

The courses last up to four days and consist of lectures and discussions led by people who have recent experience of working in the countries concerned, experts on the area, and nationals of the countries. There are also opportunities to meet others on an informal basis and to experience some aspects of the country's/ region's culture, e.g. its cuisine. The courses are normally based around the following themes:

- understanding the region and its people (historical, political and economic factors, religion, art, music, education, and so on)
- the country itself (geography, climate, politics, infrastructure, customs and social conventions)
- the working environment (economic and manpower resources, business methods, working relationships, and so on)
- the social and domestic environment or international negotiation skills.

The Centre also has an excellent bookshop offering a mail order service with a wide range of materials available of interest to people going abroad. Its resources centre contains an extensive range of published material (books and videos) on virtually every country in the world as well as reports on living conditions in a number of places written or recorded by former participants.

Employment Conditions Abroad Ltd, Anchor House, 15 Britten Street, London SW3 3TY. Tel: 071-351 7151. ECA is a non profit-making information and advisory service for companies employing expatriates or local nationals away from their home base. Apart from advising its members on terms and conditions of service, it publishes reports on living conditions in various countries and provides one day intensive briefings for company staff due to take up assignments abroad. These courses are designed to teach the skills necessary to be effective as a foreigner. They include:

- basic preparation (documentation, contract, health requirements, and so on)
- children's education at home and abroad
- financial matters and taxation
- the changing role of the spouse
- the host country (national aspirations, value systems, customs
- cultural awareness
- coping strategies
- planning ahead—the reintegration process

Howell & Associates, Hillside House, Pinewood Road, Ashley, Market Drayton, Shropshire TF9 4PR (Tel: 063087 2555) offers open and in-company courses in understanding and working with other nationalities developed in association with the Institute for Training in Intercultural Management in the Hague.

ITIM, Hillside House, Pinewood Road, Ashley, Market Drayton, Shropshire TF9 4PR. Tel: 063087-2555.

School of Oriental and African Studies (External Services Division), Thornhaugh Street, Russell Square, London WC1H 0XG. Tel: 071-637 2388. This can offer 'tailor-made' briefings on various countries in Africa, Asia and Eastern Europe—the latter in collaboration with the School of Slavonic and East European Studies. A language training component can form part of the course, if required.

Local Language and Export Centres. The Government has set up a national network of centres which offer country briefings, language courses and advice to businessmen planning to go overseas. The Adult Training Promotions Unit of the Department of Education and Science can provide you with the address of your local contact. Room 2/2, Elizabeth House, York Road, London SE1 7PH. Tel: 071-934 0888.

Women's Corona Society, Commonwealth House, 18 Northumberland Ave, London WC2N 5BJ. Tel: 071-839 7908. This organisation provides briefings, publishes a series of booklets entitled *Notes for Newcomers* on individual countries, and runs one day courses on living overseas for women who are about to go abroad to live.

FOCUS Information Services, 47-49 Gower Street, London WC1E 6HR. Tel: 071-631 4367. FOCUS can put employers in touch with recently returned expatriates to help them in the briefing of staff who are being posted abroad.

Christians Abroad, 1 Stockwell Green, London SW9 9HP. Tel: 071-737 7811. This organisation can arrange meetings with someone who has recently returned from the country you are going to.

Moran, Stahl and Boyer, 136 New Bond Street, London W1. Tel: 071-629 8222. MS&B is an American consultancy specialising in corporate relocation, and one of its divisions provides a service to help individuals and their families adjust to new locations, particularly overseas. It provides individually tailored expatriate training programmes.

Management Games Ltd, Methwold House, Northwold Road, Methwold, Thetford, Norfolk IP26 4PF. Tel: 0366 728215. This organisation has designed a half day training package entitled 'Working Abroad'. The aim of the exercise is to help participants improve their ability to adjust rapidly to a foreign environment and work more effectively with people in a foreign culture.

It is not always possible to arrange a full-blown briefing session before you leave however desirable this may be. In such cases you will have to rely on other sources of information such as bi-national cultural associations (such as the Anglo Austrian Society or the Society for Anglo Chinese Understanding), the Commonwealth Institute, the Royal Commonwealth Society, university departments specialising in particular regions of the world, and the national tourist offices.

Written information

Briefings and visits need to be supplemented by notes on living conditions in the country to which you will be posted. Some embassies in the UK provide notes or booklets along these lines, while certain organisations, such as the FCO and the British Council, produce such information for their own staff and appointees— but it may not be easy for members of the general public to get hold of these.

A series of 30-40 page booklets entitled *Expatriate Briefings* is produced and distributed by the Royal Commonwealth Society, 18 Northumberland Avenue, London WC2N 5BJ. Each booklet deals with a particular country and is updated every other year. The series covers countries in the Third World, but not North America or Europe.

Expatriate Briefings cover such topics as: background information on the economy, geography, history and climate; rules and regulations on immigration, work permits and health requirements; living conditions; working conditions; finance and money matters; family and domestic matters; education; health and insurance; transport and communications; culture and society; leisure and sport; basic facts; where to go for further information; a list of representative prices; a personal checklist.

Another worthwhile source of information is *Working Abroad*, G. Golzen (Kogan Page), which contains reports on over 40 different countries.

Location reports are also published by Inside Tracks, 10 Hartswood Road, London W12 2GQ.

The Department of Trade and Industry publishes a range of booklets on different countries entitled *Hints to Exporters*. Although not ostensibly for expatriate employees, they include some useful information on the countries in question (1 Victoria

Street, London SW1H 0ET). Finally, the following periodicals contain country reports and it might be worth trying to get hold of back issues dealing with the country you are off to:

The Expatriate, First Market Intelligence Ltd, 56A Rochester Row, London SW1P 1JU.

Home and Away, Expats International Ltd, 62 Tritton Road, London SE21 8DE. Tel: 081-670 8304.

The Multinational Employer (editor: Clare Hogg), Tolley Publishing, Tolley House, 2 Addiscombe Road, Croydon CR9 1AF.

CONTRACT CHECKLIST

Overseas employment contracts can be formidable documents and there is no standard format. You are advised to read through your contract carefully and, if necessary, take legal advice before signing. Generally speaking, a comprehensive set of terms and conditions is preferable to a short agreement which offers scope for different interpretations or misunderstandings. British employment legislation does not cover British people working in foreign countries; you are subject to the laws of the land you are working in. The following checklist may prove useful, although it does not claim to cover every eventuality:

- What is the name and address of my employer?
- Where precisely will I be working?
- What is my job title?
- What are the responsibilities of the job?
- Who am I directly responsible to?
- What is the commencement date and duration of my contract?
- Is the contract renewable (in the case of fixed contracts)?
- What is my net salary and how frequently is it paid?
- What other remuneration may I receive (e.g. overtime pay, bonuses, gratuity)?
- What hours will I normally be expected to work?
- What provision is there for paid leave?
- What provision is there for absence due to sickness?
- Do I have to work for a probationary period before being confirmed in the post?
- What are the accommodation arrangements (rent allowance, free housing, none)?
- How much notice does either side have to give to terminate the contract?

- What arrangements apply in the event of the premature termination of the contract by either side?
- What extras can I expect (fares paid to and from post, family allowance, company car or transport, and so on)?
- Which country's laws is this contract governed by (UK, USA, the country of employment)?

'... and what special skills can you bring to Canada, Mr Jackson?'

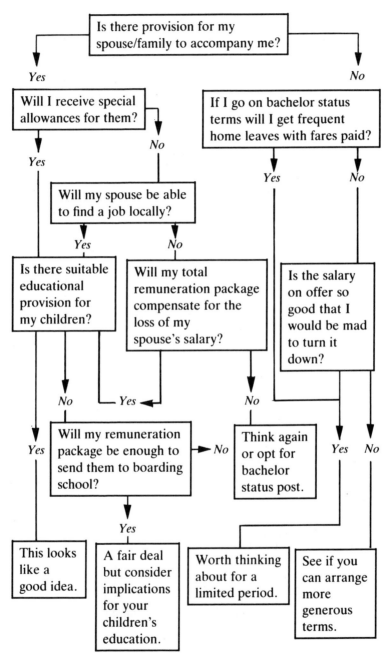

The decision-making process for a married person.

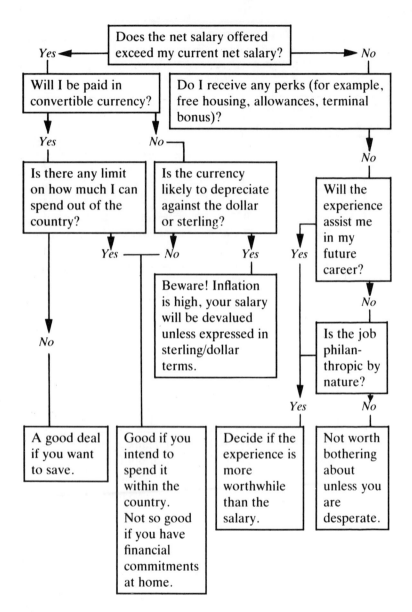

The decision-making process for a single person.

5
Preparations Before Leaving

If all you have had to prepare for in the past has been a holiday by the sea, the length of this particular chapter may seem daunting. Yet, just as you have to prepare for a holiday in Devon with care—especially if a whole family is involved—so you cannot perform all the groundwork necessary for an extended stay in foreign parts in just a few hours.

The shorter the time you will spend abroad and the fewer dependants that accompany you, the less preparation you will have to make. So I would suggest that you first skim through the chapter, make a note of all matters that will concern you, and jettison those that you can safely disregard. Then work out a timetable for the weeks between now and your date of departure.

Banking
Will you need a bank at your overseas posting? If so, it could save time on arrival if your own bank provides you with a **letter of introduction** to one in the country concerned. Whatever the case, you will need to visit your bank to:

- inform the bank that you are leaving the country
- leave a contact address
- obtain foreign exchange, travellers' cheques, or any other form of money both for your journey and to tide you over for the first few days in your new posting. Can you obtain cash with your credit card or charge card? Also, consider Eurocheques if you are going to Europe.
- transfer money
- make arrangements for the payment of bills and other financial commitments
- obtain financial advice (alternatively, you may prefer to

approach an independent financial adviser who is not connected with your bank. See the section on Finance.

Car

It always helps to have your own transport if you are going to be abroad for a long time, especially in a place where public transport is poor.

Begin by finding out if your employer will provide you with a company or official car at post, and, if so, whether the vehicle will be available for your own personal use. If the answer to both questions is 'no', then you should look into the following possibilities:

- **Buying a car** (either new or second hand) in the country of your posting. This is perfectly feasible in certain countries, but you need to find out about the state of the local car market before you leave! If on arrival you find there are no bargains to be had, it may be too late to opt for alternatives.

- **Taking your own vehicle**. This is quite sensible if your vehicle is in good condition and does not contravene any of the country's legislation—e.g. with respect to emission controls, and so on. The manufacturer or local agent should be able to put you wise on this. The position of the steering wheel might prove a problem for some people in countries which drive on the right, though the difficulties are not really as bad as some people would claim.

- **Buying a new vehicle in Britain and shipping it out.** This can be a sensible idea, since you can buy one in the UK free of VAT and may also be able to negotiate a discount. However, first you will have to find out about freight charges and import duties.

  When you choose a model, make sure that it will be suitable for the country you are going to. There is no point in buying a low slung sports saloon if you are going to a country where the roads are little more than tracks. Find out, too, which are the most popular makes of car in the country and which manufacturers are represented, so that you can obtain spares if necessary.

While on the subject of cars, it is also a good idea to apply to the AA or RAC for an international driving licence. While some countries accept a British licence—notably European Community countries—there are others that do not. *The Travellers Handbook* has details.

Clothing
If you are going to live in a country where the climate is markedly different, you will have to make changes to your wardrobe. Bear in mind that your clothing needs to be:

Comfortable
In warmer climates this means lightweight outfits, short-sleeved shirts, lightweight shoes, sandals, etc. If you are likely to spend a lot of time out-of-doors under the blazing sun, headgear is essential.

Appropriate
In many countries people dress more formally than we do in Britain, with suits commonly worn even in hot countries. In certain parts of the world women should avoid short dresses and skirts, and short-sleeved dresses and blouses, as these may offend.

Sufficient
In tropical countries, for instance, people tend to change their clothes more frequently, and you can never have too many items of underwear, shirts, dresses, pairs of trousers, etc. In cold climes, where the temperature may reach -25°C or less you will clearly need plenty of warm clothing.

Should you buy your clothes in the UK before you go, or wait until you get there? Clothing in the UK tends to cost less than in many other countries of Europe and shops offer considerable variety. However, in many Asian countries, for example, where wage rates are lower, you may well be able to have clothes made to measure more cheaply than in Britain.

Generally speaking it is easy to buy ready-made clothing in Europe, North America and Australasia. Elsewhere it is sometimes difficult to find garments in your particular size, particularly if you are well built. This is less of a problem for children.

Education
By now you should have decided on what provision you are to make for your children's education. If they are to move from their current educational establishments, you will need to search for appropriate schools either at home or abroad and send in an application as quickly as possible. If you delay, you may find the school is unable to accommodate your offspring (see Chapter 4).

FINANCE

Money matters are a very big topic, particularly if you are being offered what seems like a very good salary. But in order to benefit to the full from your time abroad you must keep two objectives in view:

- Minimise tax liability.
- Maximize the return on your investments.

Tax

The people that recruit you should be able to give you a general idea of your liability to tax in the UK and abroad, based on past experience. However, you need to do your own homework. Taxation is a complex matter and your liability for tax depends on a number of factors such as:

- how long you will spend abroad
- whether you will be abroad for a complete financial year
- who your employer is—UK based or overseas based
- taxation practice in the country of your posting.

In order to find out your precise UK tax position, the best course of action is to:

- Contact the **Inland Revenue**—either the local office or The Claims Branch, Foreign Division, Merton Road, Bootle L69 9BL—for information. The IR publishes a number of leaflets of relevance, notably Booklet IR 25 which sets out the rules governing the taxation of income from jobs overseas.
- Read **up-to-date books** on personal finance for expatriates, such as *The FT Guide to Working Abroad*, D. Young, (Financial Times Business Information), and articles in expatriate journals such as: *Expatxtra, The Expatriate, Home and Away, Resident Abroad, Middle East Expatriate, Far East Expatriate,* and *Investment International.* A number of expatriate finance advisers, including banks, also produce booklets which explain the expatriate's tax liability, such as *The Allied Dunbar Expatriate Tax Guide*.
- Seek **advice**, preferably before you go. A good adviser may be able to suggest ways of modifying your compensation package in order to reduce liability to tax. Make sure, however, that your adviser has experience in advising expatriates. Many such advisers advertise in the various expatriate magazines, but a colleague or your employers may be able to recommend one.

Remember: good advice is likely to save you money in the long run.

Investment

Many people find that they are able to put away money during an overseas assignment. If this is the first time in your life that your earnings will exceed your expenditure, you will want to find a sensible way of investing the surplus. You need to think along the following lines:

Short-term investments
You need to have some reserves in ready cash in case of emergencies, and this generally means an investment account with a building society, bank or other reputable financial institution. Go for an account which offers a high rate of interest and withdrawal facilities on demand.

If your salary will not be subject to UK income tax, go for an expatriate account where interest is not taxed. Banks in offshore tax havens, such as the Isle of Man and the Channel Islands can provide such services, but your own bank or building society may well have the facilities you require.

Long-term investments
If you reckon that you will have cash that will not be needed for a few years, it will probably be worth your while to invest it in equities. This is, of course, riskier—but the rewards can be much greater, and this definitely holds true the longer you keep your investment. In any case, risks can be minimised by achieving a spread of investments—in unit trusts, investment trusts, personal equity plans or managed currency funds, for instance. Investment in property, commodities, and individual companies is not to be recommended to a beginner. The exception is if you are buying your own home, but you need to make sure that it is fully insured and looked after in your absence.

Investment advice

Unless you are already a sophisticated investor, you should ideally get advice on investments right from the start rather than pick them out with a pin. The reason for this is that individual needs differ, and an investment package which is ideal for a bachelor in Bahrain might be inappropriate for a married couple in Malawi.

People heading abroad for the first time do not usually begin considering investment until they have already built up reserves, and this is perfectly understandable. But rather than rely on local expertise, try and find an investment adviser either based in a country where the financial services industry is tightly regulated (such as the UK, Jersey, Guernsey or the Isle of Man) or who is associated with a firm of international repute. It is important to understand the difference between an independent adviser and one who is tied to the products of a particular company:

- An **independent** adviser is committed to offering a client the best buy over a whole range of competing products and therefore needs to be particularly knowledgeable.

- The **'tied'** adviser will only offer you the products of his particular company. Most of the banks in the UK, for instance, only offer their own range of investment plans.

Outside the UK one needs to beware of offshore investment companies that claim to be independent, but tend to recommend the products of the company offering them the best commissions, regardless of whether these products are also the best on the market for their clients. One needs also to beware of so-called 'telephone salesmen' who sell non-existent shares to expatriates.

It is better to be safe than sorry, so my advice is to *check the credentials* of any investment adviser or firm before you take the plunge. Approval by the Securities and Investment Board is a good sign, and the *Financial Times* listings specify which offshore funds have SIB authorisation. Organisations such as the Expatriates' Association may also be able to advise on advisers.

Health

To be beset by poor health for the duration of your tour is no joke, but with careful preparation you can avoid such problems. For, while in many countries health standards are as high as they are in the British Isles, in others they may leave much to be desired. Here are a few suggestions:

- Obtain a copy of Leaflet SA40, *Before you go*, and Leaflet SA41, *While you're away*, from the Department of Health. If you will be travelling through an EC country you should also obtain Form E111.

- Make sure you are fit and properly equipped; have a dental check, a sight test (or a spare pair of spectacles made), a chest X-ray, and a medical check up. Several employers insist on this as a condition of employment. Even if they do not, it may be wise to consult your GP as to your general state of fitness.

- Have a prescribed course of vaccinations. Smallpox vaccinations are no longer required, but for certain parts of the world you will need to be vaccinated against:
Cholera (two injections at least 10 days apart)
Yellow fever (a single injection)
Typhoid (two injections a month apart)
Infectious Hepatitis (a single injection just before you leave).

For details of which vaccinations you need you should consult:
The Department of Health leaflets
The Traveller's Handbook (WEXAS)

Medical Advisory Services for Travellers Abroad Ltd (MASTA).
This organisation can provide details of your vaccination and other medical requirements for a modest fee. (Address: Bureau of Hygiene and Tropical Diseases, Keppel Street, London WC1E 7HT. Tel: 071-631 4408).

Your General Practitioner will probably be able to vaccinate you, but you may find it more convenient to use one of the following:

British Airways Vaccination Unit, 75 Regent Street, London W1R 7HG. Tel: 071-439 9584. In addition BA in conjunction with MASTA operates the British Airways Advisory Service for Travellers Abroad (BAMSTA) with travel clinics throughout the UK, including one at the Hospital for Tropical Diseases. Tel: 071-831 5333.

Thomas Cook Vaccination Centre, 45 Berkeley Square, London W1A 1EB. Tel: 071-499 4000.

- Arm yourself with items of medicine which you may possibly need such as:

anti-diarrhoea pills	sun lotion
indigestion pills	antiseptic cream
travel tablets	anti-insect cream (e.g. Flypel)
anti-malarial pills	basic dressings
aspirin	

Advice on which you will need is given in the literature mentioned above.

- Buy a book on how to keep healthy. Examples are:

Travellers' Health, Dr Richard Dawood (OUP).
Preservation of Personal Health in Warm Climates (Ross Institute).
The Tropical Traveller, John Hatt (Pan).

Your house

If you are going abroad for only a brief period, your main concern will be to ensure that it is properly looked after while you are away. These days, alas, it is inadvisable to leave a house empty for any length of time because of the possibility of break-ins and worse; so if possible, ask a neighbour or friend to keep an eye on it for you, and perhaps inform the local police that the residence will be empty. If you are going to be away for a year or more, there are two options that you might think about:

Find a tenant

Many expatriates plump for this solution, since it ensures that the house is occupied and it provides income which will cover the rates, mortgage repayments, upkeep, and so on. It also provides a base that you can return to.

However, remember that some tenants are far from perfect; they can cause damage, withold rent, and may try to stay put when you return. Also beware of letting agents; whilst most are fine, not all of them are reliable. Take out a legal protection insurance policy if you have qualms about letting your house.

Sell the house

If you do this, you are at least spared the worry of what may be happening to your property, and can invest the proceeds. In the past, however, people have usually found that the rise in the value of their investments has not kept pace with house price inflation. So whether you benefit or lose on the deal is very much a matter of timing.

Insurance

There are four types of insurance that you need to consider:

1. **Health and accident insurance**—this is particularly vital if there is little social security provision in the country where you will be working and your employer does not provide it. There are a number of organisations specialising in expatriate health care, among them:
   BUPA Expacare, 102 Queen's Road, Brighton BN1 3XT. Tel: 0273-23563.

Citihealth International, Citycorp Insurance Brokers, 30-33 Minories, London EC3N 1DD. Tel: 071-488 1388.

Europea IMG, Fivash House, 9 Denne Parade, Horsham RH12 1JD. Tel: 0403 63860.

Exeter HAS, 5 & 7 Palace Gate, Exeter EX1 1UE. Tel: 0392 75361.

PPP, Crescent Road, Tunbridge Wells TN1 2PL. Tel: 0892 40111.

2. **Personal effects insurance.** Loss or damage to personal effects.

3. **Car insurance**, if appropriate. Note that your current insurer may not be equipped to provide cover for you on some distant shore and you may either have to look for one that does or use a local insurance company.

4. **Life insurance**, if you have dependants. The basic 'no frills' type is quite adequate.

For all of these it pays to consult a good financial adviser or broker who specialises in insurance for expatriates. Many advertise in the expatriate magazines mentioned in the Finance Section, or can be recommended by organisations such as the Expatriate Association.

Language learning

If you are going to a country where English is not widely spoken you may find it frustrating that so few people understand you. One solution is to try and learn the local language before you arrive. There are various ways of doing this:

Teach yourself

You can buy a **language teaching manual**. Increasing emphasis is put on the spoken language these days, and many manuals are accompanied by cassettes. If you cannot find a suitable course at your local bookshop, try an academic bookshop or one of the following organisations that either publish or distribute language courses:

Hugo Language Books Ltd, Old Station Yard, Marlesford, Woodbridge, Suffolk IP13 0AG.

Audio Forum, 31 Kensington Church Street, London W8 4LL. Tel: 071-937-1647.

BBC Books, 80 Wood Lane, London W12 0TT. Tel: 081-576 2536.

Linguaphone, St Giles House, 50 Poland Street, London W1V 4AX. Tel: 071-734 0574.

Programmed Instruction Language Learning (PILL), World of Learning, Springfield House, West Street, Bedminster, Bristol BS3 3NX.

Teach Yourself Books, Hodder & Stoughton Educational, Mill Road, Dunton Green, Sevenoaks, Kent TN13 2YA. Tel: 0732-450111.

Routledge, 11 Fetter Lane, London EC4P 4EE. Tel: 071-583 9855 (*The Colloquial Language* Series).

Mind Management, 23 Sycamore Avenue, Hatfield, Herts AL10 8LZ. Tel: 07072-64163.

Take a course
Many local colleges provide part-time courses in the more common languages. In London and other large centres the range of languages taught is quite considerable. If you have difficulty finding the course you need, contact the coordinating office for the Government sponsored Language Export Centres—PO Box 1574, London NW1 4NJ. Tel: 071-224 3748.

A number of universities and polytechnics have their own language centres which offer facilities for casual students, including the School of Oriental & African Studies (External Services Division), Thornhaugh Street, Russell Square, London WC1H 0XG. Tel: 071-637 2388, and the Language and Communication Centre of King's College, Strand, London WC2R 2LS. Tel: 071-836 5454 ext 2890.

Countries like Austria, France and W Germany have their own cultural institutes in London and elsewhere which offer language tuition; and there are many private language schools which offer courses as well. Among the best known with branches around the country are:

Berlitz, 321 Oxford Street, London W1A 3BZ. Tel: 071-580 6482.
Linguarama, 53 Pall Mall, London SW1Y 5JH. Tel: 071-930 7697.
British Language Institutes, Broome House, 152 Palatine Road, Didsbury, Manchester M20 8QH. Tel: 061-434 7475.

However, there are several smaller language training organisations dotted around the UK which can provide a tailor-made service, including the Centre for International Briefing. Your local *Yellow Pages* will offer details of the one nearest you.

Alternatively, you could consult *Where and How*, an international guide to language centres published by the Wie and Wo Verlag, Postfach 2464, D-5300 Bonn 1, W Germany (UK Agent:

Geoffrey Kingscott, Praetorius Ltd, 5 East Circus Street, Nottingham NG1 5AH. Tel: 0602-411087).

The National Institute of Adult Continuing Education, 19B De Montfort Street, Leicester KE1 7GE, Tel: 0533-551451, publishes a list of residential language courses in the UK.

Find a tutor
Many colleges can put you in touch with private tutors while private language schools may be able to provide one-to-one tuition on their premises which may form part of an open-learning package.

For further information on language learning consult the Centre for Information on Language Teaching and Research. This organisation publishes Language and Culture Guides which contain information on courses in less commonly taught languages and a leaflet entitled *Part-time and Intensive Language Study*. Address: Regent's College, Inner Circle, Regent's Park, London NW1 4NS. Tel: 071-468 8221.

Luggage and personal effects
If you are travelling by air you will normally find that you can't take everything with you, unless your employer happens to be remarkably indulgent. Some of your luggage can probably be sent by air-freight in advance—which is much cheaper than the excess baggage rate—while the rest may have to be sent by sea or overland—which works out even cheaper.

Don't forget that however good your planning is, there is little likelihood of you and your personal effects all arriving at the same time. So make sure that you take with you essential household items and clothes which will keep you going for the initial period.

If you intend to sell the house and disappear from these shores for a number of years, then you will have a full-scale removal operation on your hands. You will need to take some of your things with you; others will have to be put into storage. You may decide that certain items are not worth the cost of storage, in which case it would be wise to sell them. For advice on removals and freight forwarding contact:

British Association of Removers (Overseas Group), 277 Grays Inn Road, London WC1X 8SY. Tel: 071-837 3088.
Institute of Freight Forwarders Ltd, Redfern House, Browells Lane, Feltham, Middlesex. Tel: 081-844 2266.

National Insurance

Will you have to make National Insurance contributions while you are abroad, or will you be expected to contribute to the social security fund of the country in which you will be working? You will have to find out before you go.

The best plan is to contact the Overseas Branch of the Department of Social Security, Newcastle upon Tyne NE98 1YX, or your local office, stating where you are going and for how long. The Department will then send you the relevant leaflets, such as leaflet NI 38, *Social Security Abroad.*

If you are going to work within the European Community, Leaflet SA 29 explains your social security and pension rights in the other countries of the Community. There are other leaflets dealing with individual countries with which Britain has reciprocal social security agreements. These include several European countries, North America, Australia, New Zealand, Jamaica and Mauritius. The European Scene is also covered comprehensively in Howard Foster's *Employment Benefits in Europe.*

Passport

Make certain that your passport is still valid. If it isn't, get an application form from your local post office, but remember that you and your dependants who are accompanying you will need a *full* passport, not just a visitor's one. If the passport expires in a matter of months it is sensible to renew it anyway. Time may be pressing, in which case to avoid delay you may have to pay a visit to your regional Passport Office. Their addresses are:

Greater London: Clive House, 70 Petty France, SW1H 9HD.
Scotland: 1st Floor, Empire House, 131 West Nile St, Glasgow G1 2RY.
Northern Ireland: Marlborough House, 30 Victoria St, Belfast BT1 3LY.
Northern England: 5th Floor, India Buildings, Water St, Liverpool L2 0QZ.
Wales and Western England: Olympia House, Upper Dock St, Newport NP1 1XA.
Midlands and Eastern England: 55 Westfield Rd, Peterborough PE3 6TG.

Pension

Is your job pensionable? In the case of many contract posts it probably isn't, but you will receive a gratuity at the end of your term in lieu of a pension contribution. You should therefore consider taking out a personal pension scheme which offers maximum flexibility with payments. Whether it should be a UK-based scheme or an international plan will depend on how long you are likely to remain abroad. As for your state pension, you can continue to make contributions on a voluntary basis (see National Insurance Leaflet NI 38).

If you are a permanent employee in a company pension scheme, you may wish to continue the arrangement. However, you need to find out whether this is your best option when discussing the terms and conditions of your posting abroad. Not all company schemes cover expatriate employment—particularly extended assignments—and in some circumstances you could benefit by opting out of the company scheme and making your own pension contribution arrangements.

David Harrison, of Hall Godwins (Overseas) Consulting Co, suggests that individuals look for the following features when assessing expatriate pension plans:

- **Security**. You require a reputable insurer and fund manager.
- **Contributions**. There should preferably be no limits at all with maximum flexibility to increase, reduce or stop contributions.
- **Build Up**. This should be gross of tax on investments—preferably 100 per cent or with major relief.
- **Benefit Design**. Complete flexibility is required with 100 per cent cash or annuity/cash options. Provision for irregular payments is useful.
- **Tax on benefits**. Ideally there should be some relief on benefits.
- **Investment choices**. Although a wide range of choices is useful, some people prefer the security of a *with profits* or *guaranteed* fund.
- **Charges**. These should be as low as possible, but it is unrealistic to expect none.

Mr Harrison goes on to point out:

'If you are looking for high quality independent advice on pension planning matters, you will need to take great care in selecting an adviser. The following questions for your adviser may help you to distinguish genuine specialists in retirement planning:

- Does your firm work for employers as well as for

individuals? If an adviser is working for an employer that is a good sign.

- Does your firm employ or have access to actuaries? The actuary does not have to be employed directly by your adviser—but his willingness to call on one is an important test of his quality.
- How large or long established is your firm?
- Can I pay fees? In retirement planning it is a good sign if you can pay fees for professional advice, usually with a rebate of commission.
- Does your firm employ expatriate financial planners? What is their experience? You need to be sure that your adviser combines a pension capability with general expatriate financial planning.'

Clearly it is not always possible to track down a firm which fulfils all these criteria. Nevertheless, a financial adviser is not a person to be chosen lightly, otherwise you could be the loser.

Shopping

Some prospective expatriates go on a wild shopping spree before they leave as if they are going off to a remote corner of the world where shops do not exist. When they arrive, they realise that a good many of their purchases were not really necessary and that some of the items are actually cheaper locally.

A seasoned expatriate, on the other hand, finds out what he *really* needs to buy before he takes the plunge. There are basically three reasons for buying items before you go:

- They are unavailable or in short supply in your adoptive country.
- They are much more expensive there than at home.
- They are going to be needed immediately upon arrival.

To avoid unnecessary purchases, it makes sense to find out about the availability and price of goods at your posting if possible. Consult someone who has recently returned from the country, or the lists available from Expatriate Briefings, the Women's Corona Society, the British Council, ODA, and the relevant foreign embassies or high commissions based in London.

If you are buying expensive items, you will probably be able to get them free of VAT provided you deal with a store which is au fait with the tax-free export scheme. Certain items, such as cameras, radios, or cassette players could be purchased en route at an airport duty-free shop. But do make sure that you will not be subjected to hefty customs duties on entry, otherwise your bargains may not seem such bargains!

Below is a rough list of items which you might find useful but which are not always readily obtainable abroad, and may therefore be worth taking with you:

- corkscrew/bottle opener
- mug and plate
- clothes line and pegs
- electric kettle/boiling jug
- torch
- knife, fork and spoon
- portable radio capable of receiving short-wave broadcasts
- thermos flask
- electric plug adapter
- universal bath/washbasin plug
- can opener

Travel

Most overseas employers will provide you with an economy class air ticket, and many will also provide tickets for your dependants. If your employers are reluctant to do this, ask for the fare equivalent in cash and contact an agency like WEXAS which sells fares at a discount. Many of them advertise in the classified columns of national dailies.

Other modes of travel—by sea or overland—are normally out of the question, except in the case of Europe and perhaps North Africa—unless you have plenty of time at your disposal. In Europe sea and rail travel have one advantage over air insofar as you can take much larger amounts of luggage with you, at little or no extra cost.

If you have a car, car travel is another very sensible option within Europe. Even distant locations such as Turkey can be reached easily in a few days. But if your insurance policy is limited to the British Isles, inform your insurance company; you will either need a green card before you go, or long-term alternative arrangements for your insurance may be necessary.

Visas and work permits

Unless you intend to do only casual work, or are bound for a European Community country, you will need to get a visa before you go. In the case of some countries this can be a time-consuming process, so it makes sense to find out well in advance exactly what you have to do to get one. Generally speaking, you will have to use one of the two following systems:

System 1: You take your employment contract or a letter of appointment from your employer to the consular section of the appropriate Embassy together with your passport and several passport size photographs. You may also need some or all of the following:

- birth certificate
- marriage certificate
- educational documentation—diplomas, certificates, and so on
- a certificate of good conduct
- a medical certificate

In order to avoid a wasted journey, ring the consular section in question to enquire precisely what is needed. This process can be a lengthy one if the embassy has to contact the immigration department or labour department back home.

System 2: Your employer applies for the work permit which he sends to you. You take this to the consular section with other relevant documentation for processing. Theoretically, this is a much speedier method, but do not count on it!

If you have any sort of official status (for example, if you are going to be employed directly by the government of the country or an international organisation there), the visa application is little more than a formality.

If you plan to travel overland or stop en route, check whether you will also need visas for the countries you pass through. *The Traveller's Handbook* (WEXAS) contains information on this score. If you have any problems getting visas for travel, your travel agent may be able to assist you for a fee.

XYZ—A FINAL CHECKLIST

- Cancel the milk, newspapers, subscriptions, and so on.
- Pay the water, telephone, electricity, and gas bills and inform the companies of what is happening.
- Make your will.
- Arrange for the redirection of mail—by the post office (for a fee) or by your tenants.
- Ensure that you have made provision for your pets. The local RSPCA may be able to advise. If you are planning to take them

with you, contact the International Society for the Protection of Animals for advice (106 Jermyn Street, London SW1Y 6EE). Remember that on their return to the UK they may be subjected to a period in quarantine.

- Inform your next of kin, bank manager, solicitor, tenants, insurance company and other interested parties of your new address.
- Get plenty of passport photos made of yourself and your dependants.
- Confirm arrival arrangements and ask for contact telephone numbers at your destination in case of emergency.
- Buy a phrase book, guide books and maps of the country. *The Traveller's Handbook* (WEXAS) is useful if you will be travelling around.
- Prepare an inventory of your personal effects for customs.
- If you are not taking your car with you make arrangements for storage with a friend or garage.

(Insert artwork 1 here)

6
The First Month Abroad

Your first few weeks in your new posting are crucial ones, and will set the tone for the rest of your stay. It is a time of hectic activity when you are busy making arrangements and meeting new faces. Not only are you getting to grips with your new job, but you are also trying to adapt to new social and domestic arrangements. It's not surprising, therefore, that it is also a time when less seasoned expatriates experience a measure of stress!

Stress caused by a sudden change of location is often described as **culture shock**. However well you prepare for your overseas assignment, the sudden change of environment could well have unpleasant repercussions, albeit temporary ones.

CULTURE SHOCK

Culture shock can take a number of forms:

- **Strain**. Adapting to your new environment often involves considerable effort.
- **Sense of loss and deprivation**. You miss familiar faces, places and objects and suffer from a sense of anonymity. You feel homesick.
- **Feeling of rejection**. You reject your new environment or the new environment seems to be rejecting you. You refuse to learn the language or adapt to local customs.
- **Confusion**. You are confused as to your identity and how to behave in a culture with different values and customs to your own.
- **Anxiety, disgust, and indignation**. As you develop awareness of the cultural differences, you react negatively to the way people behave. You get angry about bureaucratic delays.
- **Feelings of impotence**. You feel unable to cope with your new environment and shut yourself off from it.

Culture shock can manifest itself in the form of head-aches, lassitude, and even rashes, but it should eventually pass. However, it is no use expecting your bout of shock to disperse of its own accord. It is up to *you* to make a positive effort to come to terms with your new surroundings.

Adaptation: a five phase process

It is not uncommon for newcomers to go through five phases before they begin to feel at ease:

1. The honeymoon stage. The beginning of your tour is rather like a holiday. You are fascinated by the novelty of your new surroundings and are enthusiastic about the people you meet.
2. Crisis and disintegration. After a while the initial euphoria wears off and you may start to feel inadequate and depressed.
3. Reintegration. You regain your self-esteem, but only by rejecting or finding fault with the surrounding culture.
4. Autonomy. As you develop an ability to cope with the new culture socially, and perhaps linguistically, you become more relaxed and empathetic.
5. Independence. You feel at home in your new surroundings, and accept the differences.

THINKING POSITIVELY

To counter or overcome the worst effects of culture shock you need to concentrate from the outset on creating a friendly personal environment. You will find that you settle down more easily if you strive for:

* a comfortable home base
* a satisfying job with good interpersonal relationships
* good companionship ―Get laid ✓!
* a full range of leisure interests.

Let's look at these one by one.

Accommodation

Many people are put up in hotels on arrival, but hotel life—even if you are put in the Hilton—tends to jar after only a short time. The best plan, therefore, is to move into more permanent accommodation as soon as possible, if your stay is to be an extended one, and especially if you are accompanied by your family.

Some people can choose their accommodation; others have no

choice. Instead they are allocated housing, perhaps in a company compound, which will vary from the luxurious to the downright seedy. It has to be admitted that housing standards depend greatly on the location; while in one country you might have a villa with a swimming pool, in another you might have to be content with a small flat. If you are dissatisfied with your accommodation, find out what the normal standard is for expatriates in similar jobs to yourself before you complain.

If you have to find your own accommodation, so much the better. However, it is a good plan to ask fellow expatriates for advice on the most suitable areas to live, and then proceed with care. That elegant residence you take a liking to at first sight could prove to be a nightmare when it rains, when the water pipes run dry, or at night when you find your residence is in the red light district. Points to check are:

- How safe is the area?
- Where are the nearest shopping facilities?
- (If you have children) How far is it from an expatriate school?
- How easy is it to get to your workplace?
- Are the utilities good—are there likely to be any power cuts, water cuts and so on?
- What is included in the rent—furniture, telephone, and so on?
- What extras do you have to pay for—for example, night watchmen, or a concierge?
- How good is the heating/air conditioning?
- Is it large enough to entertain visitors in?
- Is the area liable to flooding or other environmental hazards?

If possible, get your employer to sign the contract and pay the rent direct to the landlord. Otherwise, you could find yourself having to pay a hefty premium in order to secure the house or flat.

The main consideration is: *Do you feel comfortable and at ease in the accommodation?* At times you will need a refuge from the pressures you have to face—a place where you can relax and be yourself. Make an effort to select the right sort of accommodation first time round. If you keep on chopping and changing your residence, as some expatriates do, you will never feel at home.

Your job

Starting work in a foreign environment has certain similarities with starting a new job in a new organisation at home. Your first objectives therefore must be to find out:

- how the organisation works
- who is responsible to whom
- the extent of your responsibilities
- what support is available to you
- when and how you are to be paid.

Sooner or later, however, you will recognise that there are differences—sometimes subtle, sometimes glaring—between the way the foreign organisation operates and what you would regard as normal practice back home. So in order to start off on the right foot you need to get rid of any preconceptions you may have, and apply yourself to learning the ropes.

In some organisations, you will experience a happier landing than in others; you may be offered an induction period as a matter of course. On the other hand, you could find yourself tossed into the hurly-burly right from the start with little or no explanation of how things work and what is expected of you. If you are in a senior position, your subordinates may well assume that you know it all, and so no induction is considered necessary.

Unless you *do* happen to know everything, try and find some-one who can put you into the picture. If, for example, there are other expatriates in the outfit who have been through the same process in the past, you may be able to turn to them for advice. However you would be wise to follow Polonius' counsel to Laertes:

'Give every man thine ear, but few thy voice;
Take each man's censure but reserve thy judgement.'

If you are the only expatriate in the organisation, you may feel you have no-one to turn to. Local staff are often hesitant to provide the information you really need until they have got to know you well, and it takes time to build bridges between cultures. But you will build your bridges more quickly and effectively if you approach the task in the right way. Employment Conditions Abroad offers seven useful tips designed to facilitate cross-cultural communication, which will also apply to any accompanying dependants trying to fit in:

- **Communicate respect.** Demonstrate a positive regard for the country and its people, be encouraging and show interest in them.
- **Be non-judgemental**. Don't make moralistic, value-laden, evaluative statements.

- **Personalise knowledge and perceptions**. Recognise that values, perceptions and knowledge (including your own) are relative rather than absolute.
- **Display empathy**. Try to understand the other person's point of view by putting yourself in his or her position.
- **Practise role flexibility**. Try to reach your goals in a manner and time-scale appropriate to the other culture.
- **Demonstrate reciprocal concern**. Take turns in talking and thus promote circular communication.
- **Tolerate ambiguity**. Accept a degree of frustration in order to deal with different circumstances and culture.

Companionship

Man is a social animal, and few people set off abroad intending to live the life of a hermit. The luckiest people are those who have a partner or family that they can take with them, as they will have someone to confide in, and share their experiences with.

An unattached person, on the other hand, needs to find companionship. However, if you have lived in the same locality for years you may have lost the knack of striking up new friendships. So what do you do?

The answer is to build on existing relationships if you can. Normally if you spread the word at home that you are off to Helsinki or Honolulu, someone you know is bound to recall that he has a cousin three times removed who has been living there for years, and will suggest that you look him up. Don't hesitate. Take his address and drop by at the earliest opportunity.

Making casual visits may sound out of keeping to anyone brought up on the principle that an Englishman's home is his castle. However, you will probably find that in foreign climes most British people drop their reserve and positively welcome visitors, while many other nationals are used to spontaneous fraternisation as a matter of course. Strike up a few acquaintances and it will not be long before you find yourself on the party circuit. Your first friends are likely to be expatriates, just like yourself, and you are most likely to meet them:

- at work
- in local hotels
- in clubs
- at church.

Even if you do not have strong religious feelings, you may well find that expatriate life revolves around the church, and the local parson may be a useful contact or, if needed, a source of comfort. The church may also provide a welcome for newcomers. For example, if you have Anglican leanings, you could contact the Overseas Resettlement Secretary, Board for Social Responsibility, Church House, Dean's Yard, London, SW1P 3NZ, and the board can provide a contact for you at your destination. Christians Abroad can also suggest contacts.

The local expatriate community can be tremendously supportive, but try not to restrict yourself to expatriate circles and remain aloof from the world about you; life will be more rewarding if you can strike up friendships with local people as well. However, it is wise to study local etiquette first of all to avoid making any embarrassing *faux pas*.

Some people go to the other extreme and 'go native', dressing up in national costume and trying to emulate their lifestyle to the letter. Such behaviour seldom finds favour with other expatriates or, indeed, with the local people themselves. Far from being flattered that you are trying to adopt their ways, they might turn suspicious or give you the cold shoulder.

One of your best plans is to make contact with local people who have lived or studied in Britain. Most will be able to observe their country through British eyes and will therefore be well placed to help you adapt to your new circumstances. They will be keen to hear of the latest trends in Britain and be only too happy to regale you with their own experiences.

Don't be so eager to establish friendships that you throw caution to the wind. In camp type situations, especially, you need to be circumspect. There is usually a bad apple or two who can cause problems, for example through borrowing money from all and sundry and then disappearing on leave with his debts unpaid.

Women abroad
Many countries of Southern Europe and the Third World have not really come to terms with the idea of the liberated woman yet, so women—especially single women—need to be careful in their relationships with the opposite sex. Perhaps the two most important or basic tips are:

● Dress modestly.
● Avoid looking men straight in the eye.

If you can, find out from other expatriate women with experience of the country exactly how you should behave to avoid trouble. You may find it safer to stick with the stuffy expatriate community than embark on adventures of your own. One compensation in expatriate communities is that single women are much in demand at parties. *Travelling Alone—A Guide for Working Women* by Roberta Bally (Macdonald Optima) has some useful general advice for women.

Leisure interests

Some people never get beyond the second or third phase of culture shock. For them an overseas posting is a penance, and they spend long hours wishing they were back home.

It's true that not every job abroad is a dream posting, but even if it is dull and tedious, there are usually some benefits to be derived from the experience. If you have plenty of leisure time at your disposal—and this is especially valid for accompanying partners—make sure you do not waste the opportunity. By keeping active mentally, physically and socially your posting abroad might turn out more rewarding than you ever imagined it could be. Here are a few suggestions as to how you might use your spare time:

Get to know the country.
Travel around it, read about it, attend lectures and cultural events. There are plenty of good guide books on the market these days including the *Fodor, Baedeker, Insight* (Harrap), *Michelin* and *Rough Guides* (RKP) series. Lonely Planet, c/o Roger Lascelles, 47 York Road, Brentford TW8 0QP (Tel: 081-847 0935) and Bradt Enterprises, 41 Nortoft Road, Chalfont St Peter, Bucks SL9 0LA, publish a selection of books on off-beat destinations.

Learn the local language.
There are usually language courses on offer for expatriates, at least in the capitals. Otherwise you should be able to find a private tutor. Not only will this help you to communicate effectively, it will keep the little grey cells working.

Do a course.
This could stand you in good stead in the future. Contact distance learning organisations such as the Open University or Association of Correspondence Colleges in the UK to find out what is available. Alternatively, you may find that there are part-time courses at institutions in the country to which you have been posted.

Join a club.
There are all kinds of clubs from the ubiquitous British Clubs with their own premises (that have usually seen better days) to international clubs and special interest clubs with no premises of their own. Dramatic societies, choral societies and Rotary Clubs seem to exist everywhere.

Take up a sport or other outdoor activity.
It is important to keep fit and active, and there are sporting opportunities even in the most unpromising circumstances. You will come across improvised golf courses in the desert and tennis courts with barely a passing resemblance to Wimbledon. A number of expatriates use the opportunities afforded by their surroundings by taking up hobbies such as bird-watching or archaeology.

Communications
Fortunately, life is much easier than it was, for example, three generations ago. Even if you are in a very remote spot you are not cut off completely from the world outside—that is, unless you want to be. Communications have improved. No longer does mail take months to reach you—except perhaps in the case of St Helena—and telecommunications have progressed in leaps and bounds.

Many expatriates tune into the broadcasts of the BBC World Service, Voice of America or Radio Australia, all of which can be received clearly on short wave transistor radios. The local British Embassy or British Council office should have the BBC's monthly programme bulletin—entitled *London Calling*—or you can subscribe to the publication by applying to the BBC World Service, Bush House, Strand, London WC2.

Other matters
There will be plenty to do shortly after arrival, and it is sensible to make a checklist of all the matters that you will need to attend to. This is likely to include some of the following:

- register with the embassy/consulate in case of a future emergency and to secure your voting rights at home
- arrange banking facilities
- register your children with a school
- notify the police/local authorities of your place of residence
- obtain a residence visa/work permit

- register your car (if imported)
- obtain a directory of local services
- enquire about language course facilities

Your employer should be able to advise you on bureaucratic matters. If not, try other expatriates, the Embassy, or your landlord.

Experienced expats recognise the benefit of expending plenty of effort in the initial stages in order to get their affairs straightened out quickly. If you manage to launch yourself successfully, you will find that your life will turn out to be relatively trouble-free. You are less likely to be troubled by culture shock ... or dypsomania!

WHEN THINGS DON'T WORK OUT

Dissatisfaction with the job

This book has tried to help you avoid the pitfalls associated with employment abroad, urging you to do some soul searching and to look closely at what is involved *before* you take up a position. Yet however much care you exercise as you prepare, you have to face up to the possibility that things will not turn out as planned.

Your duties may prove to be very different from what you had been led to expect. Your employer may not seem to be fulfilling some of the clauses in your contract. Your accompanying spouse may find it impossible to come to terms with the new environment. You may have reservations about how the organisation is run. What should you do in circumstances like these? You have certain simple choices:

- Carry on regardless.
- Walk out.

Clearly, if you find your work a thankless chore, you are unlikely to give of your best, and a period of stagnation is not going to help your career. On the other hand, breaking a contract can prove costly, both from your point of view and from that of your employer. At worst you might have to forfeit your salary, pay your fare home and face a compensation claim.

Try, instead, to find a solution to these problems. Contact the people that recruited you—or your boss in the UK (if you are on secondment), explain what is wrong, and ask if they can mediate on your behalf. If the answer is 'no', then you will have to go it alone—not always an easy task.

This means talking matters through with a person in authority and attempting to reconcile your differences. If you have been genuinely misled as to the nature of the work, you may well be given a sympathetic hearing. If, on the other hand, you complain about terms and conditions that are not even mentioned in the contract, then you will find yourself on less firm ground.

If you do decide to leave your post prematurely, make sure you have reasonable grounds for doing so. These would include:

- Ill health
- Failure by the employer to honour the terms of your contract
- Job is not compatible with your experience or status
- Domestic problems

Try, above all, to have the contract terminated by *mutual agreement*, if only to avoid costly litigation procedures.

Dismissal

The fact that you are working abroad is no guarantee that sooner or later you will not lose your job, whether you are on contract or have a 'permanent' position.

As in the UK, firms periodically reorganise their staffing structures to achieve greater efficiency, and this sometimes means slimming down the organisation and making people redundant; and, as in Britain, firms—particularly newly established ones—sometimes go bust.

Such occurrences can be particularly worrying when you are working in an unfamiliar environment far from home. Most importantly, you will probably expect some form of compensation—and ideally terms should be mentioned in your contract. If, on the other hand, the company or organisation for which you are working goes into receivership, you may find no payment at all is forthcoming.

Another eventuality you have to face up to is that your employer may be dissatisfied with you for some reason. Common grounds for dismissal are:

- absenteeism
- professional misconduct
- insubordination
- poor workmanship
- activities incompatible with your status.

If you believe you have been unfairly dismissed, you may well want to take the matter to court. Keith Edmonds of Expats International recounts how an EI member working in Libya was dis-

missed by his Libyan employer and took his case to the local
People's Court. He conducted his own case against the employer,
using an interpreter, and won, though Edmonds admits he was
very lucky; don't assume that all court judgements decide in the
employee's favour. Indeed, employment legislation in some countries is heavily weighted in favour of the employer, and so you
would be wise to seek advice before embarking on costly litigation.

The local British Consulate will be able to provide you with a
list of English speaking lawyers, but will not be able to offer legal
advice itself or institute legal proceedings on your behalf. Members of Expats International and the Expatriate's Association
should contact these organisations for free advice on problems of
this nature. You might also try your trade union or professional
association back in the UK to see if they have a sister organisation
in the country that can help you.

If possible, try to leave your ex-employer on reasonably
friendly terms. You may require a reference from him in future or
in certain countries a letter of release from his employ.

Other problems

In a foreign location problems often seem more complicated to
resolve than they do at home. This might be because you are
unfamiliar with the way things work, because there is a language
problem, or because you feel isolated from the people and institutions you know best.

If something serious happens, it is vital to inform the nearest
British Consulate which should be able to advise you or offer
assistance (citizens of other countries should contact their own
national consulate). Such help can be invaluable in situations such
as:

- Entanglement with the law. If you are arrested on any charge,
  you should insist on the British Consulate being informed.
- Civil disturbance and war. It is advisable to register with the
  Consulate on arrival. Then, if violence breaks out, the Consulate can try and keep you informed of the situation and, if
  necessary, arrange for your evacuation.
- Death or accidents. The Consulate can arrange for the next of
  kin to be informed and advise on procedures.
- Financial emergencies. Consulates can offer advice on the
  transfer of money, cash a sterling cheque supported by a
  banker's card and—as a last resort—make a repayable loan for
  repatriation to the UK.

- Theft. This should be reported to the police and a statement obtained. If your passport is lost or stolen, report the loss to the Consulate right away so that an emergency passport can be issued.
- Illness. The Consulate can provide a list of local doctors and hospitals. However, it is in no position to reimburse medical costs.
- Voting. Under the Representation of the People Act 1989 UK citizens may register as overseas voters in constituency in which they or their family were registered before leaving UK. The qualifying period is up to 20 years and the consulate will have forms and an explanatory leaflet. The consulates of other countries provide similar services to the above mentioned for their citizens.

It might well be a good idea to get hold of a leaflet entitled *Consular Assistance Abroad*, published by the Foreign and Commonwealth Office.

The staff of the British Consulate will usually be able to
help out in an emergency.

7
Moving On

Some years ago it was normal for a person to stay at his posting for most of his life and return to England for good only when the time came to retire. Nowadays, that kind of job is practically extinct, and a person who thought he had landed a permanent position in Tahiti or the Bahamas gets a shock when he learns, two years later, that he has been transferred to London or Timbuctoo.

If you *are* on the permanent staff of an international company or organisation, don't become too attached to a particular country or region. In this age of the international executive, many head offices take the view that a long posting in one place is bad for an employee's career. Contract staff are only too aware that if they become too closely associated with one particular country or part of the world, they could have difficulty in moving on. In the Third World in particular, expatriate jobs have a finite life, and when after several extensions your contract finally does come to an end, you could find it hard to land a new one elsewhere. The fact that you have spent 15 years in the Yemen may not impress selectors if you apply for a position in Derby or Dortmund.

Returning home can be every bit as traumatic as leaving Britain for some foreign land was; so this chapter examines the problems that a person may encounter at the end of a foreign tour and offers a few words of advice.

The career employee
The permanent employee has one advantage over the contract expatriate: his job and salary do not terminate when the posting abroad finishes. Yet the advantage does not lessen the problems of what is technically known as 're-entry'—your return to home base.

Not only will your outlook be broader than that of most of your colleagues, but you will also have the problem of adjusting to no

106

longer being a big fish in a small pond. As Clare Hogg of *The Multinational Employer* observes:

> 'Temperamentally, those employees who cope with the challenges of a foreign assignment often do not function equally well within the security of headquarters.'

...and, furthermore:

> 'The new head office position may well not have the same status and autonomy as the overseas posting.'

Clearly, the problem of readjustment is worse for people who have been away for several years. Some companies and organisations have schemes for reintegrating expatriate staff, but many more still need to address themselves to this problem.

Whether you are to get help with 're-entry' or not, the International Committee of the Institute of Personnel Management has some useful suggestions. The key is to think ahead and consider the problems you could face. Here are some key tips:

Take time to wind down properly.
Don't rush things. It will take time to acclimatise yourself and find your feet. A holiday or a training course might be sensible options.

Assess and review the change in yourself and those at home.
The likelihood is that the Britain you knew has changed. Perhaps the topics of conversation are different, the fashions have altered or a new political climate may have emerged.

Gradually re-establish relations with friends, relatives and professional contacts.
People you once knew may regard you as a stranger, and have formed new friendships of their own. They could be startled if you appear as a bolt from the blue.

Plan long and short-term goals along with strategies for achieving them.
These could include setting up a new home, improving your qualifications, or even changing career direction.

Accept that you will probably suffer from some reverse culture shock, particularly of an organisational, financial and psychological nature.
For example, your income is likely to go down, you will have to face the horrors of the British climate, and the outfit you have worked for may have changed beyond all recognition.

(The key points come from the Institute of Personnel Management, the comments are the author's.)

What if you don't want to return or move on? This is a dilemma which faces certain people who become very attached to the country where they have been working. One solution is to resign and join another company or organisation that will allow you to stay on.

For younger people this is quite a sensible step; the modern trend is for employees to chop and change jobs rather than to stay with one organisation for the whole of their career. But if you are older, there could be disadvantages, particularly financial ones, and you should consider your position very carefully. One way out could be to persuade your organisation to offer you early retirement; you might even then be able to branch out on your own.

The contract employee

If you are on a contract, you could have similar problems of adjustment. Perhaps the Britain you knew has disappeared for ever; perhaps the place is dirtier than you expected it to be; perhaps the people seem less friendly and outgoing than your colleagues in foreign parts.

But you also may have one other problem; you have to find a job. Even if you have amassed a small fortune during your contract, you will probably manage to spend it more quickly than you imagined, particularly if you do not qualify for 'perks' like unemployment benefit.

Plan ahead to avoid such problems. You need to embark on your job search some six months before your contract comes to an end. This involves:

- Perusing the job advertisement columns in newspapers and specialist journals. You may be able to inspect a few of these at your local Embassy/Consulate or at a British Council Library.

- Contacting recruitment agencies and asking to be placed on their register of candidates.

- Sending off speculative applications to companies and organisations you know.

- Writing off to contacts—colleagues, professional associations, trade unions, former employers—indicating that you are thinking of making a move and inviting suggestions.

- Taking out a subscription to a bulletin of vacancies, such as those mentioned in Chapter 2 and the Bibliography. If you are interested mainly in UK jobs, the *Intel Jobs Abstract* may prove helpful.

- Advertising your forthcoming availability in a few carefully chosen periodicals.

OPTIONS AT THE END OF A CONTRACT; STAYING OVERSEAS

The contract employee has one advantage over a permanent employee; he can choose where to go next. However, his choice will be determined to a certain extent by what work is actually available. A contract employee is much more likely to be affected by fluctuations in the job market than his colleague with a permanent job. You may be keen to continue working abroad, in which case you have the following options:

Renewing your contract

If you have been successful at your work you will probably be encouraged to renew your contract, especially by the locals who have got used to you. From your point of view, you will be spared the upheaval of moving on, and so will your family (if you have one).

But you need to look at your contract extension in terms of your long-term career—particularly if you are young and need to gain varied experience. Is there any benefit in staying on—in the form of a pay rise or increased responsibility? If you stay too long in one place, you could get stuck in a rut and find it impossible to relocate successfully if a time comes when you have to.

Finding another job in the same country

During your time in your current posting you should have made many useful contacts and become familiar with the local economy and jobs market. You may well be aware of opportunities that you could try.

Don't be put off by the fact that the job is in a slightly different field, or that your qualifications are lower than those specified for a particular vacancy. Such deficiencies are compensated for by your knowledge of local conditions, which an outsider could not possibly have.

Finding another job abroad

If you enjoy the expatriate life, but feel the need for a change, this could be your best option. There is much to be said career-wise for gaining experience in a completely different part of the world—perhaps moving from South America to Japan, or from Africa to Europe.

However, from the personal point of view, a move like this means considerable upheaval, and you will have to come to terms with a new way of life and experience culture shock all over again. Fortunately, you should be better able to cope with this the second or third time round, and when you are briefed on your new location, you will know exactly what sort of questions to ask.

Setting up your own business

In certain countries this is a possibility, though in many countries you may need a local partner. Some expatriates have been known to solve this problem by marrying a local, although you do not necessarily have to go to such extremes!

Make sure, however, that you are aware of all the legal implications. In certain countries the red tape that would-be foreign entrepreneurs have to cope with is horrendous; you will also have to remember that if your chosen country is politically unstable you risk having your assets seized.

RETURNING TO BRITAIN

On the other hand, you might decide that your roving days are over—at least for the time being—and opt to return home. If so, you have the following choices:

Finding a job in Britain

If you happen to be on leave in Britain a year or six months before your contract terminates, it is sensible to begin your job search then. Visit organisations and agencies that might be interested in your experience or would be able to help, or write to them suggesting an interview with no obligation on their part. Remember that employers and agencies will often be much more willing to deal with a person writing from an address in the British Isles than someone in far away Kiribati.

If you have not fixed yourself up with a job before your return, don't panic! You should have made some contacts by now and perhaps received invitations for a few interviews. If not, you will need to really get down to the job hunt in earnest.

Having a sabbatical

If you have spent the past few years in an isolated spot you may well have lost touch with some of the latest advances in your particular discipline, and need to catch up. Alternatively, you may decide that you want to change career direction altogether. In both cases, you will probably need a period of study.

If you do not feel you can manage a full-time course, remember that there are many alternatives, such as a correspondence course with the Open University, a part-time course at Birkbeck College, London University, or a part-time/correspondence MBA course organised by Warwick University and Wolsey Hall.

British Council offices around the world have a good deal of useful information on educational courses like these, and either the librarian or education officer should be able to help you. Local university and college libraries are another source of such information. Among the useful reference books are:

Higher Education: Finding your Way (Department of Education and Science).
University Entrance—The Official Guide (Association of Commonwealth Universities).
Opportunities in Higher Education for Mature Students (CNAA).
Training and Educational Opportunities for Adults (COIC, Moorfoot, Sheffield S1 4PQ).
Second Chances, A. Pates and M. Good (COIC).
Part-time Degrees, Diplomas and Certificates (CRAC, Bateman Street, Cambridge CB2 1LZ).
Gabbitas-Thring Guide to Independent Further Education in the UK (Northcote House).

If you are keen to do a full-time course but are uncertain whether you will have enough money, find out if there are any grants you can apply for. Send off for the Department of Education and Science leaflets *Grants to Students* and *Postgraduate Awards* or consult *The Grants Register* (Macmillan). Here are some useful addresses:

Council for the Accreditation of Correspondence Colleges, 27 Marylebone Road, London NW1 5JS. Tel: 01-935 5391.
City and Guilds of London Institute, 76 Portland Place, London W1N 4AA. Tel: 01-580 3050.
The Open College, Suite 470, St James's Buildings, Oxford Street, Manchester M1 6FQ. Tel: 0235-555444 in England, 041-334 3141 in Scotland.

University Central Council on Admissions (UCCA), (PO Box 28), Cheltenham, Glos GL50 1HY.
Polytechnic Central Admissions System, (PO Box 67), Cheltenham, GL50 3AP.
Educational Guidance Services for Adults, ECCTIS, (PO Box 88), Walton Hall, Milton Keynes MK7 6DB.
Birkbeck College, Malet Street, London WC1E 7HX. Tel: 01-637 9563.
Secretary for External Students, University of London, Senate House, Malet Street, London WC1E 7HU.
The Open University, Walton Hall, Milton Keynes MK7 6AA. Tel: 0908-74066.

Setting up in business

This is the age of the entrepreneur as far as Britain is concerned, and a number of people returning to Britain consider going free-lance or starting their own business. However, running a business is never as easy as it looks and you need to be adept at matters such as marketing and book-keeping. You also need to begin with sufficient capital to keep you going for at least a year. It can be a struggle at first, and a substantial proportion of small businesses fail.

Don't be afraid to get advice, which is freely available from a variety of sources, including your local enterprise board and the Small Firms Business Unit of the Department of Trade and Industry (Telephone: 'Freephone Enterprise'). One of the following books would also be useful:

Going Freelance, G. Golzen (Kogan Page, 1989).
The Entrepreneur's Complete Self Assessment Guide, D. Gray (Kogan Page, 1987).
Starting a Business, R. Hargreaves (Heinemann, 1987).
The Little Business Book, P. Hingston (Hingston, 5 The Roundel, Auchterarder, Perthshire PH3 1PU, 1988).
A Guide to Franchising, M. Mendelsohn (Pergamon, 1984).
Is Self Employment Right for You? (Open College, 1988).
Starting the Business (Open College, 1988).
Occupation—Self Employed, R. Pettit (Wildwood House, Gloucester Mansions, Cambridge Circus, London WC2H 8HD, 1981).
The Co-operative Bank Guide to Running Your Small Business, A. Porter (Holyoake, 1988).

Starting Your Own Business, Edited by E. Rudinger (Consumers Association, 1988).
Small Business Kit, D. S. Watkins (National Extension College, 1981).
The Guardian Guide to Running a Small Business, C. Woodcock (Kogan Page, 1987).

Guidance for the returnee

What if you are not sure what to do? If you have lived outside Britain for a number of years, your homecoming could prove a perplexing experience, and you might suffer culture shock in reverse.

If you are employed on a permanent basis, ask your organisation whether there are any counselling services available. The personnel departments of several large organisations employ qualified counsellors who should be able to help you re-acclimatise. If not, you could look into the possibility of finding your own professional counselling. The British Association for Counselling, 37A Sheep Street, Rugby, Warwickshire CV21 3BX, Tel: 0788-78328, may be able to suggest someone from its Counselling at Work Division. There are also the 'Back to Britain' conferences organised by Christians Abroad, designed to assist people with their repatriation.

The type of counselling you need will depend very much on your age and circumstances. Younger people may need an idea of the career choices open to them or of how to improve their career prospects. More mature people need to review their current situation and establish what they should or could be doing in the future. There are various forms of careers counselling/guidance available including:

- Job Clubs and Executive Job Clubs organised by or on behalf of the Department of Employment's Training Agency. Contact Job Centres for details.
- Local authority careers offices (most of these are only equipped to deal with school leavers)
- Careers Guidance departments in universities, colleges and polytechnics (some offer counselling or counselling courses to outsiders)
- Independent careers counsellors. The British Association for Counselling may be able to suggest a suitable person in your locality, or you could try *Yellow Pages* under 'Careers Advice'.

Careers counsellors for private clients include the following:

Career Analysts, 90 Gloucester Place, London W1H 4BL. Tel: 071-935 5452.

Career Assessment Services, Melbourne House, Melbourne Street, Brighton BN2 3LH. Tel: 0273-675299.

Careers Advisory and Business Services, 223 Prescot Road, Aughton, Ormskirk, Lancs L39 5AE. Tel: 0695-423576.

Career Counselling Services, 46 Ferry Road, London SW13 9PW. Tel: 081-741 0335.

Career Development Centre for Women, 97 Mallard Place, Twickenham, Middlesex TW1 4SW. Tel: 081-892 3806.

Chusid Lander, 25-37 Fitzroy Street, London W1P 5AF. Tel: 071-580 6771.

Connaught Executive Management Services Ltd, 32 Savile Row, London W1X 1AG. Tel: 071-734 3879 (Contact: J. F. Hyde Blake).

Executive Management International, Landseer House, 19 Charing Cross Road, London WC2H 0ES. Tel: 071-930 5041.

Fletcher Hunt & Associates, Premier House, 77 Oxford Street, London W1R 1RB. Tel: 071-434 0511.

GHN, 16 Hanover Square, London W1R 9AJ. Tel: 071-493 5239.

Independent Assessment & Research Centre, 17 Portland Place, London W1N 3AF. Tel: 071-935 2373.

Mainland Executive Services, Elizabeth House, 22 Suffolk Street, Queensway, Birmingham B1 1LS. Tel: 021-643 2924.

Mid-Career Development Centre, 77 Morland Road, Croydon CR0 6EA. Tel: 081-654 0808.

MSN Career Services, 18 Lloyd Street, Manchester M2 5WA. Tel: 061-834 8104.

SAS Methven Ltd, 32A Weymouth Street, London W1N 3FA.

SCS, Chislehurst Business Centre, 1 Bromley Lane, Chislehurst, Kent BR7 6LH. Tel: 081-467 0267.

Styra Partnership Ltd, 51 Lincoln's Inn Fields, London WC2A 3LZ. Tel: 071-831 8772.

Vocational Guidance Association, 7 Harley House, Upper Harley Street, London NW1 4RP. Tel: 071-935 2600.

This list is by no means complete and inclusion on the list does not imply recommendation. Note also that some of these organisations also operate a job finding service, sometimes called 'outplacement or inplacement'. Also worth mentioning in this context is Intex Executives, Chancery House, 53–64 Chancery Lane, London WC2A 1QZ, an agency specialising in temporary assignments for retired executives, independent consultants, people between jobs, and so on.

Preparing to leave

This is in many senses a re-run of Chapter 5—only in reverse. Yet that does not mean it will be any easier! There are the same practical matters to attend to before you start your homeward trip—removals, travel arrangements, coping with bureaucratic matters, and so on—and it will again pay you to plan your moves with care. Do not forget the following points:

- Give advance notice to the tenants of your house in Britain if you intend to use it as your base.
- Give notice to your current landlord, if necessary.
- Put your financial affairs in order so as to avoid paying UK tax on your return. If, for example, you have non resident status in the eyes of the Inland Revenue, try, if possible, to remain out of the country until the end of the financial year—usually early April.

- Pay bills, any income tax due, and so on. You may be unable to leave certain countries unless you can satisfy the customs that you have discharged all your debts.
- Obtain an exit visa, if necessary.

8
Short-Term Opportunities (Up to One Year)

'I'd like to work abroad but...'

There are plenty of people who are tempted to become expatriates, but are hesitant to take on a lengthy commitment in a foreign country. Are you one of them?

If you are young and committed to a career in the UK, you feel you will lose out if you stay out of the country too long. On the other hand, your work and family obligations may make it impossible for you to uproot yourself for anything more than a brief period. But the idea of living and working abroad for a while still appeals to you—not necessarily for monetary reasons, but as a means of broadening your experience.

Perhaps you should be thinking about a *short-term assignment.* It does not involve any great upheaval, and if you have little or no experience of working abroad, it offers an opportunity to decide whether you are cut out for this type of life. If, after testing the water, you find that you are, you may then decide to opt for a longer spell in a foreign land (in which case, you will need to read the following chapters).

Young people who have yet to start on their careers proper should have no hesitation about getting temporary work in a foreign country, no matter how humdrum or unimportant it might seem. National boundaries are starting to tumble, particularly in the case of Europe, and the top managers of the future will be those people who have a well engrained international outlook, perhaps gained back in their student days.

More mature employees can also benefit from international exposure. Indeed, a short-term overseas assignment can be a sensible career step for virtually anyone, provided you are adequately prepared.

It is also an option for people who may have retired, but who do not want to turn their backs on the world of work entirely. Mention that you are interested in short-term assignments abroad to your former employers or your other contacts, and there is a chance that they will remember you if something urgent crops up.

Many people find the best short-term jobs through personal contact rather than through advertisements. If you have business or professional contacts abroad, ask them to keep an eye open for you. Alternatively, find out if your locality has any twinning scheme with a town or region in another country. Such schemes usually operate an educational exchange programme and may foster business and employment links as well.

WORKING HOLIDAYS FOR YOUNG PEOPLE

The majority of advertisements for jobs abroad lay great stress on the need for experience, and this may seem unfair to anyone who is only just starting in the world of work.

However, there are ways round the difficulty. If you are in your teens or early twenties there are a number of schemes designed to help you travel and live in other countries for a short while without having to go through masses of red tape to get in. Most of them are vacation jobs, and none of them pays well. Indeed, you may well have to make some financial contribution yourself; the idea is that the experience you gain is more important than the pay.

For a fairly comprehensive list of such opportunities, your best bet is the **Central Bureau for Educational Visits and Exchanges**, or **Vacation Work International**.

The Central Bureau, Seymour Mews House, Seymour Mews, London W1H 9PE, publishes an annual guide entitled *Working Holidays* and recruits for exchange programmes in a number of countries.

Vacation Work International, 9 Park End Street, Oxford OX1 1HJ, publishes two summer jobs bulletins which are sent free to members. This organisation also arranges working holidays and publishes and distributes a number of other handbooks on jobs overseas aimed at students and young people. These include:

Directory of Summer Jobs Abroad (edited by David Woodworth)
Summer Employment Directory of the US
Emplois d'Été en France

Vacation-work opportunities can be summarised according to the following categories.

Domestic work

During the holiday season hotels, restaurants and holiday centres in the major resorts take on extra staff as kitchen assistants, cleaners, waiters and chambermaids. This can be hard work, with long hours, and poor pay, but tips or bonuses could compensate for the drudgery. When looking for such jobs, you could try these sources:

- advertisements in the job directories mentioned above
- local tourist boards who can put you in touch with establishments which take on extra staff
- a friendly travel agency

Vacation Work International can place you in jobs in German and Swiss hotels. But if you turn up in a European resort on spec early in the holiday season there is always a chance that somebody will take you on.

Farm work

At harvest-time farmers need to take on casual staff for fruit picking and other agricultural work. The work is often physically tough and the accommodation basic, but you are likely to find yourself working with people from all parts of the world. While it is certainly possible to turn up 'on spec' in the hope that there will be jobs going, it might be more sensible to arrange something in advance. Among the organisations that can arrange placements are:

British Universities North America Club (BUNAC), 232 Vauxhall Bridge Road, London SW1V 1AU.
Vacation Work International (grape picking in France and Switzerland).
GAP Activity Projects, 7 King's Road, Reading, Berks RG1 3AA. Tel: 0734-594914.

Work camps

'International work camps are a form of short-term voluntary service providing an opportunity for people of different racial, cultural and religious backgrounds to live and work together on a common project providing a constructive service to the community.' (The Central Bureau)

Normally, they are for young people aged 16 plus, and the work can include building, gardening, decorating, conservation, constructing adventure playgrounds, and providing roads and water supplies to villages in the Third World. They offer opportunities in places as far apart as Canada and Cape Verde, Bulgaria and Bangladesh. A typical workcamp will have between 10 and 30 volunteers from several countries, and participants usually have to arrange and pay for their own travel. Contact:

Concordia Ltd, 8 Brunswick Place, Hove, W Sussex BN3 1ET. Tel: 0273-772086.
Christian Movement for Peace, Hilton's Chambers, Roushill, Shrewsbury, Salop. Tel: 0743-65983.
International Voluntary Service (a branch of Service Civil International), 3 Belvoir Street, Leicester LE1 6SL. Tel: 0533-541 862.
Quaker Work Camps, Friends House, Euston Road, London NW1 2BJ. Tel: 071-387 3601.
Tear Fund, 100 Church Road, Teddington, Middlesex TW11 8QE. Tel: 081-977 9144.
United Nations Association, International Youth Service, Welsh Centre for International Affairs, Temple of Peace, Cathays Park, Cardiff CF1 3AP. Tel: 0222-28549.

For information on work of this nature in Israel, consult *Kibbutz Volunteer*, John Bedford (Vacation Work Publications).

Children's holiday camp leaders
Opportunities exist in both North America and Europe for camp leaders/camp counsellors at children's holiday camps. This involves looking after the general welfare of the children and organising activities for them. Useful addresses include:
BUNAC (see above)
Camp America, 37 Queen's Gate, London SW7 5HR. Tel: 071-589 3223.
TOC H, 1 Forest Close, Wendover, Aylesbury, Bucks HP22 6BT. Tel: 0296-623911.
YMCA International Camp Counsellor Programme, Fairthorne Manor, Southampton SO3 2GH. Tel: 04892-5228.
Euroyouth Ltd, 301 Westborough Road, Westcliff on Sea, Essex SS0 9PT.

Au pair work
The primary purpose of this arrangement is to enable single women aged 18 plus to live with a family in another country in

order to study their language and way of life. In return for doing certain household chores, you are offered accommodation and pocket money. While some arrangements are for 6 months or a year, there are also holiday au pair posts which often involve accompanying the family on a vacation. If you like children, are prepared to cope with light domestic chores, and possess a certain amount of maturity, you could find the experience well worth while.

An invaluable guide to the 'ins and outs' of these arrangements is given in *The Au Pair and Nanny's Guide*, Susan Griffith & Sharon Legg (Vacation Work Publications, 1989).

Other opportunities for young people

Some young people find they have a gap to fill between school and college; the option of a 'year off' is becoming increasingly popular. At one time it was possible to join an organisation such as VSO, but today volunteer organisations tend to recruit only people with qualifications and experience.

The more sophisticated may decide to travel the world, in which case Susan Griffith's *Work your Way around the World* (Vacation World Publications) will prove a useful guide. On the other hand, you might want to stay in one place. The following books also contain useful advice:

A Year off (Careers Research and Advisory Centre/Hobsons Ltd, Bateman Street, Cambridge CB2 1LZ).
Jobs in the Gap Year (Independent Schools Information Service, 12A-18A Princess Way, Camberley, Surrey GU15 3SP).

Finally, here are a few organisations you might contact:

GAP Activity Projects Ltd, 7 King's Road, Reading, Berks RG1 3AA. Tel: 0734-594914. Work opportunities abroad for 250 school leavers annually lasting, from 4 months to 1 year, in conservation, farm work, domestic work, general office work and as teachers' aides in Europe, India, South America and Australasia.

The Project Trust, Breacachadh Castle, Isle of Coll, Argyll PA78 6TB. Tel: 08793-444. A scheme for 130 British school leavers under which they spend a year abroad in the Third World and Australia as teachers, teaching aides, health workers or 'jack-aroos' at sheep and cattle stations.

Youth Exchange Centre, Seymour Mews House, Seymour Mews, London W1H 9PE. Tel: 071-486 5101. Offers the opportunity to do

6 months' voluntary work in hospitals, old people's homes, community projects, and so on, in Germany.

Britain-Australia Vocational Exchange Scheme. Administered by CRAC (address above).

Exchange schemes

Exchange schemes are intended to be both educational and a form of career development. Some of these are run by professional associations, while others are more official in nature.

The Central Bureau for Educational Visits and Exchanges (see address above) offers the following schemes:

- Language Assistant Exchange Scheme: This is a scheme which sends students (usually modern language students) and young teachers abroad to work in schools and colleges in Europe and certain countries in South America and Africa.

- Teacher Exchange Scheme: These are exchanges for experienced teachers for one, two or three terms in various European countries and the USA. The positions in Europe are usually for modern language teachers.

The League for the Exchange of Commonwealth Teachers, Commonwealth House, 7 Lion Yard, Tremadoc Rd, London SW4 7NF, arranges exchanges for teachers in all subjects with Commonwealth countries.

The Royal College of Nursing, 20 Cavendish Square, London W1M 0AB, Tel: 071-409 3333, also has a scheme to enable its members to gain experience abroad under the ICN Exchange Programme (See **Medical Services** in the reference section).

The Young Farmers' Centre, National Agricultural Centre, Kenilworth, Warwickshire CV8 2LG, Tel: 0203-29645, organises a scheme for young farmers called the International Farm Experience Programme. The International Agricultural Exchange Association, at the same address, has a similar scheme (see **Agriculture** in the reference section of this book).

Seasonal work

When you talk of seasonal work, you are often thinking in terms of the travel and tourism industry which experiences a personnel explosion during the holiday months.

Many of the posts are taken up by students since they happen to be available during late June, July and August, but there are certainly opportunities for more experienced people as well—particularly those who are available for the whole season. It may even be possible to arrange two consecutive seasonal jobs to keep you occupied through the year—for example, at ski resorts in the winter and at summer resorts for the rest of the year.

Remember that Europe is not the only place for seasonal work. You can pick up work on a casual basis in places like Australia at harvest time or in hotels and restaurants for part of the antipodean summer—which is our winter! For more information, turn to the sections on **Tourism and Travel** and **Hotels and Catering** in the reference section of this book.

Relief work

A number of organisations require skilled professionals at comparatively short notice to assist with disaster relief operations often only for a matter of months. The following list gives an idea of what skills are needed:

British Red Cross Society, International Aid Department, 9 Grosvenor Crescent, London SW1X 7EJ. Tel: 071-235 5454. This organisation needs experts in health, engineering, logistics, development work, and so on.

Bureau for Overseas Medical Service, Africa Centre, 38 King Street, London WC2E 8JT. Tel: 071-836 5833. This is not a recruitment agency as such, but maintains a candidate register and acts as a clearing house for various relief agencies that need medical personnel at all levels. Many of the posts on offer are at mission hospitals. The Bureau also offers medium-term opportunities and publishes a bi-monthly newsletter, *News and Jobs*.

Oxfam, 274 Banbury Road, Oxford OX2 7DZ. Tel: 0865-56777. People are needed for emergency relief operations and as advisers in community health, agriculture, engineering, social studies, and so on. Contracts last for three to six months.

Save the Children Fund, Mary Datchelor House, 17 Grove Lane, London SE5 8RD. Tel: 071-703 5400. The chief need here is for medical personnel.

REDR—Engineers for Disaster Relief, 25 Eccleston Square, London SW1V 1NX. Tel: 071-828 2600. REDR maintains a register of experienced engineers in all fields who can be called upon at short notice to fly out to a disaster area to provide technical support for relief agencies. Contracts are from two weeks to six months. As the organisation's brochure explains:

> 'REDR engineers must be adaptable to tough living conditions and ingenious in their approach to problem solving. They must have proven patience and tenacity and be sensitive to other people's different attitudes and cultures.'

Volunteer work

Volunteer agencies such as VSO and IVS tend to recruit for a minimum of two years. However, other organisations are prepared to accept volunteers—even inexperienced ones—for a much shorter period, and some of these are listed below:

Action Health 2000, 35 Bird Farm Road, Fulbourn, Cambridge CB1 5DP. Tel: 0223-880194. International voluntary health association operating in South Asia and Africa; contracts for three months and longer; age range 18 plus.

Help the Aged, St James's Walk, London EC1R 0BE. Tel: 071-253 0253. Requires 20 volunteers (principally medical specialists) annually to work in Africa for 6 months.

United Kingdom Foundation for the Peoples of the South Pacific, Edward King House, The Old Palace, Lincoln. Tel: 0522-28778. Sends personnel off to help with village development projects, health and nutrition programmes, small business and co-operative development. Six to twelve months.

Universities' Education Fund for Palestinian Refugees. Helping in children's homes and kindergartens for a minimum of three months. Age range, 20 to 40.

World Community Development Service (Educational Visits Scheme), 27 Montagu Road, Botley, Oxford OX2 9AH. Tel: 0865-725607. Rural development in India and Sri Lanka; six to twelve months; no academic qualifications necessary.

Short assignments

Short assignments tend not to be advertised, since it is not particularly cost-effective for an organisation to do so. Besides, companies of any size probably have a network of contacts or a register of candidates to fall back on. One way in, therefore, is to send details of your experience and availability to such organisations, or approach an agency that specialises in the recruitment of temporary staff for abroad.

Computer personnel, nurses, doctors and secretaries are in particular demand for short-term placements, see **Appendix B** for details of specialist recruitment agencies.

Short-term consultancies

For experienced people opportunities arise to do consultancy work, and this is often a matter of being in the right place at the right time...or on someone's register. Your professional association may keep such a register. Otherwise try getting in touch with organisations operating in your field to see if they have any freelance work. Useful organisations include the following:

British Executive Service Overseas, 10 Belgrave Square, London SW1X 8PH. This is a voluntary sector organisation that sends retired businessmen on two to six month assignments to developing countries to advise small and medium sized businesses. The organisation which is funded by ODA, industry, and commerce, pays all expenses plus a small allowance.

Consult Project Research, 110 Underwick Road, Crouch End, London N8 9JY. This is an organisation which operates a database of consultants for projects in a wide range of subjects in the Third World (see **Consultancy**).

Overseas Development Administration

In addition to offering one and two year contracts, the ODA (see next chapter) sometimes has a requirement for highly qualified experts to go out for short assignments to different parts of the Third World. Such opportunities may also occur with organisations such as the British Council (education), UN agencies and Crown Agents.

9
Medium-Term Opportunities (One to Three Years)

The majority of people who go to work abroad do so on contract terms, and the most common contract is for between a year and three years. Some contracts are on projects that have a finite life—construction projects, aid schemes and the like. Other contracts may be more open-ended with a possibility of renewal until the time comes when a local national is able to take over responsibility.

It is possible to make a career out of a succession of contracts, in the same way that an actor does; but there is an inherent insecurity in this way of life, and as a consequence people with growing families often prefer a position offering greater permanence and security. In the following sectors a high proportion of the jobs on offer are on contract terms:

- **Education**. A very high proportion of teaching and training jobs are on contract terms—and this is particularly true in the case of teaching English as a foreign language.

- **Construction**. Construction projects by their very nature are temporary. They consist of teams of people recruited for a particular project—the Channel Tunnel, for instance—and while some of the top managers may well be permanent members of their companies, the majority of jobs are contract posts.

- **Technical cooperation**. Virtually every job connected with aid programmes, whether you are working for one of the voluntary organisations or as a technical expert with the UN, will only last for a finite period of time.

- **Health care**. There are opportunities for doctors, nurses and others involved in the medical field throughout the world—administrators, paramedics, medical technicians, and so on.

- **Oil and gas industries**. This is a very wide field which includes exploration, production and refining both on land and offshore. A wide range of talents is needed.

- **Mining**. This is another important sector employing a wide range of skills, though the opportunities—certainly at the tradesman level—have diminished in recent years.

The major recruiters for contract posts include the following organisations.

Government organisations
Overseas Development Administration, Abercrombie House, Eaglesham Road, Glasgow G75 8EA. Tel: 03552-41199. The ODA, which is responsible for administering Britain's aid programme, recruits around 225 people annually from a wide range of disciplines for contracts in the Third World. Normally a good degree is required plus substantial postgraduate experience gained in a Third World environment. Its terms of employment normally follow one of two arrangements:

- **BESS—British Expatriate Supplementation Scheme**. You are employed by an overseas government or institution, and the salary you are paid is supplemented by the British Government. In 1987 some £27 million was disbursed on supplementation schemes.

- **Technical cooperation**. Your contract is with the British Government and your salary is normally subject to UK income tax. Expenditure on technical cooperation officers exceeded £30 million in 1987. Appointments are normally for two or three years, but there are occasionally short-term specialist assignments.

In addition, the ODA has a Corps of Specialists consisting of individuals whose knowledge and experience is of particular value to developing countries. They receive long-term holding contracts providing a guarantee of employment for a specified period of years.

Crown Agents, St Nicholas House, St Nicholas Road, Sutton, Surrey SM1 1EL. Tel: 081-643 3311. Crown Agents is a statutory public corporation providing supply, financial and technical support services to overseas governments and public sector bodies, for the most part in the Third World. These include ports authorities, railways, central banks, electricity authorities, broadcasting corporations and police forces. Most contracts are for two or three years. In addition to advertising vacancies, Crown Agents maintain a 2,500 strong candidate database.

The British Council, 10 Spring Gardens, London SW1A 2BN. Tel: 071-930 8466, and 65 Davies Street, London W1Y 2AA. Tel: 071-499 8011. The British Council, funded jointly by the Foreign and Commonwealth Office and the Overseas Development Administration, recruits some 500 people per year for contract posts throughout the world. The majority of the vacancies are for teachers, particularly specialists in teaching English as a foreign language. The main types of posts are:

- ODA sponsored posts, which are senior posts often in universities, teacher training institutes and ministries of education funded by the British Government.
- Posts in the Council's own language schools.
- Posts in Communist bloc countries. The British Council is often the only organisation recruiting for such countries. The positions are usually at the tertiary level, and may well be subsidised.
- Posts for which the Council operates solely as a recruitment agency.
- Opportunities may also be available under the **Know How** fund for Eastern Europe operated by the Foreign & Commonwealth Office.

International organisations
These include:

Commonwealth Secretariat (Commonwealth Fund for Technical Cooperation), Marlborough House, Pall Mall, London SW1X 5HX. Tel: 071-839 3411.

The United Nations and its Agencies. Apart from recruiting for its own bi-lateral aid programmes, the ODA recruits technical experts through its International Recruitment Unit for assignments with the UN and some of its agencies. The assignments tend to be in Third World countries, and are on a contract basis offering good conditions of employment and tax-free salaries. Highly experienced personnel are needed, and will normally be 35 or older. The requirements are as follows:

- **United Nations:** Opportunities exist in the following fields: economics, mineral resources, public finance, statistics, transport, electric power, housing, town and country planning, public administration, data processing, social welfare, community development, tourism. Very occasionally specialists in energy conservation, cartography, land surveying, museums and libraries are required.

- **UNIDO (United Nations Industrial Development Organisation):** Experts are needed to assist in all stages of industrial development over a wide range of basic and manufacturing industries.

- **ILO (International Labour Organisation):** Experts are required in the fields of manpower planning and utilisation, labour statistics, social security, vocational training, management development, organisation of co-operatives, work study, personnel management, and so on. There is a constant demand for specialists in apprenticeship training, vocational training and instructor training.

- **FAO (Food and Agricultural Organisation):** Highly qualified personnel are needed in agriculture, irrigation engineering, forestry, fisheries, nutrition, economics and statistics who are able to plan and execute work independently, train local personnel and advise national authorities.

- **IAEA (International Atomic Energy Agency):** Vacancies occur in such fields as the application of radio-isotopes, reactor physics and engineering, beta and gamma spectrometry.

Other UN agencies which recruit staff on a contract basis are the World Health Organisation (WHO), UNICEF and UNESCO—of which Britain is not currently a member. However in cases like this it is necessary to apply to the agency itself rather than through ODA (See **UN Work**, Chapter 17).

Volunteer agencies and similar organisations
These include:

Christians Abroad, 1 Stockwell Green, London SW9 9HP. Tel: 071-737 7811. This organisation provides advice about openings overseas—mainly in Third World countries—through voluntary secular and Christian recruitment agencies. It publishes a jobs bulletin, *Opportunities Abroad* which lists current vacancies on offer from about 40 such bodies. It also does some teacher recruitment in its own right for both voluntary and salaried posts.

The British Volunteer Programme, which receives financial support from the British Government, comprises four organisations:

Voluntary Service Overseas (317 Putney Bridge Road, London SW15 2PN. Tel: 081-780 1331) is the largest of these agencies. It recruits about 600 people a year to work in more than 40 Third World countries, and some 1100 volunteers are at post at any one time.

The profile of volunteers has changed radically over the past 25 years. Whereas some of the first volunteers were school leavers, the average age is now 30 and some volunteers are in their sixties. Volunteers must be experienced, skilled and highly motivated.

Opportunities exist in a wide range of sectors, including: agriculture, forestry and fisheries, education and librarianship, health, business and commerce, technical trades, crafts and engineering, community and social development.

Accommodation and payment based on local rates are provided by the community, organisation or government requesting volunteers. VSO for its part provides training and pays for air fares, national insurance, medical insurance and equipment grants. As the VSO brochure points out:

> 'Every volunteer...often leaves secure employment in the UK with little anticipation of any real material reward for the two years' tough and unpredictable experience ahead.'

The organisation recruits for posts in Africa, the Caribbean, China, SE Asia, the Pacific and Eastern Europe. VSO also recruits on behalf of United Nations Volunteers, Palais des Nations, 1211 Geneva 10, Switzerland. Tel: 010-4122 985850.

Skillshare Africa (formerly part of IVS), 3 Belvoir Street, Leicester LE1 6SL, Tel: 0533-541862, is a branch of Service Civil International and works mainly in Botswana, Lesotho, Mozambique and Swaziland.

United Nations Association International Service (UNAIS), 3 Whitehall Court, London SW1A 2EL. Tel: 071-930 0679. This is the volunteer programme of the United Nations Association which also runs an unofficial volunteer coordinating committee to which all volunteer recruitment agencies belong. It recruits mainly agricultural and health specialists for programmes in Brazil, Bolivia, Paraguay, Burkino Faso, Mali and Cape Verde.

Catholic Institute for International Relations (CIIR), 22 Coleman Fields, London N1 7AF. Tel: 071-354 0883. This recruits mainly agricultural, technical and health specialists for Latin America, Somalia, North Yemen and Zimbabwe.

Other volunteer organisations include:

Green Deserts Ltd, Rougham, Bury St Edmunds, Suffolk IP30 9LY. Tel: 0359-70265. This organisation recruits skilled volunteers aged 18 plus on two year contracts to establish a forestry system at the southern edge of the Sahara in Sudan.

Institute of Cultural Affairs, 277 St Ann's Road, London N15 5RG. Tel: 081-802 2848. 65 to 80 volunteers are recruited annually to work in community development in Africa, Asia, Europe and Latin America. Contracts are between nine and twelve months.

The Richmond Fellowship, 8 Addison Road, London W14 8DL, Tel: 071-603 6373. Volunteers aged 24 plus and preferably with experience of dealing with the mentally disturbed are recruited for one year to work with former mental patients in half-way houses in Hong Kong, Israel, India and the USA.

The following booklets and books would be of interest to anyone considering working as a volunteer in the Third World:

Volunteer Work, H. Sewell (Central Bureau).
Thinking about Volunteering? (Returned Volunteer Action, 1 Amwell Street, London EC1R 1UL. Tel: 071-278 0804).
Handbook for Development Workers Overseas, G. Roberts (The Alver Press—obtainable from RVA).

Missionary organisations
It's not always easy to draw a distinction between the work of volunteer agencies and that of religious groups. In most of the organisations mentioned below, volunteers are recruited for their practical skills rather than their evangelical prowess. For a fuller list of missionary societies turn to **Missionary Work** in Chapter 17.

Bible and Medical Missionary Fellowship International, Whitefield House, 186 Kennington Park Road, London SE11 4BT. Tel: 071-735 8227. Health, agriculture, engineering and teaching professionals are needed for Asia and the Middle East. Three years minimum.

Bible Churchmen's Missionary Society, 251 Lewisham Way,

London SE4 1XF. Tel: 081-691 6111. Teachers, doctors and people with experience in bookselling and the media are recruited for a minimum of two years.

Christian Outreach, 34 St Mary's Crescent, Leamington Spa, Warwickshire CV31 1JL. Tel: 0926-315301. This agency is involved in primary health care in refugee camps and the support of disadvantaged children in homes. Contracts are for one year.

Concern, 1 Upper Camden Street, Dublin 2. Tel: 681237. Non-denominational Irish organisation which offers two year assignments in the Third World.

Medical Missionary Association, 6 Canonbury Place, London N1 2NJ. Tel: 071-359 1313. An organisation which recruits young doctors, nurses and paramedics with at least one or two years' post qualification experience to work for one year in missionary hospitals in the Third World. It acts as a central clearing house for Protestant missionary societies needing medical personnel, and positions are advertised in the Association's quarterly magazine *Saving Health*.

The Missions to Seamen, St Michael Paternoster Royal, College Hills, London EC4 2RL. Tel: 071-248 5202. 24 assistants (aged 18 to 24) are recruited annually on one year contracts to provide spiritual and moral assistance to seafarers at 20 ports throughout the world.

National Council for YMCAs, 640 Forest Road, London E17 3DZ. Tel: 081-520 5599. Counsellors aged 21 plus work as counsellors in children's and young people's outdoor pursuit camps in the USA.

Quaker Peace and Service, Friends House, Euston Road, London NW1 2BJ. Helpers to work with mentally and physically handicapped in church run centres and homes in Austria, France and West Germany.

The Tear Fund, 100 Church Road, Teddington, Middlesex TW11 8QE. Tel: 081-977 9144. This evangelical organisation offers two and four year contracts in the fields of health care, technical training, agriculture, and so on.

Viatores Christi, 9 Harcourt Terrace, Dublin 2. Tel: 763050. Recruits volunteers for the Third World and British Columbia working with the Indian population.

Voluntary Missionary Movement, Shenley Lane, London Colney, Herts AL2 8AR. Tel: 0727-248853. This organisation sends lay missionaries from a wide range of disciplines to Papua New Guinea and seven countries in Africa.

International charities

These normally require well qualified personnel who are paid a salary, rather than a volunteer's allowance. Most of the opportunities are contract posts but there are usually a limited number of permanent staff posts as well. For all positions, qualifications and experience are vital.

Euroaction ACORD (Agency for Co-operation and Research in Development), Francis House, Francis Street, London SW1P 1DQ. Tel: 071-828 7611. Euroaction is not strictly speaking a charity but an international consortium of 23 European and Canadian non-governmental organisations which recruits some 25 experienced and qualified professional development workers per year for agricultural, training and rural development projects in Africa. Two year contracts.

Oxfam, 274 Banbury Road, Oxford OX2 7DZ. Tel: 0865-56777. This organisation offers contracts of one to four years in relief and development work.

Save the Children Fund, 17 Grove Lane, Camberwell, London SE5 8RD. Tel: 071-703 5400. SCF is involved in community health programmes, medical care for refugees, nutrition and feeding programmes in addition to disaster and famine relief.

World Vision, Dychurch House, 8 Abington Street, Northampton NN1 2AJ. Tel: 0604-22964. This is an interdenominational Christian humanitarian organisation operating in 70 countries. It is run through local churches and community leaders in cooperation with the UN and international relief agencies. Medical staff, engineers, logistics experts, and vocational instructors are the main categories in demand.

The private sector

It would be an impossible task to list all those companies which offer overseas contracts. Some recruit themselves, but many also use intermediaries—employment agencies, recruitment consultants, executive search consultants and the like. So it makes sense to get in touch with any which specialise in your particular field and ask to be put on their candidate register—if they operate one.

On the other hand you mighty apply to firms direct; but you need to approach companies who employ the bulk of their employees on short-term contracts, so, for example, banks, insurance companies and law firms would probably be a waste of time.

By contrast, construction projects last for only a certain number of years, as do hospital management contracts, so companies in these sectors prefer not to make a long-term commitment to the staff they recruit.

Take the example of British Aerospace, whose chief activity is making planes. Some years ago BAe won a contract to supply fighter planes to the Saudi Arabian Air Force, and the deal included a training and maintenance package. This meant that the company had to provide English and technical teachers, pilot instructors, maintenance engineers, and so on, to support the contract—people that it does not employ in the normal course of events. It has therefore set up a special organisation to recruit contract staff for the project (British Aerospace Saudi Arabian Support Section, Warton Aerodrome, Preston, Lancs PR4 1AX).

Construction work by its very nature is of limited duration. Once the dam, refinery or chemical plant is built the assignment is complete. However, a large scale project can last years, and if the firm is well-entrenched in a particular country, there is always the possibility that it will win new projects there. (For addresses see **Recruitment Organisations** and individual job sector sections in the appendices of this book.)

Extending the contract

A person on a contract has the best of both worlds. If the posting proves tiresome and unpleasant you know that it will all be over after a certain time, and there could be a carrot in the form of a terminal bonus to look forward to if you can stick it out. On the other hand, if you enjoy your work and the location, there is usually a possibility of extending it—often on better terms and with greater responsibility.

Some people manage to build their careers on a succession of contracts, and if your particular skill is sought after you will be presented with an extensive choice of locations and jobs as one contract draws to a close. (See Chapter 7). If you go for this type of career, remember the following points:

- You must take responsibility for upgrading your knowledge and skills (contract jobs rarely offer in-service training).
- You need to make provisions for your future, such as a pension and insurance for illness or loss of salary—what if you experience a period of unemployment between contracts?

However, successful completion of one or two contracts will often lead to more permanent job opportunities for those who want them.

10
Long-Term Opportunities

(More Than Three Years)

If you have lived and worked abroad for a while—on contract or as a volunteer, for instance—you have probably already decided if you want to choose this way of life on a long-term basis.

While it is possible to have a career which consists of a succession of contracts, there are disadvantages such as:

- the possibility of long periods of unemployment between one job and the next (actors call it 'resting')
- missing out on 'perks' such as company pensions or training.

A job which offers security of tenure is therefore a great attraction. Here you need to decide what kind of job you want:

- A UK-based job with opportunities for short visits and postings abroad.
- A career where you may be seconded to a foreign location
- A career where for a substantial amount of time you will be based abroad
- Permanent relocation

UK base with visits abroad

The idea of being based in the UK appeals to many people who are interested in foreign countries but do not relish the prospect of uprooting themselves completely. If you are part of the international sales force of a company, a consultant, or a highly qualified specialist in certain fields, you may well be accustomed to making short business visits.

Another trend, thanks to improved communications, is the increasing number of people living in one country and working in another. If you have a job on the European continent, it is perfectly feasible to work abroad during the week and spend weekends and public holidays at home in the UK. Your weekly routine would thus be similar to that of a person who divides his time between his office in London, say, and his weekend cottage in Cornwall, or between a North Sea oil-rig and a home on the mainland. If the country you have in mind is near enough, this is certainly worth a thought.

Admittedly, in both cases you would not enjoy all the perks of expatriate life—allowances, tax-free salaries, and so on. But on the other hand if you are a 'dual career' family, your spouse will not have to sacrifice her (or his) career and salary in order to follow you to the ends of the earth—a move which could result in financial loss overall. It would also mean less disruption to the rest of the family.

Secondment abroad

Secondment is likely to happen in a firm which has subsidiaries, partners or clients abroad. It is also possible within the public sector; for example, civil servants in the Overseas Development Administration may be posted to one of the department's regional offices around the world. Similarly, police officers are sometimes seconded to train overseas police forces. Secondments can turn out to be quite lengthy—for up to five years in some cases—and they generally fulfil one or more of the following purposes:

- to fill a vacancy where no local staff are suitably qualified
- to train local nationals
- to create an international cadre of managers
- to increase understanding between head office and subsidiaries
- to set up a new venture
- to exercise control over an overseas operation
- to create a development opportunity for a high-flier
- to increase mobility within the organisation.

Secondment is very similar to going abroad on contract terms, and so all the same advice applies concerning adequate preparation, renumeration, guidance on overseas removal, personal taxation, house-letting, and so on. A special contract may need to be drawn up covering your period abroad.

Not all secondments are successful—you and your firm need to consider very carefully whether you are really suited to a lengthy assignment in another country. Although you may have enjoyed a successful career up till now in the UK, there is no guarantee that you can repeat this success in other parts of the world. If you do not have the right personal qualities—and the Overseas Assignment Inventory should be able to help you decide (Chapter 1)—it might be better for both sides for you to opt out, even though this might mean turning down a promotion.

The Institute of Personnel Management makes another valid point:

> 'Communication with the home base is particularly important for secondees overseas. Because they may be in frequent contact on business matters, the need to maintain general contact with the UK organisations may be overlooked.'

This can be achieved through:

- the regular despatch of journals and company newsletters
- meetings with visitors from the UK
- frequent contact with UK based line personnel or career managers where appropriate.

The IPM also points out the importance of planning for your return well in advance. (*The IPM Secondment Code*, Institute of Personnel Management, IPM House, Camp Road, Wimbledon, London SW19 4UW. See also *Personnel Management Fact Sheet 8—Expatriates* (Personnel Publications Ltd, 1 Hills Place, London W1R 1AG.))

UK base with postings abroad

Although there is a distinct trend away from the career expatriate who spends the greater part of his working life abroad, there are still certain sectors that offer truly international careers where perhaps only a third of an employee's working life is spent in Britain. Periodically, you find yourself transferred to some new location where you are able to gain new vistas and enjoy new experiences.

Such careers normally offer good remuneration, free accommodation and ample allowances. But these advantages have to be set against potential disadvantages:

- **Rootlessness**. Your life is not as settled as that of your contemporaries back home, and you may have to relocate at a moment's notice.

- **No choice of destination**. You may be posted to a place which you find uncongenial. However, you have to grin and bear it in the hope that your next posting will be more satisfactory.

- **Family disruption**. If your children follow you to different locations there is a chance that their education will suffer. Boarding school is sometimes the only solution despite the periods of separation it entails.

- **Potential loss of income**. This could be true of dual career marriages where the accompanying spouse has no chance to pursue an uninterrupted career of their own.

- **Losing touch**. If you have a succession of two or three postings abroad you may find you lose touch with your home base and developments in your field.

It is often helpful to see a career of this nature in terms of a succession of contracts. No two postings will be the same, and each time you arrive in a different place, you will have to adjust to a new environment, even when you are posted back to Britain.

The public sector has a number of organisations where an employee must be prepared to spend a substantial part of his life in an overseas location. This is true of the Diplomatic Service, the British Council and the Services.

It is also true in industry and commerce. At one time a company with extensive overseas interests might have posted an executive to a foreign location virtually for life. Nowadays, such a person is more likely to be changed around on a regular basis.

Certain companies are more likely than others to send people abroad—particularly if their activities tend to be based overseas. This is true, for instance of British overseas banks, international mining companies and oil firms.

Permanent relocation

Since the days of the Pilgrim Fathers people have left the UK in search of a better life elsewhere. Some realise their dream, while others drift back home, having found that their new life is no better than the one they left behind.

We have already seen that going abroad on a short assignment is quite different from shooting off for a two year contract. Uprooting yourself completely belongs to yet another category, and a good deal of soul searching is essential before taking such a step, particularly if you have no experience of living outside the UK.

To be a successful emigrant requires a number of personal qualities:

- a sense of adventure
- a belief in yourself
- a mood of optimism
- a will to succeed.

No matter how strange or inhospitable your destination seems to be, you must be able to see it through rose-coloured spectacles—recognising the opportunities it offers and ignoring the drawbacks.

Admittedly, it is more normal nowadays for people to test the water before committing themselves irrevocably to spending the rest of their days abroad. If you start off with a contract posting and find the place is not to your liking, you know that at the end of the contract you will receive an air ticket home.

There are two main options for anyone deciding to reside permanently overseas.

Emigration
These days, most countries have restrictions on entry which will discriminate against the unqualified and unskilled; they prefer to let in people who have skills which are needed or are in short supply. Computer specialists and nurses, for instance, are generally welcomed with open arms.

If you have close relations residing in the country in question, it may well prove easier for you to gain entry. The same is true if you plan to set up a business in the country and have sufficient capital to invest.

Australia, Canada, New Zealand, South Africa and the USA are the most popular destinations for UK migrants. However, that is not to say that there are no others. A large number of countries, in fact, accept immigrants—usually according to a quota system—provided certain conditions, usually involving the applicant's qualifications or skills, are met.

There will soon be no restrictions at all on permanent residence for UK nations in EC countries. Indeed, to all intents and purposes countries like Italy, Germany or France will be our home ground.

A job with an international organisation
If you get a job on the permanent staff of an international organisation, you will find that you are exempt from immigration restrictions. You become a citizen of the world, as it were, while retaining your original nationality.

The United Nations, for example, has offices and regional

offices in a number of locations. The UN Secretariat is in New York, and the organisation has offices in Geneva and Vienna. In addition, there are the various UN agencies and sister organisations. For example, it has an information office in London at 20, Buckingham Gate, SW1E 6LB. Tel: 01-630 1981.

The Europa Yearbook lists the addresses of a great many international bodies.

A final option: working for yourself

These chapters have concentrated on finding employment. But there is one final option for anyone wishing to live and work abroad—and that is to work for yourself.

Entrepreneurship can be a hazardous business even in familiar surroundings; this can be even more of a problem within a strange environment. Before you even contemplate such a move, you need to acquaint yourself thoroughly with business practices within the country concerned, and understand how company law and labour law operate there. Assume that everything is quite different from the UK unless proved otherwise.

If you are determined to press ahead, remember there could be other obstacles. Before you can be issued with the required visa, you will need to satisfy the relevant Embassy or High Commission on a number of counts. Here are some of them:

- Do you have a minimum amount of capital to invest in your project?
- Can you demonstrate that you have proven business skills?
- Is your project a viable proposition?
- Would it endanger the livelihood of existing locally owned businesses?
- Do you have sufficient resources to cover your living costs until you begin to make profits from your business?

Regulations will depend on the country. The best plan is to meet the relevant officers of the Embassy or High Commission to find out precisely what is required of you. The commercial attaché or immigration officer should be able to put you on the right track.

Alternatively you might look on self-employment as a long-term aim—in which case, you could start off doing contract work, and wait until you are well-established in the foreign location before branching out on your own.

The World by Regions and Countries

This section examines job opportunities for expatriates region by region and attempts briefly to indicate the differences a person needs to prepare for. There is a reference section giving useful addresses as well as directories and other books relevant to anyone looking for employment in that particular part of the world.

Each regional survey is complemented by sources of information on different countries. Typically these sources consist of:

- address of Embassy/High Commission.
- address of British Embassy/High Commission in the country.
- address of British Council in the country—this would be of particular interest to people working in education.
- addresses of chambers of commerce or specialist trade and cultural associations connected with the country concerned.

11
Europe

Some of the most promising opportunities for overseas employment lie right on the doorstep. As Europe becomes more integrated, national barriers will no longer affect job seekers, and citizens of European Community countries, at least, will have a much larger jobs market to choose from. Perhaps one day Europeans will move as freely from one country to another as US citizens move between the states of the union. Europe can be divided up into three sections:

- The European Community Countries
- Eastern Europe
- The rest of Europe

The countries of the European Community

To take up a position in many countries these days involves a good deal of red tape—visas, work permits, and the like. This is not the case, however, with the European Community which comprises Belgium, Denmark, France, West Germany, Greece, Ireland, Italy, Luxembourg, the Netherlands, Portugal, Spain, and the UK.

Nationals of all these member states have the right to go to another member state to look for work provided they comply with the laws or regulations on employment and have a valid passport or national identity card. They are then entitled to the same treatment as nations of the host country in matters of:

- pay
- working conditions
- vocational training
- income tax
- social security
- trade union rights

However, they are not normally eligible for employment in public service in that country. (In the case of Portugal and Spain some restrictions still exist, but they are gradually being phased out.)

But everything is not quite as straightforward as it seems at first sight. Although the Treaty of Rome established the principle of freedom to work anywhere in the community, up till now there have been barriers to the operation of a community-wide job market; for example, member states do not always recognise the professional qualifications obtained in another member state. This has meant, that—in theory, at least—an accountant wanting to audit everywhere in the community would have needed to spend 50 years qualifying and requalifying.

However, help is on the way for professionals. By the end of 1992 the European Community will have established a single 'common' market—'an area without internal frontiers in which the free movement of goods, persons, services and capital is ensured in accordance with the provisions of the Treaty (of Rome)'. This will mean that in future, where the education and training for a profession is substantially the same as that in the host country, their qualifications will be recognised as equivalent.

On the other hand, where the education and training are substantially different from that required for the same profession by the host state, the would-be employee will have one of two choices:

- an aptitude test—designed to assess their ability to pursue their profession in the host country; or
- a period of supervised practice not exceeding three years.

Doctors, nurses, dentists, vets, midwives, architects and pharmacists are already covered by the EC directive and the ruling is being extended to cover other professions which require at least three years' university level training or the equivalent.

The Community is also working on an agreement on the equivalence or comparability of national vocational qualifications. So far the agreement covers the hotel and restaurant trade, car repairs, the construction industry, electrotechnology, agriculture, horticulture, forestry and the textile industry.

Legislation already exists to make it easier for people to meet vocational training requirements in other member states, though this is restricted to certain jobs and trades. If you can get a **certificate of experience**, the authorities of other member states will accept it in place of their own national qualifications for the job (details are available from the Internal European Policy Division, Department of Trade and Industry, Room 418, 1 Victoria Street, London SW1H 0ET. Tel: 071-215 5354).

1992 will not only mean increased opportunities for people to apply for jobs in the European Community countries. As more Pan-European companies are formed as a result of mergers, employees of merged companies in Britain are likely to find themselves transferred to jobs on the Continent as a matter of course.

Although there are no statistics on the numbers of British citizens actually working in the EC countries, the size of the British communities in each one will give some idea of the sort of job market for English people. The largest British communities are in Spain, West Germany, Holland, France, Italy, Belgium and Greece—in order of magnitude, but note that the figure for Spain, includes a significant proportion of retired people, and that for Italy a high proportion of long-term residents.

SEDOC (The European System for the International Clearing of Vacancies and Applications for Employment) helps people find jobs in EC countries; ask at your local Jobcentre.

Eastern Europe
Eastern Europe has started to open up, and though the jobs situation is still somewhat hazy, there is clearly a need for people with business and management expertise to help with national reconstruction. The Foreign and Commonwealth Office administers a 'Knowhow Fund' for Eastern Europe for this purpose; VSO has established an East European Partnership programme which sends volunteers (principally teachers) to the area; and a number of companies are engaged in joint venture and other programmes (eg the ICL computer assembly plant in Leningrad). Qualified emigrés and others with close ties with these countries will be in particular demand from Western companies eager to move eastwards.

The rest of Europe
Austria, Finland, Norway, Sweden, Switzerland (including Liechtenstein) and Turkey are not members of the European Community, so you will need to get work permits in advance, and if you visit the country as a tourist and find a job, you will not be allowed to take up employment without prior permission. In many

cases this means leaving the country and applying for a work visa at an embassy.

Applications for work in Austria, Norway and Sweden can be made through Jobcentres and Employment offices under the International Clearing of Vacancies (ICV) Scheme. There are British communities in excess of 10,000 people in each of the Scandinavian countries and Switzerland, which suggests there are plenty of job opportunities despite the restrictions.

THE OPPORTUNITIES

Thanks to the impetus towards European integration, the European Community is one of the most promising areas for employment these days—particularly in the growing high-tech sector. Major opportunities exist for the following groups:

- British scientists, electronic engineers and computer personnel are highly regarded and much in demand—attractive salaries are often offered.
- Teachers, especially teachers of English as a second language, are always in demand, although pay is often quite low, especially in private institutes.
- Translators and technical authors are also needed, especially in the private sector, since manuals and technical documents have to be rendered in clear English for export markets.

A large proportion of the UK's trade is with Europe, and many large firms maintain permanent offices in several of the European capitals—not only manufacturing firms, but also British banks, accountancy firms, law firms, insurance companies, management consultancies, advertising agencies, and so on. Their number is likely to increase rather than diminish. However, the majority (if not all) the staff are likely to be recruited locally.

There are also opportunities in the public sector—in the institutions of the European Community, European research establishments, the Council of Europe, NATO and the different agencies of the United Nations located in Europe, who all need specialist staff and administrators, as well as secretaries.

Generally speaking, employers are on the lookout for marketable skills. However, in some of the wealthier parts of Europe it is still possible to land semi-skilled jobs, notably in construction and the hotel and catering trades—but normally you will need to speak the local language.

Don't forget the possibility of becoming self-employed. If you have specialist skills and/or cash to invest, think about setting up on your own in some European location. As in Britain, the possibilities are endless, but like any potential businessman at home you must first do a feasibility study and be prepared to spend much time and effort in getting your show off the ground. Also remember that legal requirements differ from country to country.

Language

It is merely stating the obvious to mention that the European continent is not part of the English Speaking World. While English may be used for international communication, within the country itself you will find everybody talking to one another in the national language. This contrasts strongly with parts of the Third World where English is very much the lingua franca.

So the first cultural barrier you will need to surmount is the linguistic one. While your colleagues at work may be able to communicate with you in English, for most of the time they will address each other in their own language. So to really participate, you really will have to make an effort to learn their language, especially if your assignment is likely to be a lengthy one. If your posting is away from the cosmopolitan atmosphere of the capital, the need to come to grips with the language is even greater.

The people

There are other differences to be taken account of as well. Although we inhabit the same continent, each nation can differ quite markedly in temperament and outlook from its neighbour.

The Germans have a reputation for being thorough and professional, though their legendary dedication to work is perhaps a little less marked these days. They are tough negotiators who observe a degree of formality in their personal relationships. For instance, they tend not to be on Christian name terms with colleagues. There is a strong materialistic streak in the modern day German, who often has a passion for fast and expensive cars. To a great extent men still rule the roost.

The French are proud of their culture, food and language, and if you want to curry favour you cannot do better than praise items one and two in French. Status is important, and who you are or where you have studied is more important than your actual accomplishments. They tend to dress well, but conservatively, and attach great importance to good manners. French people never mix business with pleasure, and so avoid discussing business at meal-times.

The pace of life in the provinces tends to be more sedate than in Paris.

Status is also important to Italians who often behave in an autocratic way with subordinates. Italy seems somewhat disorganised and endless red tape can be a problem. Spaniards tend to be formal in personal relationships and place great stress on personal honour. However, remember that there are considerable dissimilarities between the various regions of Spain.

Turkey represents a blend of East and West. Although it is regarded as part of Europe and European attitudes and styles predominate among the educated classes, most of the population are followers of Islam and a good many may disapprove of alcohol, women's lib and other aspects of Western life. Turks are hospitable people but Turkish society is somewhat autocratic and male-dominated.

Each country of Europe is distinctive, and your life abroad will prove more congenial and rewarding if you make an effort to familiarize yourself with national characteristics and attitudes and blend in with your surroundings.

Useful addresses:
Great Britain—East Europe Centre, 31 Knightsbridge, London SW1H 7NH.
Europages—European Business Directory, Euroédit SA, 8 rue de L'Hôtel de Ville, 92200 Neuilly sur Seine, France.

Austria
Austrian Embassy: 18 Belgrave Mews West, London SW1X 5HU. Tel: 071-235 3731.
Austrian Institute: 28 Rutland Gate, London SW7 (has reading room).
Tourist Office: 30 George Street, London W1R 0AL. Tel: 071-269 0461.
British Embassy: Reisnerstr. 40, A-1030 Wien (Vienna).
British Council: Schenkenstr. 4, A-1010 Wien.
Anglo-Austrian Society: 46 Queen Anne's Gate, London SW1H 9AU. Tel: 071-222 0366.

Addresses:
Landesarbeitsamt, Weihburgstrasse 30, 1010 Wien. There are branches of this government run labour exchange in every provincial capital. Vacancies are notified to Jobcentres in Britain under the ICV clearance of vacancies scheme.

Leading Newspaper:
Die Presse (Representative in London: Publicitas)

Austria is not a member of the EC, and work permits are necessary. You must get them from the employer in Austria who has to satisfy the regional labour office that the job cannot be done by someone already resident. International agencies are exempt from these restrictions.

Belgium
Belgian Embassy: 103 Eaton Square, London SW1W 9AB. Tel: 071-235 5422.
Tourist Office: 38 Dover Street, London W1X 3RB. Tel: 071-499 5379.
British Embassy: Britannia House, rue Joseph II 28, 1040 Brussels.
British Council and British Chamber of Commerce: Same address as British Embassy.
Anglo-Belgian Society: 46 Belgrave Manor, Brooklyn Road, Woking, Surrey GU22 7TW. Tel: 04862-72671.

Addresses:
A recruitment service is provided by the Ministry of Labour (l'Office Nationale de l'Emploi et de la Main d'Oeuvre, Boulevard de l'Empereur 7, 1000 Brussels), which is linked to SEDOC. Unemployed nationals of EC countries who go to Belgium to seek employment must register with a local ONEM office within seven days. There are also numerous recruitment consultancies with affiliates in the UK, notably Berndtson, Egon Zehnder, Heidreck & Struggles, Korn Ferry, Mervyn Hughes, TASA, Spencer Stuart, Transearch and Eurosurvey.

Useful publications:
Intermediar, avenue du Houx 42, 1170 Brussels (for recruitment).
How to Live & Work in Belgium, Marvina Shilling (How To Books 1991).

Job advertisements are published in:
The Bulletin, avenue Louise 382, 1050 Brussels—an English language newspaper.
Le Soir, Place de Louvain 21, 1000 Brussels.
De Standaard, Vlaamse Uitgevers Maatsschappij, A Gossetlaan 30A, 1720 Groot-Bijgaarden.

Belgium (and especially Brussels) is a cosmopolitan place with a number of English medium schools in the country. Knowledge of either Flemish or French will prove useful, depending on which region is to be your base. Everyone intending to take up employment must report his intended place of residence to the municipality within one week of arrival and obtain a residence certificate.

Bulgaria
Bulgarian Embassy: 186 Queen's Gate, London SW7 5HL. Tel: 071-584 9400.
Tourist Office: 18 Prince's Street, London W1R 7RE. Tel: 071-499 6988.
British Embassy: 65 Tolbuhin Blvd, Sofia.

Czechoslovakia
Czech Embassy: 25 Kensington Palace Gardens, London W8 4QY. Tel: 071-727 3966.
Tourist Office: 17-18 Old Bond Street, London W1X 4RB. Tel: 071-629 6058.
British Embassy: Mala Strana, Thunovska Ulice 14, 12550 Prague 1.

Cyprus
Cyprus High Commission: 93 Park Street, London W1Y 4ET. Tel: 071-499 8272.
Tourist Office: 213 Regent Street, London W1R 3DA. Tel: 071-734 9822.
Turkish Republic of Northern Cyprus Office: 28 Cockspur Street, London SW1. Tel: 071-837 4577.
British High Commission: (PO Box 1978), Nicosia.
British Council: 3 Museum Street, (PO Box 1995), Nicosia.

Cyprus is not part of the European Community and a work permit must be obtained in advance by your prospective employer.

Denmark
Danish Embassy: 55 Sloane Street, London SW1X 9SR. Tel: 071-235-1255.
Tourist Office: Sceptre House, 169–173 Regent Street, London W1R 8PY. Tel: 071-734 2637.
British Embassy: Kastelvej 36-40, 2100 Copenhagen.
British Council: Montergade 1, 1116 Copenhagen K.

Addresses:
Arbejdsdirektoratet, 2 Kontor, Ornevej 301, Dk 2400, Copenhagen (the state employment service), has offices throughout the country known as 'Arbejds Avisningkontor'. International

recruitment consultancies with offices in Copenhagen include Berndtson, Boyden, Egon Zehnder. National professional associations or trade unions may be able to advise on employment prospects.

Newspapers:
Politiken—Denmark's leading newspaper carries job advertisements, as do several Sunday newspapers.

EC nationals are allowed to stay in the country for up to three months without a permit, but two weeks before your stay expires it is essential to apply to the Department for Aliens, Absalonsgade 9, 1658 Kobenhavn V for a residence and work permit.

Finland
Finnish Embassy: 38 Chesham Place, London SW1X 8HW. Tel: 071-235-9531.
Tourist Office: 66 Haymarket, London SW1Y 4RF. Tel: 071-839 4048.
British Embassy: Uudenmaankatu 16-20, 00120 Helsinki 12.
British Council: Eteläesplanadi 22A, 00130 Helsinki 13.
Finno-British Trade Association: Etala Esplanaadi 2, 00130 Helsinki 10.

Finland is not a member of the EC, so it is necessary to obtain a work permit from the Finnish Embassy before entering the country. To obtain this you must provide a certificate from your Finnish employer, copies of your certificates and three passport photos. Approval usually takes a month.

France
French Embassy: 22 Wilton Crescent, London SW1X 8SB. Tel: 071-235 8080.
Tourist Office: 178 Piccadilly, London W1V 0AL. Tel: 071-491 7622.
British Embassy: 105–109 rue de Faubourg St Honoré, 75008 Paris.
British Council: 9 rue de Constantine, 75007 Paris.
Franco-British Chamber of Commerce: 8 rue Cimarosa, 75016 Paris (publishes a year book of its members).

Addresses:
The employment service of the Ministry of Labour (Association Nationale pour l'Emploi, 53 rue Général Leclerc, 92136 Issy-les-Molineaux) has branches throughout the country and is linked to

the SEDOC system. There is also an abundance of private sector recruitment agencies, notably Manpower, Bis, John Stork, Knight Wendling, Berndtson, Egon Zehnder, Korn Ferry, Mervyn Hughes, Regot, Eurosurvey, Marlar, Transearch, and so on. Other organisations which could be of help are:

Association pour l'Emploi des Cadres (APEC)—a national organisation funded by employers and trade unions which specialises in placing junior and middle managers.

Association Bernard Gregory (53 rue de Turbigo, 75003 Paris) which offers a placement service to postgraduates.

Useful publications:
Guide des Opportunités de Carrière, Editions Formation-Carrières, 9 rue Ambroise Thomas, 75009 Paris. The French equivalent of *Graduate Opportunities*.
Activités, Documentation Pratique, 13 Galerie Vivienne, 75002 Paris. A monthly magazine which publishes a special recruitment issue in June.
How to Live & Work in France, Nicole Prevost Logan (Northcote House 1990).

Leading national newspapers which carry recruitment ads:
Le Monde, 5 rue des Italiens, 75427 Paris.
Le Figaro, 25 avenue Matignon, 75380 Paris.
International Herald Tribune, an American daily published in Paris.

Germany
German Embassy: 23 Belgrave Square, London SW1X 8PZ. Tel: 071-235 5033. German Consulates General at Norwich House, 8-12 Water Street, Liverpool L2 8TA, and 16 Eglington Crescent, Edinburgh EH12 5DG.
Tourist Office: 61 Conduit Street, London W1R 0EN. Tel: 071-734 2600.
British Embassy: Friedrich-Ebert Allee 77, 5300 Bonn.
British Council: Hahnenstrasse 6, 5000 Köln 1.
British Chamber of Commerce: Heumarkt 14, 500 Köln 1.
Anglo-German Association: 17 Bloomsbury Square, London WC1A 2LP. Tel: 071-831 8696.

Addresses:
Job placement is virtually a monopoly of the Federal Institute for Labour (Bundesanstalt für Arbeit, Regenburgerstrasse 104, 8500

Nürnberg) which has produced an English language booklet on its work. The Institute's Central Placement Service (Zentralstelle für Arbeitsvermittlung, Feuerbachstrasse 42-46, 6000 Frankfurt/ Main) offers a specialist service for job hunters from foreign countries and enquiries should be directed to the Auslandsabteilung. It has a branch (Arbeitsamt) in most towns and cities.

The Zentralstelle publishes a weekly jobs bulletin in German entitled *Markt und Chance*. One edition gives details of jobs; the other details of people looking for jobs. It also produces *Uni*, a free magazine on the job market aimed at students.

A number of recruitment consultancies have offices in Germany, notably Knight Wendling, Berndtson, Boyden, Heidreck & Struggles, Korn Ferry, Mervyn Hughes, John Stork, Egor, Eurosurvey, Marlar. German firms often advertise their specialist vacancies in the British press and use UK based recruitment firms.

References:
The leading newspapers for job advertising are:
Die Welt, Kölnerstrasse 99, Bonn.
Frankfurter Allgemeine, Hellerhofstr 2-4, 6000 Frankfurt/Main.
Süddeutsche Zeitung, Sendlingerstrasse 80, München 8.
Die Zeit, Postfach 106820, 2000 Hamburg.
How to Live & Work in Germany, Nessa Loewenthal (How To Books 1991).

Greece
Greek Embassy: 1A Holland Park, London W11 3TP. Tel: 071-727 8040.
Tourist Office: 195–7 Regent Street, London W1R 8DL. Tel: 071-734 5997.
British Embassy: 1 Ploutarchon Street, Athens, GR 10675.
British Council: (PO Box 3488), 17 Plateia Philikis Etairias, Kolonaki Square, 106/73 Athens.
British Hellenic Chamber of Commerce: 4 Valaoritou Street, 106/71 Athens.

Opportunities exist with British travel firms as couriers and resort representatives during the summer. Athens is also a favourite base for representatives of foreign companies trading with the Middle East.

Hungary
Hungarian Embassy: 35 Eaton Place, London SW1X 8BY. Tel: 071-235 2664.

Tourist Office: 6 Conduit Street, London W1R 9TG. Tel: 071-493 0263.

British Embassy: Harmicad Itca 6, Budapest V.

British Council: c/o British Embassy.

Italy

Italian Embassy: 14 Three Kings Yard, London W1Y 2EH. Tel: 071-629 8200. Consulates in Edinburgh, Manchester and Bedford.

Tourist Office: 1 Prince's Street, London W1R 8AY. Tel: 071-408 1254.

British Embassy: 80 Via Venti Settembre, 00100 Roma.

British Council: Plazzo del Drago. Via Quattra Fontane 20, 00184 Rome.

British Chamber of Commerce: Courso Buenos Aires 77, 20124 Milan.

Addresses:

The only employment placement service is the government employment office, the Ufficio di Collocamento Mandopera, Via Pastrengo 16, Roma. However a number of international recruitment firms are represented, such as Berndtson, Boyden, Egon Zehnder, Tasa, Spencer Stuart, Egor.

Reference:

The principal newspapers for job advertisements are:

Corriere della Sera, Milan

Il Messaggero, Rome (London rep. for both papers is Publicitas)

The Daily American, Via San Maria, Via 12, Roma.

Setting up in Italy, Sebastian O'Kelly (Merehurst 1990).

It is important to register with the police within three days of arrival if you are looking for a job. They will issue a certificate. You must also contact the local job centre (Ufficio di Collocamento Manadopera) to register for employment. If you have come to take up a job you should also register with the police and contact the municipality for your work permit.

Malta

High Commission: 16 Kensington Square, London W8 5HH. Tel: 071-938 1712.

Tourist Office: Suite 207, College House, Wright's Lane, London W8. Tel: 071-938 2668.

British High Commission: 7 St Anne Street, Floriana.

The Netherlands
Royal Netherlands Embassy: 38 Hyde Park Gate, London SW7 5DP. Tel: 071-584 5040.
Tourist Office: 25-28 Buckingham Gate, London SW1E 6LD. Tel: 071-630 0451.
British Embassy: Lange Voorhout 10, 2514 ED The Hague.
British Council: Keizergracht 343, 1016 EH Amsterdam.
Netherlands-British Chamber of Commerce: Javastraat 96, 2585 The Hague.
Anglo-Netherland Society: (PO Box 68), Unilever House, London EC4P 4BQ. Tel: 071-353 5729.

Addresses:
The state employment service is Directoraat Generaal de Arbeidsvoorziening, Volmerlaan 1, Rijswijk ZH. It has offices all over the country, and is the only legal placement service in the country. It has a specialist office for the highly qualified—the Bureau Arbeidsvoorziening Academici, Visseringlaan 26, Postbus 5814, 2280 HV Rijswijk, which publishes a fortnightly bulletin entitled *Vacant*. Access to the service is provided via SEDOC.

For short-term employment of at least 6 weeks contact the Ministry of Social Affairs & Employment, Visseringsplan 26, 2288 ER Rijswijk.

Publications:
Intermediair Jaarboek is a directory of job opportunities for graduates, and a weekly job newspaper. The jobs periodical *Intermediair* is published by the same company (Uitgeverij Intermediair, Postbus 3434, 1001 AE Amsterdam). Among the major newspapers carrying recruitment advertising are:
De Telegraaf, NZ Voorburgwal 225, Postbus 376, Amsterdam.
Algemeen Dagblad and *NRC Handelsblad,* Westblaak 180, Rotterdam 2.
De Volkskrant, Wibautstraat 148-150, Postbus 1002, 1000 BA Amsterdam.

Norway
Royal Norwegian Embassy: 25 Belgrave Square, London SW1X 8QD. Tel: 071-235 7151.
Tourist Office: 20 Pall Mall, London SW1Y 5NE. Tel: 071-839 2650.
British Embassy: Thomas Heftyesgate 8, Oslo.
British Council: Fridtjof Nansens Plass 5, 0160 Oslo 1.
British Business Forum: c/o British Embassy.

Anglo-Norse Society: 25 Belgrave Square, London SW1X 8QD.

Addresses:
Vacancies are handled by the official government employment agency Arbeidsdirektoratet, Holbergs Plass 7, Postboks 8127, Dep., Oslo 1, but applications must be made through a Jobcentre in the UK. The agency has a special department for foreign job seekers at Trondheimsveien 2, Oslo 1.

Publications:
Employment in Norway Under the OECD Clearing Scheme, published by the Arbeidsdirektoratet.
Summer Employment in Norway, also by the Arbeidsdirektoratet.
Dagbladet, the leading newspaper.
Norsk Lysingblad, Akersgt 34, Oslo 1, which carries advertisements for lawyers, engineers and teachers.

Poland
Polish Embassy: 47 Portland Place, London W1N 3AG. Tel: 071-580 5481.
Tourist Office: 82 Mortimer Street, London W1N 7DE. Tel: 071-580 8028.
British Embassy: Al Róż, Warsaw.
British Council: Al Jerozolimskie 59, 00-679 Warsaw.

Portugal
Portuguese Embassy: 11 Belgrave Square, London SW1X 8PP.
Tourist Office: 1–5 New Bond Street, London W1Y 0NP. Tel: 071-493 3873.
British Embassy: Rua de S Domingos a Lapa 35-37, 1296 Lisbon.
British Council: Rue Cecilio de Sousa 65, 1294 Lisbon Codex.
British Portuguese Chamber of Commerce: Rua de Estrela 8, 1200 Lisbon.
Anglo-Portuguese Society: 2 Belgrave Square, SW1X 8PJ. Tel: 071-245 9738.
Recruitment Consultancy: Robert Shaw & Associates, Rua Sampaio E Pina 70-10, 1000 Lisbon.

Publications:
Anglo Portuguese News, Avenida San Pedro 25, Monte Estoril.

Until Portugal gains full membership of the European Community in 1993, you may have to obtain a visa from the consular section of the Portuguese Embassy, which can provide you with up-to-date details.

Romania

Romanian Embassy: 4 Palace Green, London W8 4QD. Tel: 071-937 9666.

Tourist Office: 29 Thurloe Place, London SW7 2HP. Tel: 071-584 8090.

British Embassy: Strada Jules Michelet 24, Bucharest.

British Council: c/o British Embassy.

Soviet Union

Russian Embassy: 13 Kensington Palace Gardens, London W8 4QX. Tel: 071-229 6412.

Tourist Office: 292 Regent Street, London W1R 6QL. Tel: 071-631 1252.

British Embassy: Naberezhnaya Morisa Toresa 14, Moscow 109072.

British Council: c/o British Embassy.

Spain

Spanish Embassy: 24 Belgrave Square, London SW1X 8QA. Tel: 071-235 5555.

Consular Section: 20 Draycott Place, London SW3. Tel: 071-584 7405. Sections in Liverpool and Manchester.

Tourist Office: 57–58 St James's Street, London SW1A 1LD. Tel: 071-499 0901.

British Embassy: Calle de Fernando el Santo 16, Madrid 4.

British Council: Calle Almagro 5, Madrid 28001.

British Chamber of Commerce: Marques de Valdeiglas 3, Madrid 4.

Anglo-Spanish Society: 5 Cavendish Square, London W1M 9HA. Tel: 071-580 7537.

Addresses:

The government employment agency is the Centro Nacional de Colocación, General Pardinas 5, Madrid. A number of international recruitment consultancies have offices in Spain, including Berndtson, Egon Zehnder, Knight Wendling, Korn Ferry, Transearch, Tasa and Egor.

References:

ABC, Serrano 61, Madrid.

El Pais, Miguel Yuste 40, Madrid.

La Vanguardia, Pelayo 28, Barcelona.

How to Live & Work in Spain, Robert Richards (How To Books 1991).

Setting up in Spain, David Hewson (Merehurst 1990).

Until Spain achieves full membership status within the European Community in 1993, it may be necessary for your employer to obtain a work permit for you before your arrival.

Sweden

Swedish Embassy: 11 Montagu Place, London W1H 2AL. Tel: 071-724-2101.
Tourist Office: 3 Cork Street, London W1X 1HA. Tel: 071-437 5816.
British Embassy: Skarpögatan, S-115-27 Stockholm.
British Council: Skarpögatan 6, S-115-27 Stockholm.
British Swedish Chamber of Commerce: Nybrokajen 7, S-111-48 Stockholm.
Anglo-Swedish Society: 5 Mansfield Street, London W1M 9FH. Tel: 071-580 5952.

Addresses:
The Swedish national employment agency is Arbetsmarknadsstyrelsen, 171 99 Solna and applications should be made through Jobcentres in the UK. A number of international recruitment firms operate in Sweden, including John Stork, Knight Wendling, Boyden, MPS Enterprises, Christopher Tilly and Transearch.

Sweden is not a member of the EC so EC nationals need to obtain a visa and work permit before they arrive. It can take up to two months to obtain the necessary documentation.

Switzerland

Swiss Embassy: 16-18 Montagu Place, London W1H 2BQ. Tel: 071-723 0701.
Tourist Office: Swiss Centre, 1 New Coventry Street, London W1V 8EE. Tel: 071-734 1921.
British Embassy: Thunstrasse 50, Bern.
British-Swiss Chamber of Commerce: Freiestr. 155, CH-8032 Zürich.
Anglo-Swiss Society: Rose Cottage, Hastingleigh, Ashford, Kent TN25 5HW (Tel: 023375 233).
International recruitment consultancies: Knight Wendling, Spencer Stuart, Canny Bowen, Tasa, Korn Ferry, Heidreck & Struggles, Boyden, Berndtson, Egon Zehnder.

Publications:
Neue Züricher Zeitung, Basler Zeitung, Tribune de Genève are all represented in the UK by Publicitas.

The Swiss Government has a restrictive immigration policy and it is difficult to obtain the residence permits that allow you to take up employment. Your prospective employer has to apply on your behalf. There are three types of residence permit applicable to employees:

A—Seasonal permit for employment in construction, hotels, and tourism.

B—1 year permit (renewable) for a specific job.

C—Permanent residence permit for between 5 and 10 years.

The British Embassy issues a useful leaflet entitled *Employment for British Subjects*.

Turkey

Turkish Embassy: 43 Belgrave Square, London SW1X 8PA. Tel: 071-235 5222.

Consular Section: Rutland Lodge, Rutland Gardens, London SW7 1BW. Tel: 071-589 0360.

Tourist Office: 1st Floor, 170–173 Piccadilly, London W1V 9DD. Tel: 071-734 8681.

British Embassy: Şehit Ersan Caddesi 46A, Çankaya, Ankara.

British Consulate-General: Tepebaşi, Beyoğlu, Istanbul.

British Chamber of Commerce: (PO Box 190), Karaköy, Istanbul.

British Council: Kirlingic Sokak 9, Gazi Osman Paşa, Ankara. There is also a branch in Istanbul.

Anglo Turkish Society: 43 Montrose Place, London SW1X 7DT.

Yugoslavia

Yugoslav Embassy: 5 Lexham Gardens, London W8 5JJ. Tel: 071-370 6105.

Tourist Office: 143 Regent Street, London W1R 8AE. Tel: 071-734 5243.

British Embassy: Ulica General Zdanova 46, 11000 Belgrade.

British Council: Ulica General Zdanova 34—Mezanin, 11001 Belgrade.

12
The Middle East and North Africa

The Middle East comprises the countries of the Arab World plus Iran and Israel. In recent years, the Arabian Peninsula and Libya in particular have offered a wide range of well paid job opportunities for expatriates with income derived principally from oil revenues.

It is an area of the world that is often a puzzle to outsiders, and not all westerners feel truly at ease. There is definitely a substantial cultural difference between Middle Eastern society and the West, and anyone planning to work in the area would be well advised to develop an understanding of and respect for the region's traditions.

THE OPPORTUNITIES

After the oil price rise in the mid-seventies the oil producing countries of the Middle East offered boundless job opportunities for expatriates in a variety of different fields. The relative decline in oil prices and cutbacks in oil production has meant that many of these countries are cutting down on their overheads. As a result, opportunities are not what they once were.

Another consideration is that in the mid-seventies to mid-eighties many of these countries invested large sums in building up an infrastructure, but now this infrastructure is more or less complete. As a consequence, there are fewer projects around and they are more carefully costed. The main opportunities continue to be in:

- the oil and gas industry—especially on the Arabian Peninsula, in Libya and Algeria
- construction
- education and training

160

- the medical sector—hospitals and clinics
- banking and financial services
- telecommunications and utilities.

It is likely that there will continue to be opportunities on the Arabian Peninsula, Libya and—to a lesser extent—in Algeria. The number of expatriates working in Egypt has increased in recent years as aid has poured in, and the range of opportunities in Iraq is also likely to increase. Theoretically, there should be a similar situation in Iran as well, if a less xenophobic regime comes to power. Israel is more or less self-sufficient in qualified personnel, but there are opportunities for young people to work on kibbutzim.

The influence of Islam
While there are a significant number of Arab Christians—among the Lebanese, Palestinians and Egyptians—the majority of Arabs and Iranians are Muslim. Islam is more than just a religion, it is a way of life, which affects people's behaviour and attitudes.

- **Prayer times.** The call of the minaret (mosque tower) summons the faithful to prayer five times a day, and the very devout may well prostrate themselves facing towards Mecca. In Saudi Arabia shops close at prayer time.
- **Weekends may be centred on Friday.** This is the holy day for Muslims, many of whom attend the mosque at midday.
- **Fasting** from sunrise to sunset takes place during the month of Ramadan. However, many people stay up for part of the night eating and merry-making, and this can mean frayed tempers and inefficiencies at work. You should avoid eating or drinking in view of a Muslim during daylight hours.
- **Abstinence from alcohol.** Many Muslims abstain from alcohol, and in certain countries it is prohibited.
- **Abstinence from pork and pork products.** Pork is regarded as unclean, and is usually unavailable in Arab countries. Even if you manage to obtain some you should avoid serving it up at a meal attended by Muslims.
- **The subordinate position of women.** Some of the more traditional Arab societies are very much male dominated. Social contact between the sexes is discouraged, and in some countries women may not be allowed to work, drive a car or leave the house unaccompanied.

There are two main branches of Islam—Sunni and Shia—and a number of sects. Conflicts sometimes arise between these different groupings, and nowhere is this more evident than in Lebanon. Arabs tend to be Sunnis, while most Iranians are Shiites. In Iraq, however, the ruling class is Sunni while the majority of the population is Shiite.

The Wahabbis are a somewhat puritanical Sunni sect whose influence is felt particularly in Kuwait and Saudi Arabia, and there are Islamic fundamentalist movements in many countries with a strongly traditionalist outlook.

Political attitudes

Avoid discussing politics in the Middle East, unless you happen to be talking to someone you know well. Politics has strong emotional overtones, and your observations, however well-meant, are likely to be regarded as criticism.

Today's Arabs have inherited a civilisation which flourished for eight centuries and then went into decline. For the following five centuries they came under the rule of the Ottoman Empire, and later under French, Italian or British control. Now the Arab countries have regained their independence, many younger Arabs aspire to the creation of a single Arab nation which could restore their civilisation to its former preeminent position. For the moment this is very much a dream, and past attempts to unite the Arab World (such as Nasser's United Arab Republic) have ended in failure. Indeed, there is considerable hostility between certain states—Iraq and Syria, for instance—and you need to be aware of such tensions. However, there is still a sense of Arab nationhood, and an outsider is unlikely to be thanked for pouring scorn on the concept.

The concept of Western democracy is alien to the Arab World, and most countries in the region are authoritarian, ruled over by kings, princes or generals. In many cases the only machinery for changing the government is a *coup d'état*. Arab socialism has very little to do with socialism as we know it in the West.

Israel and the Palestine problem

The creation of Israel in 1948 caused consternation in the Arab World, and has been a cause of tension in the area ever since. If there is one cause which unites the Arab states it is opposition to the Jewish homeland.

Israel's existence is at the root of almost any anti-Western feeling you come across. In Arab eyes, the West requisitioned a portion of Arab territory and gave it to the Jews, displacing the Palestinian Arabs. The country, rightly or wrongly, is regarded as a bastion of Western imperialism, and was at one time blamed for all the Arab World's problems. Until recently no Arab state was prepared to recognise the existence of Israel, and when Egypt did so, it was ostracised by the other Arab states.

Many Arab countries operate a blacklist of firms that trade with Israel. If you wear St Michael clothing, for instance, it is a sensible precaution to cut off the labels before you go to the Arab World to avoid confiscation by the customs.

The deep seated antagonism towards Israel is unlikely to disappear overnight, despite the signs of a relaxation of attitudes. Leaders like President Qadaffi in Libya will continue to make political capital out of the Palestinian problem; it is an extremely sensitive subject, and the best advice to Westerners is to avoid the subject completely wherever possible.

Dealing with Middle Easterners

Some of the Arabs you come into contact with will have been educated in Western countries, and will be distinctly cosmopolitan in their outlook. Others will expect you to adapt to their norms. Here are a few tips on good etiquette:

- Be patient, and don't expect quick decisions, particularly after only an initial meeting. Arabs like to build up a relationship with people and that takes time.
- Accept a flexible approach to time. People may be late for appointments and be unwilling to agree to deadlines.
- Observe social niceties before you get down to business. Accept offers of coffee or tea and converse generally before turning to business matters.
- Ask about the health and progress of the male members of the family, but do not ask after the womenfolk.
- Be prepared for interruptions to meetings and the presence of other people during your deliberations, however confidential you may regard them. An official or the director of a firm sits in his office and holds court, often dealing with a number of matters at the same time.

Iran and Israel

Since the overthrow of the Shah by the Ayatollah Khomeini and his supporters Iran has become more traditional and fundamentalist than any country in the Arab world. For Europeans, it is an uncomfortable place to live, and will probably remain so until a more tolerant régime comes to power.

Israel is very European in comparison. However, the Israelis see themselves as surrounded by hostile neighbours and have something of a siege mentality. Judaism is the binding force which has brought together three distinct communities: the Ashkenazi Jews from Eastern Europe who predominate in the urban area, the Sephardi Jews whose origins lie on the Iberian peninsula, and the Middle Eastern Jews. In addition there is a sizeable Arab minority resident in Israel.

Reference:
Middle East & Mediterranean Business Directory (Owen's World Trade Ltd, Tridon House Industrial Estate, Thame OX9 3XB).
The Arabian Year Book (Owen's World Trade Ltd).
Major Companies of the Arab World (Graham & Trotman).
Arabian Construction (Beacon Publications, Jubilee House, Weston Favell, Northampton).
Gulf Guide & Diary (World of Information, 21 Gold Street, Saffron Walden, Essex CB10 1EJ.
Middle East Review (World of Information).
UK Firms with Offices in Arab countries (Arab British Chamber of Commerce, 6 Belgrave Square, London SW1).
Arabian Government and Public Services (Matrix Publishing Group, Silbury Court, 268 Silbury Boulevard, Central Milton Keynes MK9 2AF).
Arab Industry (Whitehall Overseas Publications Ltd).
Arab Hospital Update (230 Vauxhall Bridge Road, London SW1V 1AL).
Middle East Expatriate, monthly (Hilal International, 3rd Floor, Regal House, London Road, Twickenham TW1 3QS. Tel: 081-891 3362).
Middle East Economic Digest, weekly (21 John Street, London WC1N 2BP).
The Arab Mind R. Patai (Charles Scribner's Sons, New York).
The Arabs, P. Mansfield (Pelican 1987).
Understanding Arabs, M. K. Nydell (Intercultural Press 1988).
The Middle East Handbook (Middle East Christian Outreach— 1986, 22 Culverden Park Road, Tunbridge Wells, Kent TN4 9RA).

Useful Addresses:
Committee for Middle East Trade, 33 Bury Street, London SW1Y 6AX. Tel: 071-839 1170.
Middle East Association, same address.
Anglo Arab Association, 21 Collingham Road, London SW5 0NU. Tel: 071-373 8414.
The Arab British Centre, same address.
School of Oriental & African Studies, Malet Street, London WC1E 7HP.
Centre for Arab Gulf Studies, Old Library, University of Exeter, Prince of Wales Road, Exeter, EX4 4JZ. Tel: 0392-264041.
Centre for Middle Eastern & Islamic Studies, University of Durham, South End House, South Road, Durham DH1 3TG. Tel: 0385-64971.

Algeria
Algerian Embassy: 54 Holland Park, London W11 3RS. Tel: 071-221 7800.
Tourist Office: 6 Hyde Park Gate, London SW7. Tel: 071-584 5152.
British Embassy: Résidence Cassiopée, Bâtiment B, Chemin des Glycines, Algiers.
British Council: 6 Avenue Souidani Boudjemaa, Algiers.

The main opportunities would appear to be in the oil and gas industries.

Bahrain
Bahrain Embassy: 98 Gloucester Road, London SW7 4AU. Tel: 071-370 5978.
British Embassy: (PO Box 114), Government Road, North Manama.
British Council: 21 Government Avenue, (PO Box 452), Manama 306.

Bahrain has become a major banking and financial services centre for the region. A major employer is the Bahrain Oil Corporation and its various subsidiaries (PO Box 25504, Awali).

Egypt
Egyptian Embassy: 26 South Street, London W1Y 6EL. Tel: 071-499 2401.
Consular section: 19 Kensington Palace Gardens, London W8 4QL.
Tourist Office: 168 Piccadilly, London W1Y 9DE. Tel: 071-493 5282.

British Embassy: Ahmed Ragheb Street, Garden City, Cairo.
British Council: 192 Sharia el Nil, Agouza, Cairo.

Iran

Iranian Embassy: 22 Queen's Gate, London SW7 5JG. Tel: 071-584 7141.
Consulate: 50 Kensington Court, London W8 5DD. Tel: 071-937 5225.
British Embassy: (PO Box 1513), Avenue Ferdowsi, Teheran.
Irano-British Chamber of Commerce: Bezrouke House, 140 North Forsate Avenue, Teheran.

Iraq

Iraqi Embassy: 21 Queen's Gate, London SW7 5JG. Tel: 071-584 7141.
British Embassy: Sharia Salah, Ud-din, Karkh, Baghdad.
British Council: (PO Box 298), Waziriya 301, Street 3, Houses 22 and 24, Baghdad.

Israel

Israeli Embassy: 2 Palace Green, London W8 4QB. Tel: 071-937 8050.
Tourist office: 18 Great Malborough Street, London W1V 1AF. Tel: 071-434 3651.
British Embassy: 193 Hayarkon Street, Tel Aviv 63405.
British Council: (PO Box 3302), 140 Hayarkon Street, Tel Aviv 61032.
Israel-British Chamber of Commerce: (PO Box 3540), 76 Ibn Guirol Street, Tel Aviv.
Anglo-Israel Association: 9 Bentinck Street, London W1M 5RP. Tel: 071-486 2300.

Jordan

Jordanian Embassy: 6 Upper Phillimore Gardens, London W8 7HB. Tel: 071-937 3685.
Tourist Office: 211 Regent Street, London W1. Tel: 071-437 9465.
British Embassy: (PO Box 87), Abdoun, Amman.
British Council: (PO Box 634), Rainbow Street, off First Circle, Jabal Amman, Amman.

Kuwait

Kuwaiti Embassy: 45-46 Queen's Gate, London SW7. Tel: 071-589 4533.
British Embassy: (PO Box 300), Arabian Gulf Street, Safat 13003.
British Council: (PO Box 345), 2 al Arabi Street, Manouriyah.

The Kuwait Petroleum Corporation is the major employer in the country (PO Box 26565, 13126 Safat).

Lebanon
Lebanese Embassy: 21 Kensington Palace Gardens, London W8 4QM. Tel: 071-229 7265.
British Embassy: (PO Box 60180), Jal el Dib, East Beirut.

Libya
The Saudi Arabian Embassy represents Libyan interests in the UK. Useful contact addresses for employment are:

Umm Al-Jawaby Oil Service Co Ltd, 33 Cavendish Square, London W1M 9HF.
Libyan National Oil Corporation, (PO Box 2655), Tripoli.

Libya is still an important employer of British expatriates despite the lengthy break in diplomatic relations. Entry visas are usually obtained en route (e.g. in Malta).

Morocco
Moroccan Embassy: 49 Queen's Gate Gardens, London SW7 5NE. Tel: 071-581 5001.
Tourist Office: 174 Regent Street, London W1R 6HB. Tel: 071-437 0073.
British Embassy: 17 Boulevard de la Tour, Rabat.
British Council: (BP 427), 22 Avenue Moulay Youssef, Rabat.
British Chamber of Commerce: 291 Boulevard Mohammed V, Casablanca.

Oman
Omani Embassy: 44A Montpelier Square, London SW7 1JJ. Tel: 071-584 6782.
British Embassy: (PO Box 6898), Ruwi, Muscat.
British Council: (PO Box 7090, Jibroo) Road One, Medinat Qaboos West.

Qatar
Embassy of Qatar: 27 Chesham Place, London SW1X 8HG. Tel: 071-235 0851.
Consular Section: 115 Queen's Gate, London SW7 5LP.
Tourist Office: 115 Queen's Gate, London SW7 5LP. Tel: 071-581 8611.
British Embassy: (PO Box 3) Doha.
British Council: (PO Box 2992) Ras Abu Aboud Road, Doha.

Qatar General Petroleum Co: (PO Box 3212), Doha.

Saudi Arabia
Saudi Arabian Embassy: 30 Belgrave Square, London SW1X 8QB. Tel: 071-235 0831.
British Embassy: (PO Box 94351), Riyadh 11693.
British Council: (PO Box 2701), Dabab Street, off Washem Street, Mura'aba, Riyadh 11461.

Saudi Arabia is the largest employer of expatriates in the world. One of the major employers is ARAMCO based in Dhahran, but there are opportunities in many fields, such as education, health care, and so on.

Useful publications:
How to Live & Work in Saudi Arabia, M. Nydell (How To Books, 1991).

Syria
Syrian Embassy: 8 Belgrave Square, London SW1 8PH.
British Embassy: Quartier Malki, 11 Mohammed Kurd Ali Street, Immeuble Kotob, Damascus.

Tunisia
Tunisian Embassy: 29 Prince's Gate, London SW7 1QG. Tel: 071-584 8117.
Tourist Office: 7a Stafford Street, London W1. Tel: 071-499 7679.
British Embassy: (BP 229), 5 Place de la Victoire, Tunis.
British Council: Same address as Embassy.

United Arab Emirates
(Abu Dhabi, Dubai, Ras al Khaimah, Sharjah, Fujairah, Ajman, Umm al Qawain)

UAE Embassy: 30 Prince's Gate, London SW7 1PT. Tel: 071-581 1281.
Consular Section: 48 Prince's Gate, London SW7 2QA.
British Embassy: (PO Box 248), Abu Dhabi; (PO Box 65), Dubai.
British Council: (PO Box 248), Al-Jaber Building, First Floor, Sheikh Zayed I Street, Abu Dhabi.
ADCO (PO Box 270) and ADMA-OPCO (PO Box 303)—both in Abu Dhabi—are the two oil producing companies.

Yemen
Embassy of Yemen: 41 South Street, London W1Y 5PD. Tel: 071-629 9905.

Yemeni Consulate: 57 Cromwell Road, London SW7 2ED. Tel: 071-584 6607.

British Embassy: (PO Box 1287), 13 Al Qasr al Jumhuri, San'a.

British Council: (PO Box 2157), Beir Al-Mottahar, Al-Bonia Street, Harat Handhal, Sona'a.

13
Asia and the Pacific

ASIA

It is a virtual impossibility to describe Asia in just a few words. Asia is a vast continent—both in area and population—and comprises a diversity of ethnic groups and cultures. It is a continent of contrasts: some of the countries—like Nepal, Burma and Bangladesh—belong to the Third World; while others—South Korea, Taiwan, Hong Kong, Singapore, not to mention Japan—have flourishing economies and living standards similar to those in the West. For convenience I shall divide Asia up into three regions.

- The Indian Sub-Continent
- South East Asia
- The Far East (including China)

The Indian Sub-Continent
Britain's involvement with this part of the world stretches back to the eighteenth century, and it is still possible to see vestiges of the British Raj in many of the institutions and attitudes of these countries. Nowadays countries like India and Pakistan have plenty of indigenous expertise, and opportunities for expatriates are few, except as representatives for foreign companies. In other countries—Nepal, for instance—there is a need for aid workers.

South East Asia
ASEAN countries like Thailand, Singapore, Indonesia and Malaysia have had some of the highest economic growth rates in the world in recent years, and nowadays they too are able to rely almost wholly on indigenous expertise except in certain specialist areas such as education, mining, oil exploration and drilling.

Many foreign firms have manufacturing bases in this area and those that have not often employ representatives who may be recruited either back home or locally. Singapore in particular has become a very important centre for trade, finance and banking.

The Communist countries of what was French Indo-China are perhaps the most backward in the region and at the time of writing, opportunities for expatriates there are practically non-existent, and will remain so until political attitudes soften. Burma, which has an abundance of natural resources, pursues an isolationist line, and there are few opportunities for expatriates here outside government service.

The Far East
Many of the countries of Eastern Asia have highly developed economies and can no longer really be regarded as part of the Third World. Many of the opportunities lie in the education field and as representatives for foreign companies that need a presence there.

The British Crown Colony of Hong Kong still offers many opportunities to the qualified—both in the business and the private sector—though whether this will continue after the colony's incorporation into China in 1997 remains to be seen.

China has in the past been seen to be a land of promise, but appearances are deceptive. Despite the size of the country, its per capita GNP places it in the ranks of Third World countries. There are, however, opportunities in the voluntary sector or with British companies with representation in Beijing. There are also possibilities with firms that have joint venture agreements in the special economic zones on the coast; however, in the light of recent events, it is difficult to know if the gradual process of 'opening up' to the West will continue.

Cultural differences
Many of the Asian peoples adhere to religions and cultural traditions that are very different from our own. Buddhism, Confucianism and Hinduism as well as Islam have shaped attitudes over the centuries, and in some areas these are tinged with animist beliefs. Many countries contain a mixture of religions rather than a predominant one.

Islam is strong in Pakistan, Bangladesh, Malaysia, Brunei and Indonesia. Hinayana Buddhism is the predominant religion in Thailand, Sri Lanka, Burma, Cambodia and Laos. Korea, Japan and Vietnam are predominantly Mahayana Buddhist, while the

Chinese tend to be Buddhist or Confucian. The predominant religion in the Philippines is Christianity, while India is home to a variety of religions with Hinduism predominating. In many of these countries there are sizeable Christian communities as well. It is also worth remembering that traces of Western colonial influences can still be found. Britain once controlled the Indian subcontinent, Burma, Malaysia and Singapore, and still is in charge in Hong Kong. Cambodia, Laos and Vietnam were once French possessions, Indonesia was a Dutch colony, and the Philippines came under Spanish and American control.

Many of these countries have significant racial minorities. Immigrants from China play an important role in the commercial life of several South East Asian countries. There are substantial Indian minorities, too—particularly in Malaysia and Burma.

There are certain norms of behaviour that are common to a number of Asian peoples. Here are a few of them.

- **Avoidance of confrontation.** People exercise tact. Arguments are to be avoided at all costs.
- **Fatalism.** People accept that they are powerless to change the world.
- **Superstition.** People often believe in the supernatural and often do not embark on an enterprise without consulting an astrologer beforehand.
- **Submission to authority.** It is unthinkable for a person to contradict his boss even if he knows him to be wrong.
- **Respect for age and education.**
- **Passivity.** People are not as demonstrative as Westerners. Excessive shows of affection, for instance, are often frowned on.
- **The concept of face or status.** This is very important. You must take care not to humiliate a person either directly or indirectly.
- **Politeness and discretion.** You will cause offence if you go about criticising people and speaking your mind.

THE PACIFIC

The Pacific covers a vast area but is sparsely populated. Many of the island countries in this region are small and dependent on aid. The opportunities tend to be in government service (recruited by Crown Agents or ODA) or with voluntary organisations, although there are mining interests on a few of the islands.

The Pacific Islanders have the reputation of being easy-going, friendly people. English—or rather Pidgin English—is the lingua franca on a number of the islands which can often boast a profusion of languages and dialects. On the Solomon Islands, for instance, there are no less than 60 languages and dialects amongst a population of 25,000!

On some of the smaller islands facilities tend to be somewhat restricted, and residents have to rely very much on their own resources. The native population is Melanesian or Polynesian, but in some of the larger centres there is a substantial Indian, European and Chinese presence.

ASIA: REFERENCES AND ADDRESSES

References:

Asian Oil and Gas (Publishing Resources Ltd, 12th Floor, 200 Lockhart Road, Hong Kong).

Far Eastern Economic Review, weekly (Centre Point, 181 Gloucester Road, Hong Kong).

All Asia Guide, annual (published by the *Far Eastern Economic Review*).

Asia Mining (7514 Bagtikan Street, Corner Pason Tano, Makati, Metro Manila, Philippines).

Far East Expatriate, monthly (Hilal International, Regal House, London Road, Twickenham, Middlesex TW1 3QS).

Indonesia—Malaysia—Singapore—Brunei Business Directory (Utraco Pte Ltd, Colombo Court, (PO Box 782), Singapore 9117).

Languages of Asia and the Pacific, C. Hamblin (Angus & Robertson). A phrase book covering 25 languages.

Addresses:

School of Oriental & African Studies, Malet Street, London WC1.

Centre of South Asian Studies, University of Cambridge CB2 1TN.

Centre for South East Asian Studies, University of Hull HU6 7RX. Tel: 0482-46311.

East Asia Centre, University of Newcastle upon Tyne NE1 7RU. Tel: 0632-328511.

Asian Studies Centre, St Anthony's College, Oxford OX2 2JF. Tel: 0865-59651.

Bangladesh

Bangladesh High Commission: 28 Queen's Gate, London SW7 5JA. Tel: 071-584 0081.

British High Commission: (PO Box 90), Dilkhusha, Dhaka 2.
British Council: (PO Box 161), 5 Fuller Road, Ramna, Dhaka 2.

Brunei Darussalaam

Brunei High Commission: 49 Cromwell Road, London SW7 2ED.
Tel: 071-581 0521.
British High Commission: (PO Box 2197), 5th Floor, Hong Kong
Bank Chambers, Jalan Pemancha, Bandar Seri Begawan.
British Council: Same address as Embassy.

The major private sector employer here is the Brunei Shell
Petroleum Company.

Burma (Myanmar)

Burmese Embassy: 19A Charles Street, Berkeley Square, London
W1X 8ER. Tel: 071-499 8841.
British Embassy: (PO Box 638), 80 Strand Road, Rangoon.
British Council: (c/o Embassy.)

China (People's Republic)

Chinese Embassy: 45-51 Portland Place, London W1N 3AH. Tel:
071-636 5726.
Consular Section: 31 Portland Place, London W1N 3AH.
Tourist Office: 4 Glentworth Street, London NW1. Tel: 071-235
9427.
British Embassy: 11 Guang Hua Lu, Jian Guo Men Wai, Beijing
(c/o FCO, King Charles Street, London SW1).
British Council: (c/o Embassy).
Society for Anglo-Chinese Understanding: 152 Camden High
Street, London NW1 0NE. Tel: 071-485 8236.
Great Britain China Centre: 15 Belgrave Square, London SW1X
8PG. Tel: 071-235 6696.

Reference:
The Chinese, D. Bonavia (Penguin 1982).

Hong Kong

Hong Kong Government Office: 6 Grafton Street, London W1X
3LB. Tel: 071-499 9821.
Tourist Office: 125 Pall Mall, London SW7 5EA. Tel: 071-930
4775.
The Hong Kong Association: 43 King William Street, London
EC4.
British Council: Easey Commercial Building, 255 Hennessy Road,
Wanchai.

British Chamber of Commerce: 8 Queen's Road, Central District, HK.

The job market for expatriates is largely confined to the professions or specialist posts, and most of the jobs are on contract terms. The Hong Kong Government employs some 3,000 expatriates as administrators, doctors, accountants, engineers, lawyers, surveyors, senior police officers, etc. Send enquiries about posts with the Government to the HK Government Office or the Civil Service Branch, Government Secretariat, Hong Kong.

There is also a substantial British military presence in Hong Kong with its own schools and radio station. Many firms base their Far East representatives in Hong Kong and there is a thriving banking and financial services sector. Among the leading British firms in Hong Kong are:

Inchcape Pacific Ltd, 1 Exchange Square, 8 Connaught Place.
Jardine Matheson, Connaught Centre (PO Box 70).
Swire Group, Swire House, 9 Connaught Road Central.
Wheelock Marden, Wheelock House, 23rd Floor, 20 Pedder Street.
Hutchison Whampoa, Hutchison House, 22nd Floor, 10 Harcourt Road.

The HK Govt Office can provide you with a useful booklet entitled *Coming to Hong Kong* together with fact sheets on the health services, education, housing, recreational facilities, and so on.

Reference:
The South China Morning Post and the *Hong Kong Standard* can both be consulted at the HK Government Office library.
How to Live & Work in Hong Kong, M. Bennett (How To Books, 1991).

India
Indian High Commission: India House, Aldwych, London WC2B 4NA. Tel: 071-836 8484.
Tourist Office: 7 Cork Street, London W1X 2AB. Tel: 071-437 3677.
British High Commission: AIFACS Building, Rafi Marg, New Delhi 110/001.
British Council: (c/o High Commission).
British & South Asian Trade Association: 103 New Oxford Street, London WC1A 1DU.

Indonesia

Indonesian Embassy: 10 Portman Street, London W1 9AQ. Tel: 071-499 7661.

Consular Section: 157 Edgware Road, London W2 2HR. Tel: 071-499 7661.

Tourist Office: 38 Grosvenor Square, London W1X 9AD. Tel: 071-493 2080.

British Embassy: Jalan M H Thamrin 75, Jakarta 10310.

British Council: S Widjojo Centre, 57 Jalan Jendral Sudirman, Jakarta.

Indonesia British Association: Lippo Life Building, 2nd Floor, Jalan HR Rasuna, Said Kav B-10, Jakarta 12910.

Indonesia Association: 90-93 Fenchurch Street, London EC3M 4BY. Tel: 071-480 5493.

Reference:
The main English language newspapers are *Indonesian Times, Indonesian Observer, Jakarta Post,* and *Indonesian Daily News.*

Japan

Japanese Embassy: 101-104 Piccadilly, London W1Y 9FN. Tel: 071-465 6500.

Tourist Office: 167 Regent Street, London W1R 7FD. Tel: 071-734 9638.

British Embassy: 1 Ichibancho, Chiyoda-Ku, Tokyo 102.

British Council: 2-Kagurazaka 1-Chome, Shinjuku-ku, Tokyo 162.

British Chamber of Commerce: Kowa 16 Bldg Annex, 3rd Floor, 9-20 Akaska 1-Chome, Minato-ku, Tokyo.

Centre for Japanese Studies: University of Sheffield S10 2TN. Tel: 0742-78555.

Centre for Japanese Studies: University of Stirling, FK9 4LA.

Centre for the Study of Contemporary Japan: Essex University, Wivenhoe Park, Colchester CO4 3SQ. Tel: 0206-862286.

Japan Business Consultancy, Newton Park, Bath BA1 9BN. Tel: 0225-874146.

Japan Centre: 66-68 Brewer Street, London W1R 3PJ. Tel: 071-439 8035. Specialists in books on Japan and Japanese.

Japan Recruitment, 5 Sherwood Street, London W1V 7RA. Tel: 071-734 4422. Recruits English teachers for Japanese schools and universities.

Reference:
The main English language newspapers are:

The Japan Times (5-4 2-cheni, Hirakawa-cho, Chiyoda-ku, Tokyo 10).

Mainichi Daily News, 1-1-1 Hitotsubashi, Chiyoda-ku, Tokyo 100.

Shushoku Joho, a job information magazine for Japanese studying in Europe and Europeans with a good knowledge of Japanese. (Obtainable from Recruit Europe Ltd, Berkeley Square House, Berkeley Square, London W1X 5LB. Tel: 071-495 3929.)

Jobs in Japan, J. Wharton (Global Press 1989, distributed by Vacation Work Publications).

Japanese Ethics and Etiquette in Business, Boye de Mente (Merehurst).

Japan Posting: Preparing to live in Japan (British Chamber of Commerce).

Gaijin's Guide: Practical Help for Everyday Life in Japan, J. Ashby (Japan Times Ltd 1985).

Japan Times Directory: Foreign Residents, Business Firms and Organisations.

Korea (South)

South Korean Embassy: 4 Palace Gate, London W8 5NF. Tel: 071-581 0247.

Tourist Office: Vogue House, 1 Hanover Square, London W1R 9RD. Tel: 071-408 1591.

British Embassy: 4 Chung-Dong, Choong-ku, Seoul.

British Chamber of Commerce, c/o Chartered Bank, Samsung Building 50, 1-Ka Ulchi Ro, Choong-Ku, Seoul.

British Council: Room 401, Anglican Church Annex, 3-7 Chung-Dong, Choong-ku, Seoul.

Reference:
Korean Ethics and Etiquette in Business, Boye de Mente (Merehurst).
Korea Herald, Korea Times.

Among the major corporations are:

Daewoo Group, 541, 5-ka, Namdaemun-no, Choong-ku, Seoul.
Hanjin Group, 118 2-ka, Namdaemun-no.
Hyundai Group, 140-2 Gae-dong, Chongno-ku.
Lucky Goldstar Group, 537 Namdaemun-no 5, Choong-ku.
Samsung Group, 250, 2-ka, Taepying-no Choong-ku.

Malaysia

Malaysian High Commission: 45 Belgrave Square, London SW1X 8QT. Tel: 071-491 4172.

Tourist Office: 17 Curzon Street, London W1Y 7FE. Tel: 071-499 7388.

British High Commission: PO Box 11030, 13th Floor, Wosma Damansara, Jalan Semantan, 50732 Kuala Lumpur.

British Council: (PO Box 10539), Jalan Bukit Aman, 50480 Kuala Lumpur.

British Malaysia Industry and Trade Association: (PO Box 2574), Kuala Lumpur 2307.

Malaysia, Singapore & Brunei Association: 90 Fenchurch Street, London EC2M 4BY.

Newspapers:
New Straits Times, Sabah Times, Sarawak Herald.

Nepal

Nepalese Embassy: 12A Kensington Palace Gardens, London W8 4QU. Tel: 071-229 6231.

British Embassy: (PO Box 106), Lainchaur, Kathmandu.

British Council: (PO Box 640), Kantipath, Kathmandu.

Pakistan

Pakistan High Commission: 35 Lowndes Square, London SW1X 9JN. Tel: 071-235 2044.

British High Commission: Diplomatic Enclave, Ramna 5 (PO Box 1122), Islamabad.

British Council: 23 87th Street G 6/3, (PO Box 1135), Islamabad.

The Philippines

Philippines Embassy: 9A Palace Green, London W8 4QE. Tel: 071-937 1609.

Consular Section: 1 Cumberland House, Kensington High Street, London W8.

Tourist Office: 199 Piccadilly, London W1V 9LE. Tel: 071-439 3481.

British Embassy: (PO Box 1970 MCC), Electra House, 115-117 Esteban St, Legaspi Village, Makati, Metro Manila.

British Council: (PO Box AC 168 Cubao), 73rd Street, New Manila, Quezon City, Metro Manila.

Singapore

Singapore High Commission: 2 Wilton Crescent, London SW1X 8RX. Tel: 071-235 8315.

Tourist Office: 33 Heddon Street, London W1R 7LB. Tel: 071-437 0033.

British High Commission: (PO Box 19), Tanglin Circus, Singapore 10.

British Council: Singapore Rubber House, Collyer Quay, Singapore 0104.

British Business Association: 1st Floor, Inchcape House, 450-452 Alexandra Road, Singapore 0511.

Reference:
Culture Shock Singapore & Malaysia, JoAnn Craig (Times Editions, Times Centre, 1 New Industrial Road, Singapore 1953).
The Straits Times.

Sri Lanka

Sri Lankan High Commission: 13 Hyde Park Gardens, London W2 2LU. Tel: 071-262 1841.

Tourist Office: 52 High Holborn, London WC1V 6RL. Tel: 071-405 1194.

British High Commission: (PO Box 1433), Galle Road, Killiputiya, Colombo 3.

British Council: 49 Alfred House Gardens, Colombo 3.

Taiwan (Republic of China)

Anglo Taiwan Trade Committee: 272-274 Vauxhall Bridge Road, London SW1V 1BB.

Thailand

Royal Thai Embassy: 30 Queen's Gate, London SW7 5JB. Tel: 071-589 0173.

Tourist Office: 9 Stafford Street, London W1X 3FE. Tel: 071-499 7679.

British Embassy: Ploenchit Road, Bangkok.

British Council: 428 Rama I Road, Siam Square, Bangkok 10500.

British Chamber of Commerce: Room 206, Bangkok Insurance Building, 302 Silom Road, Bangkok 5.

Anglo-Thai Society: 22 Ulster Court, Albany Park Road, Kingston, Surrey KT2 5SS. Tel: 071-546 3048.

Reference:
English language newspapers—*The Bangkok Post, The Nation.*

Vietnam

Vietnamese Embassy: 12 Victoria Road, London W8 5RD. Tel: 071-937 1912.

British Embassy: 16 Pho Ly Thuong Kiet, Hanoi.

REFERENCES AND ADDRESSES: PACIFIC

Pacific Island Society, 2 Harpsen Way, Henley on Thames RG9 1NL. Contact: The Rev. John Pinder.

Pacific Island Business & Trade Directory (Universal Business Directories Ltd, New Zealand News Centre, 360 Dominion Road, Auckland 3, New Zealand).

Pacific Islands Monthly (Fiji Times, 20 Gordon Street, Suva. UK distributor: F.A. Smyth & Associates, 23 Aylmer Parade, London N2).

Fiji

Fiji High Commission: 34 Hyde Park Gate, London SW7 5BN. Tel: 071-584 3661.

British High Commission: (PO Box 1355), Victoria House, 47 Gladstone Road, Suva (also looks after Nauru and Tuvalu).

British Council: Vanua House, Victoria Parade, Suva. Has responsibility for the whole of the South Pacific.

Kiribati

British High Commission: (PO Box 61), Bariki, Tarawa.

Honorary Consul: Maurice Chandler, Rutland House, 8 Brookhouse Street, Leicester LE2 0JB.

Papua New Guinea

PNG High Commission: 14 Waterloo Place, London SW1 4AR. Tel: 071-930 0922.

British High Commission: (PO Box 729), Port Moresby.

Solomon Islands

British High Commission: (PO Box 676), Honiara.

Tonga

Tongan High Commission: New Zealand House, Haymarket, London SW1X 4TE. Tel: 071-837 3287.

British High Commission: (PO Box 56), Nuku'alofa.

Vanuatu (formerly New Hebrides)

British High Commission: (PO Box 567), Port Vila. Also looks after New Caledonia.

British Friends of Vanuatu: 67 Beresford Road, Cheam, Surrey. Contact: Richard Dorman.

14
Africa

Africa south of the Sahara consists of 46 countries, 2,000 tribes and 750 languages. Many of the countries are artificial entities whose boundaries cut across ethnic and tribal groupings—a consequence of the 1884 Conference of the Great Powers in Berlin, which partitioned the continent among the different European governments. When conflicts break out—for instance, the Nigerian War—it is often because tribal loyalties outweigh national ones.

THE OPPORTUNITIES

Sub-Saharan Africa is very much part of the Third World, with a large proportion of the population living at subsistence level; so the Continent is a major recipient of aid. Virtually all the major aid agencies and volunteer agencies are active here, as well as many missionary groups.

Many of these bodies are involved in education, health, rural development, small industries and agriculture. In an effort to make Africa self-sufficient in food production, agriculture receives top priority, and agricultural advisers are much in demand. There is also considerable private sector involvement in mining, oil, agriculture-related industries, utilities and telecommunications. The area can be roughly divided into three regions:

East Africa
Kenya, which is one of the more successful African countries, still has a substantial expatriate population of white settlers. Its neighbour, Tanzania, is at last trying to lift itself out of the doldrums after years of economic stagnation and it looks as if opportunities will beckon there. Uganda is still recovering from the disastrous civil war and needs plenty of reconstruction. Sudan has in recent

years been a disaster area suffering from drought, flooding and a refugee problem. The major relief and aid agencies are active here and in Ethiopia, too.

West Africa

The best opportunities for British people tend to be in former British territories, rather than in Zaire and the countries of what was French West Africa. However a few British firms have operations in Francophone Africa, among them Plessey Airports.

The most promising place for work opportunities is Nigeria. This is the most populous of the African states with some 100 million inhabitants, and one of the wealthiest thanks to oil. A large number of British firms have representations there.

Central and southern Africa

Zambia has a substantial expatriate workforce in the copper mining sector, though salaries tend to be below the international average for expatriates. Conditions are better in neighbouring Zimbabwe which in recent years has had to import around 90,000 expatriates to fill gaps in its workforce left by white emigrants. Many of these work in education, agriculture, mining and commerce. Botswana also has a substantial expatriate population, many of them working with the Botswana Development Corporation.

The former Portuguese colonies of Angola and Mozambique could offer good employment opportunities in the future, once a peace settlement comes into force in southern Africa, and there are already a number of British companies involved in the diamond mining and oil sector. Mozambique is the leading producer of cashew nuts and there is a substantial British aid presence there. Namibia, when it achieves independence (anticipated in 1990) could well offer good expatriate employment opportunities in the future.

The people

Africa suffers from some of the worst problems of any part of the Third World. Poverty, disease, illiteracy, malnutrition and poor communications characterise many of the countries of the continent, and the situation is not helped by inept leadership, corruption in government and civil wars. However, that is not the whole story. Since independence a number of countries have made progress on certain fronts (in raising standards of literacy, for example) and a new generation of more pragmatic African leaders is emerging, keen to set their economies in order. There are grounds for hope that things will be better in the future.

It would be misleading to try and describe a 'typical African' since in such a vast area, there is naturally almost endless variation, not only from one country to another, but within each country. However, here are some of the factors likely to affect the outlook and behaviour of many Africans:

- **Tribal influence.** A person is obliged to help a fellow-tribesman before anyone else. Tribal allegiance is often considered more important than nationalism.

- **Colonial influences.** The manners and attitudes of the educated élite of former French territories resemble—at least superficially—those of their former colonial masters; similarly, in former British colonies, the administration still tends to run along British lines. Some of these influences have tended to hamper rather than promote a country's development. Former British territories, for instance, have in the past produced more arts graduates than people with technical skills.

- **The country's leadership.** The attitudes and political philosophy of the person (or people) in power can have a profound influence on the people of a country. Leaders who exploit their positions to their own advantage or pursue unrealistic policies that cause stagnation, often cause feelings of indifference or resignation at the grass roots.

- **The level of education.** Europeans often complain that Africans lack initiative and commonsense; this is usually because many have received only a rudimentary education, or perhaps no education at all. However, educated Africans are quite capable of holding their own with people of other nationalities.

- **Health considerations.** Health care is often developed in urban areas, but in the countryside doctors are scarce, and people can often suffer from debilitating diseases which produce lethargy.

One other problem you may encounter is a different concept of time. There is an absence of rush, and punctuality is not one of Africa's strong points. Patience and resilience are other characteristic features: Africans seem prepared to wait indefinitely and face up stoically to every eventuality. African society is male-dominated, though women do play an important role in commerce and agriculture, particularly in countries like Nigeria.

There are also significant minorities, such as the Indians in Kenya, or the Lebanese in parts of West Africa, whose importance in the economy is disproportionate to their numbers.

REFERENCE, ADDRESSES AND USEFUL PUBLICATIONS

Reference:

Africa & Asia Business Directory (Owen's World Trade, 18 Farndon Road, Oxford OX2 6RT. Tel: 0865-514378).

Braby's Commercial Directory of Southern Africa (10 Caversham Road, (PO Box 1426), Pinetown 3600, Natal, South Africa).

The Africans, D. Lamb (Methuen 1985).

New Africa Yearbook (IC Publications, (PO Box 261), Carlton House, 69 Great Queen Street, London WC2B 5BN. Tel: 071-404 4333).

Journals:

West Africa (West Africa Publishing Co, 43-45 Coldharbour Lane, London SE5 9NR. Tel: 071-737 2946).

Africa Business (IC Publications).

New Africa (IC Publications).

Africa Events (Dar es Salaam Ltd, 55 Bonner Street, London EC1Y 8PX. Tel: 071-608 1205).

Africa Analysis (Orchard House, 167 Kensington High Street, London W8 6SH).

Useful addresses:

The Africa Book Centre, 1st Floor, 38 King Street, Covent Garden, London WC2E 8JT. Tel: 071-240 6649. The centre has a wide range of journals and books devoted to Africa.

School of Oriental & African Studies, Malet Street, London WC1.

African Studies Centre, Cambridge University, Free School Lane, Cambridge CB2 2RQ. Tel: 0223-358381, ext 231.

Centre for Southern African Studies, University of York, Heslington, York YO1 5DD. Tel: 0904-59861, ext 566.

Centre for West African Studies, University of Birmingham, (PO Box 363), Birmingham B15 2TT. Tel: 021-472 1301, ext 2263.

Royal African Society, 18 Northumberland Avenue, London WC2N 5BJ.

Angola

Angolan Embassy: 87 Jermyn Street, London SW1. Tel: 071-839 5743.

British Embassy: (CP 1244), Rua Diego Cao, 4 Luanda.

Two activities employing expatriate labour are oil exploration (Gulf Oil) and diamond mining.

Botswana

Botswana High Commission: 8 Stratford Place, London W1N 9AE. Tel: 071-499 0031.

British High Commission: Queen's Road, The Mall, Gaborone.

British Council: Same address as High Commission.

Mining is important to Botswana's economy, notably for manganese, copper, nickel, diamonds.

Cameroon

High Commission: 84 Holland Park, London W11 3SB. Tel: 071-727 0771.

British Embassy: (BP 547), Le Concorde, avenue Winston Churchill, Yaoundé.

British Council: (BP 818), Les Galéries, avenue J F Kennedy, Yaoundé.

Work permits are obtainable in Cameroon where French influence is still strong.

Ethiopia

Ethiopian Embassy: 17 Princes Gate, London SW7 1PZ. Tel: 071-589 7212.

British Embassy: (PO Box 858), Dessie Road, Addis Ababa.

British Council: (PO Box 1043), Artistic Building, Adwa Avenue, Addis Ababa.

Gabon

Gabon Embassy: 48 Kensington Court, London W8 5DB. Tel: 071-937 5258).

British Embassy: (BP 476), Bâtiment Sogame, Blvd de l'Indépendence, Libreville.

Gabon's oil industry is dominated by the French, and its mining sector by US companies. The country boasts the highest GNP south of the Sahara.

Gambia

Gambia High Commission: 57 Kensington Court, London W8 5DG. Tel: 071-937 6316.

British High Commission: (PO Box 507), 48 Atlantic Road, Banjul.

Ghana

High Commission: 13 Belgrave Square, London SW1X 8PR. Tel: 071-235 4142.

British High Commission: (PO Box 296), Barclays Bank Building, High Street, Accra.

British Council: (PO Box 771), Liberia Road, Accra.

Ivory Coast (Côte d'Ivoire)

Ivory Coast Embassy: 2 Upper Belgrave Street, London SW1X 8BJ. Tel: 071-235 6991.

British Embassy: (BP 2581), 5th Floor, Immeuble Shell, Avenue Lamblin, Abidjan.

British Businessmen's Association, c/o Barclays Bank, Immeuble Alpha 2000, 01-BP-522 Abidjan.

Kenya

Kenyan High Commission: 24–25 New Bond Street, London W1Y 9HD. Tel: 071-636 2371.

Tourist Office: 13 New Burlington Street, London W1X 1FF. Tel: 071-839 4477.

British High Commission: (PO Box 30133), 13th Floor, Bruce House, Standard Street, Nairobi.

British Council: (PO Box 40751), ICEA Building, Kenyatta Avenue, Nairobi.

Lesotho

Lesotho High Commission: 10 Collingham Road, London SW5 0NR. Tel: 071-373 8581.

British High Commission: (PO Box 521), Maseru.

British Council: (PO Box 429), Hobson's Square, Maseru 100.

Malawi

Malawi High Commission: 33 Grosvenor Street, London W1X 0DE. Tel: 071-491 4972.

British High Commission: (PO Box 30042), Longadzi House, Lilongwe 3.

British Council: (PO Box 30222), Plot No 13/20, City Centre, Lilongwe 3.

Mauritius

Mauritius High Commission: 32 Elvaston Place, London SW7 5NW. Tel: 071-581 0294.

Tourist Office: 23 Ramillies Place, London W1A 3BF. Tel: 071-439 4461.

British High Commission: King George V Avenue, Floreal.

British Council: (PO Box 111), Royal Road, Rose Hill.

Mozambique

Mozambique Embassy: 159 New Bond Street, London W1Y 9PA. Tel: 071-493 0694.

British Embassy: (CP 55), A. Vladimir I Lenine 319, Maputo.

Namibia

Namibian High Commission, Centre Link, 34 South Moulton Street, London SW1Y 2BP. Tel: 071-408 2335.

British High Commission, 116A Leutwein Street, Windhoek 9000.

British Council, c/o British High Commission.

Nigeria

High Commission: 9 Northumberland Ave, London SW1. Tel: 071-839 1244; and 56 Fleet Street, London EC4Y 1JU. Tel: 071-353 3776.

British High Commission: Private Mail Bag 12136, Lagos.

Nigeria-British Chamber of Commerce: (PO Box 109), Lagos, and 69 Cannon Street, London EC4N 5AG.

Reference:

Major Companies of Nigeria, edited by M. Lawn (Graham & Trotman, 1982).

Daily Times/Sunday Times, (PO Box 139), Lagos and 52-54 Grays Inn Road, London WC1X 8LT. The leading English language newspaper of Nigeria and publisher of *Nigeria Handbook, Africa Yearbook, Trade and Industrial Directory.*

Senegal

Senegalese Embassy: 11 Phillimore Gardens, London W8 7QG. Tel: 071-937 0925.

British Embassy: (BP 6025), 20 Rue du Docteur Guillet, Dakar.

British Council: Same address as Embassy.

Sierra Leone

Sierra Leone High Commission: 33 Portland Place, London W1N 3AG. Tel: 071-636 6483.

British High Commission: Standard Bank of Sierra Leone Building, Lightboot Boston Street, Freetown.

British Council: (PO Box 124), Tower Hill, Sierra Leone.

Somalia

Somali Embassy: 60 Portland Place, London WQ1N 3DG. Tel: 071-780 7148.

British Embassy: (PO Box 1036), Waddada Zasan Geeddii Abtoow 7–8, Mogadishu.

Sudan

Sudanese Embassy: 3 Cleveland Row, London SW1A 1DD. Tel: 071-839 8080.

Tourist Office: 308 Regent Street, London W1R 5AL. Tel: 071-631 1785.

British Embassy: (PO Box 801), New Aboulela Building, Barlaman Avenue, Khartoum.

British Council: (PO Box 1253), House 60, Street 49, Khartoum 11 (East).

Tanzania

Tanzanian High Commission: 43 Hertford Street, London W1Y 7TF. Tel: 071-499 8951.

Tourist Office: 77 South Audley Street, London W1Y 5TA. Tel: 071-499 7727.

British High Commission: (PO Box 9200), Permanent House, Corner Azikiew St/Independence Avenue, Dar-es-Salaam.

British Council: (PO Box 9100), Samora Avenue, Dar-es-Salaam.

Uganda

Ugandan High Commission: Uganda House, Trafalgar Square, London WC2N 5DX. Tel: 071-839 5783.

British High Commission: (PO Box 7070), 10-12 Parliament Avenue, Kampala.

British Council: Same address as Embassy.

Zaire

Embassy of Zaire: 26 Chesham Place, London SW1X 8HH.

British Embassy: (BP 8094), 9 avenue de l'Equateur, 5th Floor, Kinshasa.

Zambia

Zambian High Commission: 2 Palace Gate, London W8 5NG. Tel: 071-589 6655.

Tourist Office: 163 Piccadilly, London W1V 9DE. Tel: 071-498 1188.

British High Commission: (PO Box 50050), Independence Avenue, Lusaka.

British Council: (PO Box 34571), Heroes Place, Cairo Road, Lusaka.

Zimbabwe

Zimbabwe High Commission: 429 Strand, London WC2R 0SA. Tel: 071-836 7755.

Tourist Office: Collette House, 52-53 Piccadilly, London W1V 9AA. Tel: 071-629 3955.

British High Commission: (PO Box 4490), Stanley House, Stanley Avenue, Harare.

British Council: (PO Box 664), 23 Stanley Avenue, Harare.

Publications:

The Sunday Mail and *The Herald* (PO Box 396, Harare), which can be read at the High Commission.

The country has a network of private recruitment consultants, including:

Kipps Personnel Consultants, 11th Floor, Michael House, Baker Avenue, Harare.

P.E. Consulting Group, (PO Box 8381), Causeway, Harare.

Valcol Employment Bureau, (PO Box 4916), Harare.

Rio Tinto, (PO Box 4490), Harare.

15
Latin America and the Caribbean

Apart from a few regions colonised by the British, Dutch and French, the whole of the land mass from Mexico southwards has come under Spanish and Portuguese influence, and the influences are still very much in evidence today in the form of religion (overwhelmingly Roman Catholic), language, institutions and attitudes.

Many people think of Latin America as a troubled region, burdened by debt, overwhelmed by inflation, beset by instability, where poverty and social injustice are the order of the day. This is something of a caricature. Dictatorships are now few and far between, although it is true that parts of the region face economic problems.

The opportunities

In the past, British expatriates helped develop the infrastructure of the region, building railways and developing the banking system, for example. Nowadays they are more likely to be involved in the aid and education sectors. In fact, the multinational companies operating in the region are more likely to recruit their staff either locally, or from the US.

It is advantageous to have connections with a particular country. Robert Herin (Egon Zehnder) cites the case of Brazil:

> 'Today the far rarer expatriate is likely to be a non-Brazilian who has joined his present employer while overseas and has well-established roots in Brazil.' (*Corporate Expatriate*, April 1987.)

One organisation which deserves to be mentioned in connection with employment opportunities in this area is the International Committee for Migration (ICM), Geneva office for Latin America, (PO Box 100), 17 route des Morillons, CH 1211 Geneva 19. The

UK office for ICM is Cranmer House, 3rd Floor, 39 Brixton Road, London SW9 5DD. Tel: 071-735 6197.

One of the Committee's aims is to help suitably qualified people who want to work or settle in Latin America to transfer there—especially those who would be able to assist in the development of that particular country in such areas as industry, the economy and education.

The ICM offices in Europe carry out the selection of the professionals and help them in their transfer in the following ways:

- providing information on the country in question
- obtaining the necessary entry visa
- defraying part of the travel cost from Europe to the country of destination
- providing orientation and special assistance on arrival
- offering a special insurance scheme, if desired

A recent jobs bulletin containing more than 100 vacancies illustrates the scope of opportunities on offer—most of them with governments or government funded bodies: for example, perhaps Chile needs a forest engineer; Costa Rica a professor of international finance; Venezuela a chemical engineer for a textile plant; Chile a lecturer in civil engineering; Honduras a librarian; Nicaragua a petrographer; Panama an odontologist; Argentina a lecturer in macroeconomics, and so on.

The people
Generally speaking, Latin Americans are easy-going people who welcome contact with expatriates. A knowledge of Spanish (Portuguese in the case of Brazil) is, however, vital for every expatriate.

Argentina, Paraguay and Costa Rica are reckoned to be the most European of all the countries of Latin America. Brazil, on the other hand, has a considerable ethnic mix: 55% white; 37% of mixed descent (European/black/Indian), 6% black and 2% native Indians. In the Andean states there is a much higher proportion of Andean Indians in the population.

South Americans take pride in their personal appearance and like to dress smartly, whether or not they can afford it. Family life and personal relationships are very important to them, and take precedence over most other matters. Punctuality is not a Latin American strong point, so try to adopt a more relaxed attitude to time. People relish compliments and praise, but personal criticism should be avoided, especially in public, as it is often regarded as rude and offensive. When speaking to people, remember to maintain eye contact.

Some Europeans are disturbed by some aspects of Latin American life, such as the wide chasm between the rich and the poor in some countries that people seem to accept rather than trying to alter. There are also Latin American male machismo attitudes that women can find trying at first until they learn to live with them.

On the whole, however, Europeans enjoy postings to the region and experience few problems of adaptation.

REFERENCES & ADDRESSES

References:
Major Companies of Argentina, Brazil, Mexico & Venezuela, S. J. Longrigg (Graham & Trotman 1982).
South American Handbook (Travel & Trade Publication, 5 Prince's Building, George Street, Bath).
Latin America Weekly Report (Latin American Newsletters, 61 Old Street, London EC1V 9HXS. Tel: 071-251 0012).
Latin American News (Latin American Trade Advisory Group, 2 Belgrave Square, London SW1X 8PJ. Tel: 071-235 2303).

Useful Addresses:
Hispano & Luso Brazilian Council, Canning House, 2 Belgrave Square, London SW1X 8PJ. Tel: 071-235 2303. This organisation has a library of some 50,000 books on Iberian and Latin American affairs which is open to the public. Although it does not have newspapers it has a special collection of background economic and trade information of interest to businessmen and possibly jobseekers.
Latin American Bureau, 1 Amwell Street, London EC1R 1UL. Tel: 071-278 2829. This is an independent, non profit-making research and publishing organisation founded and supported by church and development agencies. It has an extensive library/resource centre devoted to Latin America and the Caribbean. The library's opening hours are variable so check on the phone before visiting.
Centre for Latin American Studies, University of Cambridge, West Road, Cambridge CB3 9EF. Tel: 0223-61661, ext 66.
Latin American Centre, University of Essex, Wivenhoe Park, Colchester CO4 3SQ. Tel: 0206 862286.

Argentina

Argentine Interests Section: Brazilian Embassy, 111 Cadogan Gardens, London SW3 2RQ. Tel: 071-730 7173.

British Chamber of Commerce: Corrientes 457, 1043 Buenos Aires.

Anglo Argentine Society: 2 Belgrave Square, London SW1X 8PJ. Tel: 071-235 9505.

Newspaper:
Buenos Aires Herald (weekly).

Despite the Falklands dispute there is still a substantial British presence here.

Belize

Belize High Commission: 15 Thayer Street, London W1M 5DL.

British High Commission: Belize House, (PO Box 91), Belmopan.

Bolivia

Bolivian Embassy: 106 Eaton Square, London SW1W 9AD. Tel: 071-235 4255.

British Embassy: (Casilla 694), Avenida Arce 2734-2754, La Paz.

Brazil

Brazilian Embassy: 32 Green Street, London W1Y 4AT.

Consular Section: 6 St Albans Street, London SW1Y 4SG.

Tourist Office: 35 Dover Street, London W1. Tel: 071-499 0877.

British Embassy: Avenida das Nações Lote 8, Caixa Postal 586, Brasília DF.

British Council: (Caixa Postal 6104), SCRN 708/9 Nos 1/3, 70.740 Braxília DF.

British Chamber of Commerce: Caixa Postal 669 ZC 00, Sao Paolo.

Anglo-Brazilian Society: 35 Dover Street, London W1X 3RA. Tel: 071-493 8493.

Chile

Chilean Embassy: 33 Regent Street, London SW1. Tel: 071-734 0802.

British Embassy: (Casilla 72-D), La Concepción Av 177, Providencia, Santiago.

British Council: (Casilla 15 T), Eliodoro Yanez 832, Tajamar, Santiago.

British Chamber of Commerce: (Casilla 536), Oficina 1011, Santiago.

Anglo Chilean Society: 12 Devonshire Street, London W1N 2DS. Tel: 071-581 1271.

Colombia

Colombian Embassy: 3 Hans Crescent, London SW1X 0LR. Tel: 071-589 9177.

Consular Section: 140 Park Lane, London W1Y 3DF. Tel: 071-493 4565.

British Embassy: (Apartado Aéreo 4508), Calle 38, 13-35 Pisos 9-11, Bogotá.

British Council: (Apartado Aéreo 089231), Calle 87 No 12-79, Bogotá.

Colombo-British Chamber of Commerce: (Apartado Aéreo 4305), Cra 10 Nos 15-39, Piso 10, Bogotá.

Costa Rica

Costa Rican Embassy: 93 Star Street, London W2 1QF. Tel: 071-723 1772.

British Embassy: (Apartado 815), Centro Colon 1007, San José.

Ecuador

Ecuadorean Embassy: 3 Hans Cresent, London SW1X 0LN. Tel: 071-584 2648.

British Embassy: (Casilla 314), Gonzalez Suarez, 111 Quito.

British Council: (Casilla 8829), Av. Amazonas 1646, Quito.

Falkland Islands

Falkland Islands Government Office: 29 Tufton Street, London SW1P 3QL. Tel: 071-222 2542.

Falkland Islands Association: 2 Greycoat Place, London SW1P 1JD. Tel: 071-222 0028. (Recruitment: Crown Agents.)

Publication:
Falkland Islands Gazette (Government Printing Office, Port Stanley).

Limited stock of housing.

Guyana

Guyana High Commission: 3 Palace Court, Bayswater Road, London W2 4LP. Tel: 071-229 7684.

British High Commission: (PO Box 10849), 44 Main Street, Georgetown.

Mexico
Mexican Embassy: 60 Trafalgar Square, London SW1. Tel: 071-235 6393.
Consular Section: 8 Halkin Street, London SW1X 7DW.
Tourist Office: 7 Cork Street, London W1X 1PB. Tel: 071-434 1058.
British Embassy: (PO Box 96 Bis), Rio Lerma 71, Col Cuauhtémoc, Mexico City 06500 DF.
British Council: (Apdo Postal 30-588), Maestro Antonio Caso 127, Col San Rafael, Mexico City 06470 DF.
British Chamber of Commerce: Tiber 103, 6th Floor, Cuauhtémoc, Mexico City 06500 DF.

Paraguay
Paraguayan Embassy: Braemar Lodge, Cornwall Gardens, London SW7 4AQ. Tel: 071-937 1253.
British Embassy: (Casilla de Corréo 404), Calle Presidente Franco 706, Asunción. One of the few countries in this part of the world where—at the time of writing—work permits and visas are not required.

Reference:
Live & Work in South America—Brazil and Paraguay (Herdcroft Ltd, 18 Coulter Close, Cuffley, Herts EN6 4RR).

Peru
Peruvian Embassy: 52 Sloane Street, London SW1X 9SP. Tel: 071-235 6867.
Tourist Office: 10 Grosvenor Gardens, London SW1W 0BD. Tel: 071-730 7122.
British Embassy: (Apartado 854), Edificio Pacifico-Washington, Plaza Washington, Avenida Arequipe, Lima.
British Council: (Apartado 14-0114), Calle Alberto Lynch 110, San Isidro, Lima 1.

Uruguay
Embassy of Uruguay: 48 Lennox Gardens, London SW1X 0DL. Tel: 071-589 8835.
British Embassy: Calle Marco Bruto 1073, Montevideo.
British Chamber of Commerce: Av Lib Brig Gral Laullya 1641, Montevideo.

Venezuela
Venezuelan Embassy: 1 Cromwell Road, London SW7 2HW. Tel: 071-581 2776.

British Embassy: (Apartado 1246), Avenida La Estancia No 10, Ciudad Comercial, Tamanaco, Caracas.
British Council: (Apartado 1246), Torre La Noria, Piso 6, Paseo Enrique Eraso, Sector San Roman, Las Mercedes, Caracas.
Camero Venezolano Britanic de Comercio y Industria: Apartado 5713, Torre Britanica, Piso 11, Letra E, Av Jose Felix Sosa, Altamira, Sur Caracas.

Reference:
Living in Venezuela (Venezuelan American Chamber of Commerce & Industry, Apartado 5181, Caracas).

CARIBBEAN

'There are few regions in the world where history has been so critical in shaping the present as in the Caribbean. The key to understanding Caribbean history is slavery and the forced transportation to the region of multitudes of peoples from Africa, and to a lesser extent from Asia and even Europe. Barely a trace remains of original population: they were either killed off or absorbed. But neither is there much trace of African cultures.' (Tony Thorndike, *The Caribbean Handbook 1988*)

Of the countries that make up the area, 17 are independent, 6 are British colonies, 3 are French dependencies, 2 are Dutch dependencies, and 2 are in association with the USA. The largest is Cuba with a population of 10 million; the smallest is Anguilla with its 7,000 people. The total population of the area is more than 30 million.

The largest countries of the region are Cuba and the Dominican Republic (Spanish speaking) and Haiti (French speaking). Cuba's population alone is double that of the islands colonised by Britain, but the best opportunities for British people are definitely in the latter.

Many of these countries are slowly diversifying their economies away from primary products (such as bananas, sugar and minerals) into agro-processing, tourism, manufacturing for export, and services. One of the main growth sectors for expatriate employment in recent years has been offshore financial services, notably in the Cayman Islands, British Virgin Islands, Turks and Caicos, and Bermuda.

Many of the expatriates working in the Caribbean have been there for some time—a testimony to the attractions of the area, which include a good climate, friendly people and a relaxed lifestyle. However, the picture is not completely rosy, and there are pockets of poverty and deprivation throughout the area.

Reference and addresses:
The Caribbean Handbook (Financial Times Caribbean (PO Box 1037), St John's, Antigua).
Caribbean Business Directory (Caribbean Publishing Co, Box 1365, Grand Cayman, BWI).
The Latin American Bureau, 1 Amwell Street, London EC1, has a library which includes a section on the Caribbean.
Centre for Caribbean Studies: University of Warwick, Coventry CV4 7AL.

Bahamas
Bahamas High Commission: 10 Chesterfield Street, London W1X 8AH. Tel: 071-408 4488.
Tourist Office: 23 Old Bond Street, London W1X 4PQ. Tel: 071-269 5238.
British High Commission: (PO Box N7516), 3rd Floor, Bitco Building, East Street, Nassau.

Barbados
Barbados High Commission: 1 Great Russell Street, London WC1B 3NH. Tel: 071-631 4975.
Tourist Office: 163 Tottenham Court Road, London W1P 9AA. Tel: 071-636 9448.
British High Commission: (PO Box 676C), Barclays Building, Roebuck Street, Bridgetown.

British Virgin Islands
Government Office: 48 Albermarle Street, London W1X 4AR. Tel: 071-629 6355.

Cayman Islands
Cayman Islands Government Office: Trevor House, 100 Brompton Road, London SW3 1EX. Tel: 071-823 7613. An important offshore banking centre with more than 300 banks and trust companies.

Reference:
Cayman Islands Handbook and Businessman's Guide (Northwester Co, PO Box 243, Grand Cayman).

Cuba

Cuban Embassy: 167 High Holborn, London WC1. Tel: 071-240 2488.

Consular Section: 15 Grape Street, London WC2 8DR. Tel: 071-836 7618.

British Embassy: Edificio Bolivar, Capdevila 101-103, Morro y Prado, Havana.

Eastern Caribbean (Antigua, St Kitts-Nevis, St Lucia, St Vincent)

Eastern Caribbean Commission: 10 Kensington Court, London W8 5DL. Tel: 071-937 9522.

Grenada

Grenada High Commission: 1 Collingham Gardens, London SW5 0HW.

British High Commission, 14 Church Street, St George's.

Jamaica

Jamaican High Commission: 63 St James's Street, London SW1A 1LY. Tel: 071-629 5477.

British High Commission: (PO Box 575) Trafalgar Road, Kingston 10.

Trinidad & Tobago

Trinidad and Tobago High Commission: 42 Belgrave Square, London SW1X 8NT. Tel: 071-242 9351.

British High Commission: (PO Box 225), Furness House, Independence Square, Port-of-Spain.

Turks & Caicos

Government Office: 48 Albermarle Street, London W1X 4AR. Tel: 071-629 6355.

16
North America, Australasia and South Africa

Australia, Canada, New Zealand, South Africa and the USA have always been popular destinations for British migrants. Indeed, there are currently over 5 million UK passport holders in these countries—some on a permanent basis, others on short-term contracts. Many become naturalised citizens of their adopted countries.

At one time migration was open to virtually anyone, as these countries were keen to build up their populations. However, times have changed, and now all of them have introduced more restricted immigration policies. British people are still welcome as immigrants, but only if they can offer skills that are in short supply in that country.

What skills are these? It is difficult to generalise, since the situation constantly changes. Some years back, for instance, New Zealand badly needed TV engineers who could repair colour TV sets, and at one time Canada had a teacher shortage. Nowadays these countries tend to be self-sufficient in most skills and no longer need to import expertise from abroad.

If you want to work in any of these countries, you will normally have to obtain a visa, and this is no mere formality. In most cases you will need to produce evidence that you have a job offer. However, you may be accorded preferential status if you have close relatives resident in the country concerned. The end of this section looks more closely at current visa requirements.

Clearly the Embassy or High Commission of the country concerned is the best place to start. These organisations often have booklets and magazines that offer advice to the would-be emigrant. In the case of Australia and Canada, also try the Agent-General offices of the various states, which may be better informed on job prospects in their home state than the federal government representatives.

There are also various private organisations and associations which offer advice and assistance. One such organisation is Leeson's Employment & Accommodation Service, 4 Cranley Road, Ilford, London IG2 6AG, which offers a comprehensive package for prospective migrants. Its services include:

- lists of companies employing your particular trade or profession together with all employment bureaux and consultants in any area or location of your choice
- help in assessing your prospects
- advice on all your approaches to personnel officers and employers
- interviews in the UK on behalf of overseas companies.

Australia

Australia is fast becoming a favourite destination for young people who go to take up temporary jobs there in much the same way that young Aussies descend on London—there is casual work to be had in the catering trade at vacation time and on farms at harvest time (in the middle of the British winter). For permanent employment, however, you will need to possess appropriate skills.

The stereotype image of an Australian is of a rough, tough, unpretentious, beer-swilling pioneering type. But over the years the image has softened, and although you may still come across such characters in the outback, the majority of Australians are sophisticated urban dwellers.

The country has grown in self-confidence over the past two decades. Australian films and soap operas are shown throughout the world; Australian wines are gaining a considerable reputation; and Australian personalities—from Germain Greer to Barry Humphries—have given the country a high profile. Indeed, there is no better preparation for a working stint in Australia than acquaintance with Dame Edna Everage or Sir Les Patterson; on your arrival you will find, in contrast to these two characters, that Australians are charming, tactful and modest people.

Australian High Commission: Australia House, Strand, London WC2B 4LA. Tel: 071-379 4334. Also: Chatsworth House, Lever Street, Manchester 1 2DL; 2nd Floor, Hobart House, Edinburgh EH2 2DL.

Tourist Office: 4th Floor, Heathcoat House, 20 Savile Row, London W1X 1AE. Tel: 071-434 4371.

Agents-General:

New South Wales, 66 Strand, London WC2N 5LZ.
Queensland, 392-393 Strand, London WC2R 0LZ.
South Australia, 50 Strand, London WC2N 5LW.
Victoria, Melbourne Place, Strand, London WC2B 4LJ.
Western Australia, 115-116 Strand, London WC2R 4LG.
British High Commission: Commonwealth Avenue, Canberra ACT 2600.
Australian British Trade Association: Commerce House, 26 Brisbane Avenue, Canberra ACT 2603.

Temporary residence:
Visas are now required even for business or recreational visits. If you intend to take up employment you will need to be sponsored by your prospective employer in Australia who will need to get permission from the appropriate authorities.

There are various categories of temporary residence including

- Exchange—people participating in bi-lateral staff exchange schemes
- Independent Executive—anyone planning to establish new businesses under the Business Migration Programme
- Executive—senior management personnel
- Specialist—highly skilled workers offering skills in short supply in Australia

Working holidays:
Young people aged 18-25 can apply for a Working Holiday visa valid for 13 months which enables them to travel and take up casual work to supplement their holiday funds.

- usually for up to six months with the possibility of an extension
- usually restricted to people aged 18 to 25
- the duration of each job must not exceed 3 months
- no sponsorship is needed
- applicants must have sufficient funds to tide them over for the first weeks and to purchase a return ticket (if they do not have one on arrival)

Jobs lasting between 4 months and 4 years:

- you must be sponsored (preferably by the prospective Australian employer)
- you must offer skills which are in short supply in Australia.
- you cannot be recruited to fill an unskilled, semi-skilled or part-time post

- you must meet certain character and health requirements

Permanent migration:
There are two types of migration:

- **Family Migration.** 'Preferential' family members (such as spouses, fiancés, unmarried dependent children) need to be sponsored and meet the basic entry requirements. 'Concessional' family members (non-dependent children, certain parents, brothers and sisters, nieces and nephews) will also have to meet the 'points test'. Points are awarded for a person's skill, age, relationship to the sponsor, sponsor's citizenship, his ability to provide settlement support, and his location.

- **Economic Migration.** You may be able to migrate if you possess skills or experience and fall into one of the following categories:
  Tripartite Negotiated Arrangements—for skilled people under 55 nominated by an employer within the framework of an industry-wide agreement;
  Employer Nomination Scheme—for skilled people under 55 nominated by an employer in Australia;
  Business Migration Programme—for people able to demonstrate they have sufficient expertise and capital to set up a business either independently or as a joint venture;
  Distinguished Talent—for people with an exceptional record of achievement;
  Independent—for people whose education, skills and ready employability will contribute to the Australian economy. These people do not need to be nominated or sponsored by anyone, but are subject to the 'points test' (which takes into account one's level of skill/education, language ability and age).

Other Information:
The Commission on Overseas Professional Qualifications, Commerce House, Cnr Brisbane Avenue and Macquarie Street, Barton, ACT 2600, may well assess your professional competence before you can practice your trade or profession in Australia. The High Commission should be able to advise you on this.

The Department of Employment, Education & Training (PO Box 826, Woden, ACT 2606) offers assistance and advice to job seekers and would-be entrepreneurs on broadly similar lines to those on offer in Britain, although with different titles (e.g. New Enterprise Incentive Scheme).

The Commonwealth Employment Service handles job vacancies at all levels, and there are private recruitment consultants in most cities (listed under Employment Agencies in *Yellow Pages*). There are also Careers Reference Centres—occupational information libraries located in most large cities and listed in telephone directories. Reference:

Australasian News, Outbound Newspapers, 1 Commercial Road, Eastbourne BN21 3XQ.

Job Guide for... (State) (Dept of Employment & Industrial Relations/Australian Government Publishing Service).

Occupational Outlook (DEIR/AGPC). Employment prospects by industry and occupation.

Looking for a Job (Graduate Careers Council of Australia, PO Box 28, Parkville, Vic). The GCCA also publishes *Opportunities for All Graduates* and handbooks on particular careers.

Graduate Outlook (Hobsons Press, 491 Kent Street, Sydney, NSW 2000).

Jobson's Year Book of Public Companies (Dun & Bradstreet International).

Directory of Australian Associations (Information Australia Group, 45 Flinders House, Melbourne, Vic 3000).

The Australia & New Zealand Employment Guide (Overseas Employment Services).

How to Live & Work in Australia, Laura Veltman (Northcote House Publishers). Second edition 1990.

Successful Migrating to Australia, Ian Gale (Macdonald/Queen Anne Press 1990).

Canada

Canada is in many respects a halfway house between the US and Britain. Although the bulk of Canada's commerce is with the States, Canadians jealously guard their own identity. They tend to be more reserved than Americans. Over a million UK nationals have emigrated there since the war and found it an easy place to settle in, though some have found the climate rather harsh.

The country covers a vast area, and as a consequence the different areas of Canada have each evolved a character of their own. British Columbia is British in character as well as in name. The province of Quebec—which includes Montreal—is more reminiscent of France and continental Europe. The most cosmopolitan place of all is Toronto with its extensive ethnic mix. Multiculturalism is a cornerstone of Government policy and ethnic groups are encouraged to maintain their languages and traditions.

Canada is a country rich in natural resources. However, manufacturing is playing an increasing role in the economy now, particularly in the hi-tech field. While Canada welcomes immigrants, they must have the skills that are in demand. Entry methods:

- Obtain work in advance from a Canadian employer who in turn obtains permission from his employment centre to offer a post to a foreign national.
- Apply for an immigrant visa. It is usually necessary to have a job offer before you go.

In order to determine eligibility for a visa the Canadian Immigration Department assess people according to a points system based on the following criteria:

- education
- knowledge of English/French
- age
- area of destination
- close relatives residing in Canada
- occupational training
- occupational demand
- occupational experience
- arranged employment

The number of points needed for an independent application is currently 70. Certain occupations are regarded as priority occupations and attract a higher number of points (see *Canada News*).

If you have a relative in Canada who has submitted an undertaking of assistance on your behalf to a Canadian Immigration centre you will receive up to 15 bonus points. Similarly, if you contemplate investing in or setting up your own business in Canada, you will be allotted 45 bonus points towards the 70 you need. The Entrepreneurial Development Officer of the Immigration Section will be able to supply details of the process.

Reference:
Canada News (Outbound Newspapers Ltd, 1 Commercial Road, Eastbourne, BN21 3XQ. Tel: 0323 412001). This contains up-to-date news of interest to prospective immigrants and includes a list of the priority occupations.
The Directory of Canadian Employment Agencies (Overseas Consultants, (PO Box 152), Douglas, Isle of Man).
Directory of Canadian Employment Agencies (Overseas Employ-

ment Services, (PO Box 460), Town of Mount Royal, Quebec,
H3P 3C7).
Jobsearch Canada (Herdcroft Ltd, 18 Coulter Close, Cuffley,
Herts EN6 4RR).
Directory of Associations in Canada.
The Canadian Almanac.
Fraser's Canadian Trade Directory.
The Toronto Globe and Mail (444 Front Street West, Toronto,
Ontario). Canada's national newspaper.

Useful Addresses:
Canadian High Commission: MacDonald House, 38 Grosvenor
Street, London W1.
Canada House: Trafalgar Square, London SW1Y 5BJ. Tel:
071-629 9492 (library and national tourist office).
British High Commission: Elgin Street, Ottawa, Ontario. Between
9,000 and 10,000 immigration visas issued annually in the UK.

The offices of the various Agents General of different Canadian
Provinces may be able to provide you with information on the kind
of work available:

Alberta: 1 Mount Street, W1Y 5AA.
British Columbia: 1 Regent Street, SW1Y 4NS.
Nova Scotia: 14 Pall Mall, SW1Y 5LU.
Quebec: 59 Pall Mall, SW1Y 5HJ.
Ontario: 21 Knightsbridge, SW1Y 7LY.
Saskatchewan: 16 Berkeley Street, W1X 5AE.

Centre for Canadian Studies, University of Edinburgh, 21 George
Street, Edinburgh RH8 9LD. Tel: 031-667 1011.
Regional Canadian Study Centre, University of Leeds LS2 9JT.

New Zealand

The climate of New Zealand is similar to that of the UK, but the
pace of life is slower and the country is relatively sparsely populated. Some newcomers find the country something of a backwater
with not much going on; others are reminded of Britain as it used
to be a few decades back.

However, New Zealand is a relatively prosperous country with
a well-developed welfare state. New Zealanders tend to be more
'British' than the Australians and many families still have close
connections with the UK. The Government is keen to import

expertise from abroad, so there are certainly opportunities here for expatriates with the right kind of skills.

Further Information:
New Zealand Embassy: New Zealand House, 80 Haymarket, London SW1Y 4TE. Tel: 071-931 0368/9.
Tourist Office: (same address). Tel: 071-973 0360.
British High Commission: Norwich Union Building, 179 Queen Street, Auckland 1.
British Trade Association: Commerce House, 126 Wakefield Street, Wellington.

While a British passport holder can visit New Zealand for up to six months without the need for a visa for business or vacation purposes, you cannot take up employment—except perhaps on a casual basis, in which case you would need to apply for a work permit when you get there.

If you have already made arrangements to take up a job you must apply for a work visa, which is more than just a formality. Like all the other countries in this section, New Zealand no longer has an 'open door' policy on immigration. There are three main ways you can qualify for residence in New Zealand:

- occupational skills
- business skills
- family relationship

Occupational skills
Like other countries New Zealand operates an Occupational Priority List which identifies those skills for which employers may recruit qualified migrants overseas. If your occupation is not on the Occupational Priority List but you are offered a job, your prospective employer in New Zealand must write to the appropriate regional office of the New Zealand Immigration Service for approval to recruit overseas, showing evidence that he has not been able to recruit a suitable person in New Zealand.

Business skills
If you plan to start a business in New Zealand, you will be assessed on your potential contribution to New Zealand, your business record and skills, your intended business activities in New Zealand and the amount of investment capital you have available. In addition you will be expected to have at least NZ$200,000 available to meet housing and personal establishment costs in addition to the amount required for your intended business.

Family relationship
Family immigration covers four categories:
1. Marriage to a New Zealand citizen or resident
2. Parent, dependent children, and single adult siblings or children
3. Sponsorship of an adult sibling or child provided they have a job offer or a worthwhile skill
4. Humanitarian reasons

The Immigration Service at New Zealand House can provide up-to-date information on immigration policy and will have the latest *Occupational Priority List* which lists occupations for which there is a demand. The Service also holds current newspapers including the *New Zealand Herald* represented in London by New Zealand Associated Press, 107 Fleet Street, London EC4A 2AN.

New Zealand News UK is an independent weekly newspaper which contains coverage of events in New Zealand and items of interest to prospective migrants (PO Box 1, Berwick on Tweed, Northumbria TD15 1BW).

The Employment Service of the Department of Labour (Charles Fergusson Building, Box 3705, Auckland) provides a comprehensive job placement service and has branches at 50 locations throughout the country, but is unable to assist visitors or people overseas. Private recruitment consultants are listed under Employment Agencies in *Yellow Pages*.

Reference:
Australasian News (Outbound Newspapers, 1 Commercial Road, Eastbourne, BN21 3XQ).
The Circular advertises details of all public service jobs.
The New Zealand Business Who's Who (Fourth Estate Holdings).
The Public Service Official Circular advertises details of all public service jobs.
The Education Gazette publishes details of all teaching jobs.

Other jobs are advertised in the newspapers particularly on Wednesdays and Saturdays.

South Africa
South Africa is politically in a state of flux now that its government has abandoned the controversial apartheid policies which may have deterred some people from taking up jobs there in the past. However, plenty of expatriates have settled in the country, and South Africa seems, as always, to be keen to attract skilled immi-

grants from other countries particularly to the mining and manu-facturing sector. It offers a good climate and an excellent standard of living—for whites, at least—and is more industrialised and developed than its neighbours.

You may find that as a consequence of past history some of the locals, notably the Afrikaners, have developed something of a siege mentality, but there are many others who welcome progress towards a multiracial society. Yet South Africa's future is full of imponderables, and anyone planning to work there needs to be aware of this fact and go prepared for any eventuality.

Further information:
South African Embassy: Trafalgar Square, London WC2N 5DP. Tel: 071-839 2211.
Tourist Office: Regency House, 1-4 Warwick Street, London W1R 5WB. Tel: 071-439 9661.
British Embassy: 6 Hill Street, Arcadia, Pretoria 0002.
UK South Africa Trade Association: 45 Great Peter Street, London SW1P 3LT.

Reference:
Opportunities for Graduates in Southern Africa (MSL Publi-cations, PO Box 52518, Saxonwold 2132).
Education and Careers in Southern Africa (Erudita Publications, PO Box 25111, 2048 Ferreirasdorp).
My Career—Guide Edition (Department of Manpower, Private Bag X117, Pretoria 0001).
South Africa News, Outbound Newspapers, 1 Commercial Road, Eastbourne BN21 3XQ.
National Trade Index of South Africa (Intratex). This includes addresses of Chambers of Industries and Mines, etc.
Directory of Scientific and Technical Societies in South Africa (South African Council for Scientific and Industrial Research).

Useful Addresses:
Careers Research & Information Centre, 7 Roscommon Road, Claremont, Capetown (611058).
Careers Centre, 8642, Zone 6, Dielkloof, Box 38, Orlando, Johan-nesburg (938 1439).
Careers Information Centre, 20 St Andrews Street, Durban (301 2097).
1820 Settlers Association, 415 Union Centre, 55 Harrison Street, Johannesburg and c/o Outbound Newspapers, 1 Commercial Road, Eastbourne BN21 3XQ.

United States

For generations, the United States has attracted immigrants from all over the world and out of the melting pot a very distinctive culture has emerged. British people who expect the American way of life to be exactly the same as their own may be in for a shock.

- Americans are workaholics. They are keen to get on and take fewer holidays than Europeans.
- They express enthusiasm for what they are doing and for the organisation they work for. This enthusiasm may not be genuine.
- They are less status conscious. It is what you have achieved, not who you are, that is important.
- Theirs is an acquisitive society where success is usually measured by how much you earn.
- They are self-confident and good at selling themselves.
- There is a strong conformist element in the US. People are expected to act and think American.
- Americans tend to be restless people, impatient to get on with things. In discussions they don't like to beat about the bush.
- They tend to be more spontaneous, open and optimistic than British people.
- There is possibly less of a social conscience in the US, with little sympathy for the underdog.

The USA is an enormous place, and there are considerable differences between the people on the eastern coast and the southern states—who may seem more European in outlook—and those of California and the mid-west, for example.

In the past there has been a considerable brain drain from Europe to the United States. There are still plenty of opportunities for the well qualified, but it is considerably more difficult to get in now.

Further information:
United States Embassy: 24 Grosvenor Square, London W1A 2JB. Tel: 071-499 9000.
Visa Branch: 5 Upper Grosvenor Street, London W1A 2JB. Tel: 071-499 3443.
Tourist Office: 22 Sackville Street, London W1X 2EA. Tel: 071-439 7433.
British Embassy: 3100 Massachusetts Avenue NW, Washington DC 20009.
British American Chamber of Commerce: 275 Madison Avenue,

New York NY 10016 and 3150 California Street, San Francisco, CA 941115.

US-UK Educational Commission: 6 Porter Street, London W1M 2HR. Tel: 071-486 1098.

Visa information
Visas are no longer required for most citizens of the UK and certain other countries visiting the US for less than 90 days for business or pleasure subject to certain conditions. However they must be obtained in advance if you wish to study or work in the US.

Non immigrant visas
Non immigrant visas are categorised as follows:

- **The H (temporary worker) visa** is required by anyone going to the US to work temporarily in a specific prearranged job or to fulfil a contract.
- **The L (intra company transfer) visa** is needed for an employee who is being transferred to a branch of his current firm in the US.

In both cases the proposed employment must be approved in advance. To gain this approval the employer or agent in the US must file a petition on form I-129b (petition to Classify Nonimmigrant as Temporary Worker or Trainee) with the nearest office of the Immigration and Naturalisation Service in the US.

- **Exchange Visitor Visa.** This is for individuals who enter the US as exchange visitors sponsored by organisations such as universities, hospitals, summer camps and au pair organisations. Such a visa enables a person to work for the organisation on a temporary basis and to be paid a salary. The sponsoring organisation must issue the eligible individual with Form IAP-66 (Certificate of Eligibility for Exchange Visitor J-1 Status) which needs to be presented to the Visa Branch with the application.

Immigrant visas
These are for people who wish to live and/or work in the US permanently or for an indefinite period. Under the Immigration Act of 1990 (effective from 1st October 1991) there are no numerical limits on immediate relatives (spouses and children of US citizens and parents of citizens at least 21 years old) but there are for most other categories.

- **Family sponsored preferences**

Unmarried sons and daughters of citizens
Spouses and unmarried sons/daughters of permanent residents
Married sons/daughters of citizens
Brothers/sisters of citizens 21 years of age or over.

- **Employment-based preferences**
  Priority Workers (people of extraordinary ability in the sciences, arts, education, business or athletics; outstanding professors and researchers; certain multinational executives and managers).
  Members of the professions holding advanced degrees or persons of exceptional ability in the sciences, arts or business.
  Skilled Workers in short supply, professionals holding baccalaureate degrees, other workers in short supply.
  Certain *special immigrants* (ministers of religion, religious workers, members of international organisations, certain employees of US Government abroad).
  Investors in a new commercial enterprise which will create employment for at least 10 people other than members of the investor's family.

- **Diversity Immigrants**
  If you do not fall into one of the above categories you can maybe try your luck under this scheme whereby applicants are chosen at random on an annual basis. Only one application may be made per year.

The above information reflects changes in the US Immigration Act of 1990 and comes into effect on 1st October 1991.

Reference:
Immigration Procedures Handbook (Clark Boardman Co, 435 Hudson Street, New York NY 10014).
The National Directory of Addresses and Telephone Numbers (General Information Inc., 401 Park Place, Kirkland, Washington, DC 98033).
The Guide to over 750 of Florida's Largest Employers (Overseas Consultants).
How to Live & Work in America, Steve Mills (Northcote House 1988).
Living in the USA, Alison R. Lanier (Intercultural Press, Yarmouth, Maine 1981).

17
Job Opportunities by Profession

Accountancy

Qualified accountants are in demand in virtually every sector of commerce and industry and in the public sector, too. International accountancy firms, such as Ernst & Whinney, Price Waterhouse, Coopers & Lybrand, Arthur Anderson and Arthur Young have offices in most major capitals of the world. The Institute of Chartered Accountants operates an appointments service exclusively for its members (Chartac Recruitment Services), and some of the appointments are overseas ones. The opportunities for newly qualified Chartered Accountants are primarily from the public practice sector, principal locations being Europe, Australasia, Africa, the Caribbean and Bermuda, Hong Kong and the Middle East. For more experienced members seeking commercial positions, occasional instructions are received from a variety of sources.

Recruitment:
ASA International, Ludgate House, 107-111 Fleet Street, London EC4A 2AB.
Harrison Willis, Cardinal House, 39-40 Albermarle Street, London W1X 3FD (Offshore Specialist Appointments).

Reference:
ICA Journal.

Agriculture

The main opportunities these days tend to be in the Third World, as the governments of these countries try to become self-sufficient in food production. This means that most of the jobs are on contract terms—often with organisations such as the Overseas Development Administration, Crown Agents, the volunteer agencies, international aid organisations and FAO. For young agri-

culturalists and horticulturalists in search of work experience overseas there are the following exchange schemes based at the
National Agricultural Centre, Kenilworth, Warwickshire CV8
2LG:

- **International Farm Experience Programme** (Tel: 0203-696584).
  This is a work exchange programme for young people aged
  18-28 with at least two years' experience in agriculture administered by the National Federation of Young Farmers Clubs.
  Countries: North America, Israel, Europe (including Poland
  and Hungary).

- **International Agricultural Exchange Programme** at the same
  address offers exchanges of 7-14 months to North America,
  Australia and New Zealand (Tel: 0203-696578).

There are a number of private sector agencies and consultancies
that advertise vacancies from time to time:

International Agricultural Services, Cheapside, Waltham, Grimsby
DN37 0HU. Tel: 0472-220298.
Booker Agriculture International Ltd, Bloomsbury House, 74-77
Great Russell Street, London WC1B 3DF.
Harrisons Fleming Advisory Services, 1-4 Great Tower Street,
London EC3R 5AB (Tropical agriculture).
Hunting Technical Services, Elstree Way, Boreham Wood, Herts
WD6 1SB.
Minster Agriculture Ltd, Belmont, 13 Upper Thames Street,
Thame, Oxon OX9 3HL.
Consult Project Search, 110 Inderwick Road, London N8 9JY. Tel:
071-400 3157.

Nannies, governesses and au pairs

Nannies or governesses have usually received some kind of training and may well be possessors of the Nursery Nurse Examination
Board Certificate. They usually live in and can expect a full salary.

Au pairs are in a different category. They look after children
and are probably involved in some of the household tasks, but are
treated as a member of the family and receive pocket money
rather than a salary. Au pairing is usually considered to be an
educational experience rather than a job, and as such does not
normally require a work permit.

Reference:
The Au Pair and Nanny's Guide, S. Griffith and S. Legg (Vacation
  Work Publications 1989).
European Treaty on Au Pair Placements 1979, (Council of
  Europe). Available from HMSO, 51 Nine Elms Lane, London
  SW8 5DR.

Addresses:
For a fully comprehensive selection, check *The Au Pair & Nanny's
Guide*. However, the following list is a useful starting point:

Aaron Employment Agency, 1 Calverley Road, Tunbridge Wells
  TN1 2TE. Tel: 08892-46601.
Anglia Au Pair & Domestic Agency, 37 Old Southend Road,
  Southend on Sea SS1 2HA. Tel: 0702-613888.
The Au Pair Centre, 23 King's Road, London SW3 4RP. Tel:
  071-730 8122.
Avalon Agency, 11 Abinger Road, Portslade, East Sussex BN4
  1SD. Tel: 0273-421600.
Bees Knees Agency, 296 Sandycombe Road, Kew Gardens, Rich-
  mond, Surrey TW9 3NG. Tel: 081-876 7039.
Interlingua, Torquay Road, Foxrock, Dublin 18. Tel: 081-893876.
Janet White Employment Agency, 67 Jackson Avenue, Leeds
  LS88 1NS. Tel: 0532-666507.
Jeeves & Belgravia Bureau, 35 Brompton Road, London SW3
  1DF. Tel: 071-828 2063.
Jolaine Au Pair & Domestic Agency, 18 Escot Way, Barnet, Herts
  EN5 3AN. Tel: 081-449 1334.
Kensington & Chelsea Nurses & Nannies, 2nd Floor, Collier
  House, 163/169 Brompton Road, London SW3. Tel: 071-589
  2093.
Knightsbridge Nannies Ltd, 5 Beauchamp Place, London SW3
  1NG. Tel: 071-584 9323.
Nash Personnel Services, 53 Church Road, Hove, Sussex BN3
  2BD. Tel: 0403-711436.
Occasional & Permanent Nannies, 15 Beauchamp Place, London
  SW3 1NQ. Tel: 071-225 1555.
Universal Aunts, 250 King's Road, London SW3 5UE. Tel:
  071-351 5767.
Universal Care Ltd, 9 Windsor End, Beaconsfield, Bucks HP9
  2JJ. Tel: 04946-78811.
Westbury International Agency, 18 Saunderson Place, London
  SW8 3DG. Tel: 071-627 3046.

Banking

People sometimes forget that the major High Street banks have considerable operations abroad, and that a career with them could eventually take you off to some exotic climes once you reach a certain level of seniority. However, even if you approach the international divisions of Barclays, Lloyds, Midland or Natwest, you will be expected to spend time working in Britain first of all.

There are other banks, however, the bulk of whose operations are abroad, and you might find that overseas opportunities come more quickly if you join one of these. They include the following:

Standard Chartered Bank, 10 Clements Lane, London EC4 7AB.
Grindlays Bank, 36 Fenchurch Street, London EC3P 3ED.
Bank of London & South America, 40 Queen Victoria Street, London EC4.
British Bank of the Middle East.

There are also opportunities with foreign banks. Jonathan Wren, for instance, recruits staff for Arab banks in the Middle East. Merchant banking is a specialised branch of banking for which competition is very keen. As you make it up the hierarchy opportunities will arise for secondments and transfers overseas.

Reference:
International Bankers' Directory (Financial Publishing Group, 43 Hamilton Street, Chester CH2 3JQ. Tel: 0244-316879).
The Bankers Almanac and Yearbook (Thomas Skinner Publications, Reed Publishing Group).

Addresses:
British Overseas & Commonwealth Banks Association, 8 Old Jewry, London EC2R 8ED. Tel: 071-600 0822.
Foreign Banks Association, 4 Bishopsgate, London EC2N 4AD. Tel: 071-283 1080.

Recruitment:
William Channing, Consultancy International, Expatriate Resources Co, Christopher Little, Anthony Nevile.

Communications

'Politicians give communications a high priority in order to get their message across.'

The communications business—telecommunications, radio communications, satellite communications—is a buoyant field these days and there are a number of firms in the field that specialise in the installation and maintenance of these systems. Expatriate expertise is needed especially for projects in Third World countries that are often developing nationwide communications systems for the first time. (See **Construction** in this section).

Recruitment:
Clark Rich, Advanced Technology Recruiters, Anders Glaser Wills, BEE, Beechwood, Grange Selection, Ian Marshall, Network, Antony Nevile, Professional Employment Group, Wrightson Wood.

Computers/information technology
The information technology industry has expanded at an unprecedented rate over the past decade, and the number of competent professionals in this field has not kept pace with demand; so if you *are* a qualified and experienced computer programmer, systems analyst, systems designer or computer engineer, you certainly have an eminently marketable skill and can be quite choosy as to where you want to work.

To get an idea of where the opportunities lie, look through the vacancy columns of specialist journals such as *Computer Weekly, Computing, Computer Talk, Electronics Express, Freelance Informer, Computer Freelance.*

For a long-term career in computing with plenty of opportunities for assignments or postings abroad you could approach firms such as the following:

International Computers Ltd, Bridge House, Fulham, London SW6 3JX.
Logica, 64 Newman Street, London W1A 4SE.
Cray Research UK Ltd, Cray House, London Road, Bracknell, Berks RG12 2SY.

Recruitment:
Advanced Technology Recruiters, James Baker Associates, Barnett Consulting Group, BEE Professional, Beechwood, Benney, CC&P, Clark Rich, Cliveden, Computer Consultants Australia, Computer Search & Selection, Dalroth, Electronics Recruitment, Expatriate Resources, FM Recruitment, Forsyth Recruitment, Grange Selection, International Training & Recruitment Link, Intertech, Jenrick, MDA Computer Gp, Merton Associates, Modus, Prescot, Sabre, Selleck, Team-Sel, Vision.

Construction

A large construction project requires people with a variety of skills: site managers, site engineers, plant engineers, electricians, quantity surveyors, structural engineers, store managers, finance personnel, personnel managers, catering staff, procurement officers, and so on.

According to Expats International, many of whose members get jobs in the construction industry, staff turnover on construction projects is high—as much as 100% over a period of 15 months. There are several reasons for this:

- Personnel are ill-prepared for the camp-type atmosphere.
- Many of the jobs are bachelor status—camps rarely have facilities for dependants—and some people dislike prolonged separation from their partners.
- Some camps suffer from bad management or poor working relationships.
- Not everyone adapts to the continual changes of moving from one project to another every few months. But not all projects are short-term; construction of an oil refinery, or a port, for example, can last for years.

The construction industry is certainly very prone to economic change. In the seventies and early eighties the Arabian peninsula was an El Dorado for construction companies. However, in the eighties there has been a sharp decline in activity, and the number of opportunities for Europeans is lower than it used to be.

Also, profit margins for construction companies have grown tighter and companies are tending to recruit supervisory staff and skilled workers from Asia. A skilled Korean, Filipino, or Indian, for example, costs far less to employ than a European. On the other hand, British expertise is still highly regarded, and although openings for craftsmen and supervisors have diminished there are still ample opportunities at the middle management level and above.

A useful source of information on vacancies in this field is the vacancies bulletin which accompanies the Expats International magazine *Home and Away*. Trade newspapers, such as *Construction News, Contract Journal,* and *Building Today*, carry a number of advertisements for overseas jobs in each issue. For an overview of developments in certain parts of the world *Far East Construction* and *Gulf Construction & Saudi Arabia Review* make for useful reading (Hilal International, 3rd Floor, Regal House, London Road, Twickenham TW1 3QS).

Recruitment:
Ander Glaser Wills, ARA International, BEE Professional, Beechwood Recruitment, Grange Selection, Malla, Ian Marshall, Network Technical, Professional Employment, Team-Sel International, F J Selleck.

One alternative to these recruitment organisations is approaching a construction firm direct. Among the leading British construction firms that operate abroad are:

Balfour Beatty, Randolph House, Wellesley Road, Croydon CR9 3QD.

Kier, Tempsford Hall, Sandy, Beds SG19 2BD.

Taylor Woodrow International, Western House, Western Avenue, London W5 1EU.

John Laing Construction, Page Street, Mill Hill, London NW7 2ER.

Mowlem International, Foundation House, Eastern Road, Bracknell, Berks RG12 2UZ.

Tarmac International, Construction House, Birch Street, Wolverhampton WV1 4HY.

Costain Group, 111 Westminster Bridge Road, London SE1 7UE.

ARC Construction Ltd, Sutton Courtenay, Abingdon, Oxon OX14 4PD.

George Wimpey International, 27 Hammersmith Grove, London W6 7EN.

Consultancy

British consultants have always enjoyed a high reputation abroad, and this is a field which presents plenty of opportunities for experienced and qualified people, particularly in the Third World.

Consultancies advise and draw up plans for others to execute. Most specialise in just one or two fields: architecture, management, planning, agriculture, transport, rural development, economics, leisure, and so on. Some of the best known firms are consulting engineers, such as the Ove Arup Partnership (13 Fitzroy Street, London W1P 6BQ), Sir Alexander Gibb & Partners (Earley House, London Road, Earley, Reading RG6 1BL), Sir M MacDonald & Partners (Demeter House, Station Road, Cambridge CB1 2RS), and Sir Owen Williams & Partners (41 Whitcombe Street, London WC2 7DT).

Management consultancy is an expanding sector at the moment with a number of multi-national groups—often the offshoots of accountancy firms—catering for a range of multi-national clients. However, you can also work on a self-employed basis, or find jobs as advisers to governments or government organisations—often in the Third World.

Addresses:

The British Consultants Bureau, (1 Westminster Palace Gardens, 1-7 Artillery Row, London SW1P 1RJ) publishes an extensive handbook of around 500 UK based consultancy firms that operate internationally. Tel: 071-222 3651.

Consult Project Search (110 Inderwick Road, London N8 9JY. Tel: 071-400 3157) is an organisation which finds agriculturalists, engineers, economists, accountants, health personnel, sociologists, project managers, management consultants, export promoters, and so on, for assignments in the Third World.

Association of Consulting Engineers, Alliance House, Caxton Street, London SW1H 0QL.

Management Consultancies Association, 11 West Halkin Street, London SW1 8JZ. Tel: 071-235 3897.

Diplomacy

Diplomatic service

The job of the diplomat is to see that his or her country's interests are properly represented abroad and to achieve this the UK has some 200 embassies, high commissions and other missions in over 160 countries run by the Foreign and Commonwealth Office. It has a budget of over £400 million to run its affairs and around 4,700 of its staff spend two thirds of their careers at a posting abroad, involved with:

- embassies (high commissions)
- consulates
- delegations (to the United Nations, European Community, and so on)

A typical medium sized embassy will be headed by an Ambassador (High Commissioner) followed by a Counsellor. The Embassy is divided into sections, which may be combined in smaller representations:

- **Consular section:** This issues passports, visas, and looks after the interests of British citizens in that particular country.

- **Chancery:** This deals with political matters—reporting on political developments in the country and dealing with its government. In the developing world it is also involved in the policy and administration of British aid.

- **Commercial Section:** This section helps British companies to sell in the local market, gathers commercial intelligence and ensures that British commercial interests are protected.

- **Information Section:** This section is concerned with explaining British policy and presenting a positive image of Britain abroad.

- **Administration Section:** This section looks after the running of the mission and the well-being of its staff.

- **Support sections:** These include security officers, registry clerks, secretarial staff and communications officers.

The work of the diplomatic service is varied and demanding, but generally speaking the FCO looks after is employees well, particularly in the more difficult postings. Staff, particularly at the more senior level, will need to think of their duties more as a way of life than a job, since they may well be required to attend functions at any hour of the day. Although staff are subjected to UK income tax, they also receive generous overseas allowances and free accommodation during their posting abroad.

Entering the service
There are various ways of getting into the Diplomatic Service:

- **Administrative Entry:** This is the entry to the senior management levels of the Diplomatic Service with work offering a high policy content. The possession of a degree is essential, and applicants must be under 32. Some 20-25 staff are recruited annually.

- **Executive entry:** Officers entering at this level will be involved in a wide range of tasks at the middle management/junior management level, including consular work, accounts, and administration. The upper age limit for entry is 50, and although two 'A' Levels are the minimum qualification, a very high proportion of entrants these days are graduates. You may be able to transfer to the administrative grades. Some 35 to 40 people are recruited by this method each year.

- **Clerical entry:** Clerical officers normally start off in registry work, but may move on to do administration, accounts or visa work. the minimum qualification is 5 'O' levels or GCSEs, and between 80 and 100 appointments are made annually. There are opportunities for promotion to the executive grades.

• **Secretarial branch:** The minimum requirement is a typing speed of 30 wpm and there are opportunities for promotion to the position of Senior Personal Secretary or transfer to the executive branch by means of special competitions. Some 80 to 100 appointments to the 670 strong branch are made each year.

• **Communications branch:** This branch requires people with communications expertise.

Further information and applications forms are available from the Recruitment Section, Personnel Policy Department, Foreign and Commonwealth Office, 3 Central Buildings, Matthew Parker Street, London SW1H 9NL. Tel: 071-233 5244.

The British Council
The British Council could almost be called the cultural wing of the FCO, although it prides itself on its independence. Originally set up in the 1930s in order to counteract Nazi propaganda, the Council is involved in 'promoting a wider knowledge of our United Kingdom and the English Language abroad and developing closer cultural relations with other countries.' It achieves this through its network of libraries, its scholarship programme, the promotion of cultural events, its language institutes and its educational advisory services. It also helps the ODA administer the Government's aid programme.

In addition to recruiting contract staff the Council has a permanent number of overseas career service personnel who spend some two thirds of their working lives overseas as science officers, librarians, accountants, English language specialists and as generalists. Around 300 of the Council's overseas careers service officers are at a foreign posting at any one moment. The British Council also recruits for contract posts at various levels, normally in the education field (see Chapter 9). Contact the Staff Recruitment Department, The British Council, 65 Davies Street, London W1Y 2AA.

Education and training
There are opportunities for teachers, lecturers and training personnel all over the world, and though there are some posts that

offer security of tenure, most of the jobs are on contract. There are four main categories:

- **EFL teachers (teachers of English as a foreign language).** There are opportunities in virtually every country of the world (including Eastern Europe) in both the public and private sectors and at all levels. Positions are advertised mainly in the *Times Educational Supplement*, the *Education Guardian* (Tuesdays), *EFL Gazette* (Loop Format Ltd, 10 Wright's Lane, London W8 6TA), the *Vacancies Bulletin* of Christians Abroad, and so on. The main recruitment agencies are the British Council, volunteer agencies such as VSO, and a number of private agencies such as ILC Recruitment, Inlingua, International House and Specialist Language Services.

- **Teachers of other subjects.** Opportunities occur particularly in the international school sector, mission schools, in bi-lingual schools in the Middle East and in service schools. Positions are advertised in the *Times Educational Supplement*, the *Education Guardian*, in teaching union journals and sometimes in church newspapers and magazines (e.g. *Church Times*). The main recruitment agencies are Gabbitas Truman & Thring, the volunteer and missionary organisations and the Service Children's Educational Authority (Court Road, Eltham, London SE29 5NR). The European Council for International Schools operates a placement service for subscribers, and a few organisations are involved in teacher exchanges, notably the Central Bureau for Educational Visits and Exchanges (Seymour Mews House, Seymour Mews, London W1H 9PE) and the League for the Exchange of Commonwealth Teachers (Commonwealth House, 7 Lion Yard, Tremadoc Road, London SW4 7NF).

- **University and College Lecturers.** Positions are advertised in the *Times Higher Education Supplement*, the *Education Guardian* and in specialist journals. The Association of Commonwealth Universities (36 Gordon Square, London WC1H 0PF) helps members recruit staff by advertising positions and circulating details of them to universities, but is not equipped for speculative applications. Some embassies and high commissions recruit teaching staff on behalf of their governments, notably those of Singapore and Zimbabwe.

- **Training Staff.** Positions are advertised mainly in the relevant professional and trade journals. Among the organisations recruiting personnel of this nature are the volunteer and missionary organisations, ODA, petroleum, construction and hospital operating firms in the Middle East, and firms such as British Aerospace (Saudi Arabian Support Division) and Airwork.

Reference:
How to Teach Abroad, R. Jones (Northcote House, 1989).

Electronics
Demand for specialists in electronics and other hi-tech manufacturing applications seems to be exceptionally buoyant, particularly for opportunities in Europe and the US.

Reference:
Electronics Express, Electronics Times, Electronics Weekly.

Recruitment:
Advanced Technology Recruiters, Cliveden, Electronics Recruitment, Ingineur.

Engineering
See under **Communications, Computers, Construction, Consultancy, Electronics, Mining, Oil and Gas** in this section.

European Community jobs
British people tend to be overrepresented in most international organisations, so it is a surprise to find a body where we are actually underrepresented. However, this is true in the institutions of the European Community. These are:

The European Commission, 200 rue de la Loi, B-1049 Brussels.
The Council of the European Communities, 170 rue de la Loi, B-1048 Brussels.
The European Parliament, Bâtiment Robert Schuman, Plateau du Kirchberg, L-2920 Luxembourg.
The Court of Auditors of the European Communities, 29 Rue Aldringen, L-2920.
The European Court of Justice, C. Postale 96, Plateau du Kirchberg, L2920 Luxembourg.
The Economic and Social Committee of the European Communities, rue Ravenstein 2, B-1000 Brussels.
The Secretariat for Selection Committees—Research, 35 rue

Montoyer, Brussels. This recruits for the different European research establishments.

The European Commission is the largest of the Community's institutions with some 14,000 officials including:

- 2,500 administrative staff
- 1,000 linguists
- 2,000 technical and scientific staff.

Many of them work in Brussels or Luxembourg but the majority of technical and scientific staff work in the Community's joint research centres at Ispra (Italy), Karlsruhe, Petten (Netherlands), Geel (Belgium) and Culham in Oxfordshire. Many of the latter are employed on contract terms. There are five grades:

Category A: Graduates engaged in policy formation and administration and also advisory duties, often of a political nature
Category LA: Graduates who work as translators or interpreters
Category B: Executive officers with 'A' Levels
Category C: Clerical and secretarial staff
Category D: Manual and service staff

Information on translation and interpreting jobs can be obtained from the Joint Interpreting and Conference Service or the Translation Service (Resources and Professional Development Service) at the Commission's Brussels Headquarters.

The opportunities are very good, particularly for lawyers and economists, and employees receive good pay and allowances. There are opportunities for training and transfers between departments, and career development of this nature is positively encouraged. The main problem is *getting into* the Community institutions since the entry procedures are rigorous. For the top grades you will usually have to take a written examination and later, if successful, an oral test.

The different institutions of the European Community are responsible for their own recruitment and do indeed recruit separately. But the number of institutional competitions is increasing, and successful candidates are placed on a reserve list open to all the institutions involved.

Details of upcoming competitions are published in the 'C' series of the *Official Journal of the European Communities* which are distributed by Her Majesty's Stationery Office in the UK and the Government Publications Sales Office in Ireland and to which one may subscribe (HMSO, 51 Nine Elms Road, London SW8 5DR.

Tel: 01-211 5656. Govt Publications, Sun Alliance House, Molesworth Street, Dublin 2. Tel: 710309). Such competitions are also advertised widely in the newspapers of the member countries.

The European Commission has published a useful document entitled *A Career in the Commission of the European Communities* obtainable from either the Recruitment Division in Brussels or from the national offices of the commission:

8 Storey's Gate, London SW1P 3AT.
Windsor House, 9-15 Bedford Street, Belfast BT2 7EG.
4 Cathedral Road, Cardiff CF1 9SG.
7 Alva Street, Edinburgh EH2 4PH.
39 Molesworth Street, Dublin 2.

These offices may also have information on competitions planned for the next twelve months. If you happen to be in Timbuctoo or Honolulu at the time of a competition, don't despair; the community is prepared to conduct its examinations virtually anywhere in the world.

Finally, there is a graduate trainee scheme, recruitment for which takes place twice a year in February and September. Address your enquiries to the Bureau des Stages at the Commission's Headquarters.

Financial services

Financial services are a growing sector, and many of Britain's major financial institutions have branches throughout the world. While some of these branches are manned by locally recruited staff, the more important centres which have a corporate clientele often have at least one British person among their senior staff. However, you will usually need UK experience before you are sent abroad.

Opportunities on the sales side may be easier to come by— particularly in places where there is a substantial expatriate community who prefer to do business with their fellow Brits—for example, Southern Spain, or the Gulf States. You might also look into the possibilities of offshore financial services in places such as the Cayman Islands.

Reference:
Financial Times World Insurance Yearbooks (Longman).

Recruitment:
William Channing, Consultancy International, Expatriate Resources Co, Anthony Nevile, Offshore Specialist Appointments, Wrightson Wood.

Hotels and catering

At one end of the spectrum you can find casual jobs in hotels and restaurants in Europe, Australasia or the Americas, particularly during the holiday season—including ski and summer resorts. Such jobs are not hard to find but you could face long working hours during the height of the season for relatively little pay.

The speculative approach is as good a way as any of landing such jobs, but it makes sense to fix up your employment before you arrive. Certain agencies, such as Vacation Work, can arrange placements, and job advertisements in this sector occur from time to time in British newspapers.

At the other end there are management posts in top rated international hotels throughout the world. Many of these belong to major hotel chains and therefore continuity of employment can be assured.

There are also good opportunities worldwide in institutional catering. For example, you could try the major hospital groups operating in the Middle East, with oil and gas companies abroad and in construction camps, on merchant ships and cruise liners. Jobs abroad are advertised regularly in *Caterer & Hotelkeeper* and other specialist publications. Alternatively, you might shoot off speculative applications to one of the large international chains, such as Grand Metropolitan or Hilton International.

Recruitment:
Angel International; VIP International.

Reference:
ABC Worldwide Hotel Guide lists leading hotels throughout the world (ABC International, World Timetable Centre, Church Street, Dunstable, Beds LU5 4HB) and is particularly helpful for experienced personnel.

Agents' Hotel Gazetteer (CHG Travel Publications, Waterside House, West Common, Gerrards Cross, Bucks) lists a much wider range of hotels at different resorts and locations: Mediterranean (Vol 1); Cities of Europe (Vol 2); USA (Vol 3); Alpine Resorts (Vol 4). This is a useful reference for people seeking seasonal work.

National tourist offices can often supply lists of hotels in specified resorts for you to contact, while tourist information bureaux at resorts may be able to put you in touch with hotels that require staff.

Law

There are opportunities for lawyers throughout the world—in international companies and organisations, with international law firms, and with foreign governments. However, you will encounter differences in the practice of law in different parts of the world. You may also find that there are restrictions placed on foreign lawyers designed to protect members of the local bar. *The Legal Practice Directorate (International)* of the Law Society can provide up-to-date information on conditions within a member state of the European Community. The Directorate also publishes notes to guide solicitors applying for admission to a bar or law society outside England and Wales. The Directorate's address is: The Law Society, 50 Chancery Lane, London WC2A 1SX.

A useful reference work is *Regulation of Foreign Lawyers* (American Bar Association—1984). This deals with the jurisdictions in 11 American states, Australia, Belgium, Brazil, Canada, China, France, West Germany, Hong Kong, Israel, Italy, Japan, Mexico, the Netherlands, Nigeria and Singapore.

Recruitment:
The following recruitment consultants recruit for international posts:

Meredith Scott Associates, Legal Selection Consultants, 17 Fleet Street, London EC4 1AA. Tel: 071-353 7085.

Law Personnel, 95 Aldwych, London WC2B 4JF. Tel: 071-242 1281.

Harding Management Consultants Ltd, 2 Queen Anne's Gate Buildings, Dartmouth Street, London SW1H 9BP. Tel: 071-222 7733.

Chambers & Partners, 74 Long Lane, London EC1 9ET. Tel: 071-606 9371.

Reuter Simkin Ltd, 26-29 Bedford Row, London WC1R 4HE.

The Overseas Development Administration sometimes recruits for legal posts with Third World governments.

Medicine

Doctors, nurses and paramedics are much in demand all over the world, and while in some countries (notably the USA) you have to take an examination before you are allowed to practice, most countries are very ready to accept British qualifications. Some of the best paid jobs are in hospitals in the countries of the Arabian Peninsula, many of which are managed by British or American companies. British nurses are also much sought after in North America, Canada and on the European continent.

Medical staff are also needed in industrial and construction projects, on MOD bases, for emergency relief operations, and in mission hospitals around the world. In countries where there is a large British community there may be opportunities in clinics and medical practices that cater for the expatriates.

Reference:

Overseas positions are advertised in the relevant professional journals, such as *Lancet, British Medical Journal, British Dental Journal, Nursing Times, The Gazette* (Institute of Medical Laboratory Sciences), and so on. Some of the relevant professional organisations may be able to help with overseas jobs either by operating a placement service themselves or by putting you in touch with sister bodies abroad. Most of them are able to offer advice to their members. The BMA, for instance, offers 'Notes and Contracts for appointments overseas'.

Recruitment:

A number of recruitment firms operate candidate registers, among them Angel International Recruitment, ARA International, British Nursing Association, Dorothy J Hopkins, Hospital Doctor Locum Service, INS International Recruitment, International Training & Recruitment Link and Medic International.

Alternatively, you could apply direct to one of the hospital management groups which operate hospitals in the Middle East. These include:

Allied Medical Group, 12-18 Grosvenor Gardens, London SW1W 0DZ.

HCA International Ltd, 4th Floor, 49 Wigmore Street, London W1H 9LE.

International Hospitals Group, Stoke House, Stoke Green, Stoke Poges, Slough, Berks SL2 4HS (or FREEPOST 35, London W1E 5LY).

Gama International, 7th Floor, Glen House, Stag Place, London SW1E 5AG.

Opportunities also exist with the Overseas Development Administration, the World Health Organisation and other UN bodies such as UNICEF. Many charities, missionary groups and volunteer organisations need medical personnel, notably:

Volunteer Missionary Movement
British Red Cross Society
Save the Children Fund
Action Health 2000 (The Bath House, Gwydir Street, Cambridge CB1 2LW. Tel: 0223-460853).
Health Unlimited, 3 Stamford Street, London SE1 9NT. Tel: 071-928 4809.
International Medical Relief, 98 Eversholt Street, London NW1. Tel: 071-387 8447.

If you are interested in working in the voluntary and missionary field your first port of call would be the Bureau for Overseas Medical Service (Africa Centre, 38 King Street, Covent Garden, London WC2E 8JT. Tel: 071-836 5833). The Bureau, founded in 1979, acts as a clearing house for medical vacancies in the voluntary sector and publishes a monthly bulletin called *News and Jobs*. The Medical Missionary Association performs a similar service for the missionary organisations. Their quarterly magazine *Saving Health* includes a vacancies section. Christians Abroad publishes a vacancies bulletin *Opportunities Abroad* which includes medical and other vacancies with both voluntary, missionary and other aid organisations.

Military
One of the services' main selling points for recruitment is the opportunities they afford for foreign travel. These opportunities, of course, also have a downside—considerable strain can be placed on family relationships by frequent changes of residence (in the case of army personnel) and prolonged periods of separation (in the case of Royal Navy personnel).

Nevertheless, if you can accept the rigours of military life, the forces offer a good deal in terms of travel opportunities, though they are not as extensive as they were two or three decades ago. Most service people spend part of their service life in Germany, and there is a possibility of being based in Hong Kong, Belize, the

Falklands, Gibraltar or Cyprus for a while. Other opportunities include:

- serving with NATO forces in Europe
- serving with a UN peace-keeping force
- training forces in certain areas of the Third World
- shore leave in various exotic places for navy personnel.

If you plan to become an officer, it is best to start young. The cut-off age for graduates applying for commissions tends to be around 25, and for non-graduates a year or so earlier. An exception may be made if you have specialist skills or only plan to apply for a short service commission. The cut-off age for NCOs, privates and RN ratings is 33, while the RAF accepts people aged up to 38½ in the case of air traffic control officers and fighter control officers. The nearest careers office of the service you are interested in will be able to offer more precise details of what qualifications and attributes are required. Alternatively, you could write to:

Ministry of Defence, Lansdown House, Berkeley Square, London
    W1X 6AA (Army).
Ministry of Defence, Old Admiralty Building, Spring Gardens,
    London SW1A 2BE (Navy).
Ministry of Defence, Adastral House, Theobalds Road, London
    WC1X 8RU (RAF).

Opportunities occur from time to time with the armed forces of foreign countries, usually in a training or maintenance capacity. Currently there are opportunities in Saudi Arabia with British Aerospace (Saudi Arabia Support Department) and Oman with Airwork Ltd, Hurn Airport, Christchurch, Dorset BH23 6EB.

If you are attracted to life abroad with the services, but prefer to remain a civilian, you could consider:

- teaching in service schools (Service Children's Education Authority, Court Road, Eltham, London SE9 5NR)
- working in the NAAFI (Navy, Army & Air Force Institutes, 160 Kennington Lane, London SE11 4BR)
- community care (Soldiers', Sailors' and Airmen's Families Association, 27 Queen Anne's Gate, London SW1H 9BZ).

Mining
In recent years opportunities for British expatriates in the mining sector overseas have diminished considerably, and opportunities for skilled craftsmen have virtually dried up altogether.

Employees at this level tend to be recruited either locally or from other parts of the world—notably the Far East.

Where there is a demand, it is for graduate geologists and engineers with four years' previous experience. The only exception is perhaps South Africa which still seems prepared to take on inexperienced graduates. There are a few opportunities in Australia, Canada and elsewhere in Africa—on the Copper Belt in Zambia, for instance.

In the future there could be opportunities in countries such as Namibia and Angola as they start to exploit their resources. Europe is another promising area—particularly Spain and Portugal—but remember that you will be competing for jobs against graduates from all over Europe when barriers to job mobility come down after 1992.

Half of the 5,000 or so members of the Institution of Mining and Metallurgy work overseas, many in mining camps or settlements in remote locations. But the pattern of employment seems to be changing. While many mining engineers and geologists continue to be employed by prospecting companies and producing mines, more and more work for companies undertaking the development and management of mines for others, notably foreign governments. Don't forget that a career in mining brings plenty of responsibilities:

'There is no room in a prospecting team, a mine, a mill or a smelter for those who depend on routine, nor for the nine to fiver watcher. Mining is full of surprises, sometimes pleasant, usually not. You will be expected to cope with changing conditions, occasionally with emergencies. You will be expected both to think and act.' (The Mineral Industry Manpower and Careers Unit.)

Addresses:

Gencor Recruitment, 30 Ely Place, London EC1N 6UA. Recruits for General Mining Union, South Africa.

ACIS Recruitment. Recruits for Anglo-American and De Beers Consolidated Mines, South Africa.

Hunter Personnel, (PO Box 564), Verwood, Wimborne, Dorset BH21 6YB.

British Mining Consultants, Mill Lane, Huthwaite, Sutton in Ashfield, Notts NG17 2NS.

Reference:
International Mining: A Career for Professional Engineers (Mineral Industry Manpower & Careers Unit, Prince Consort Road, London SW7 2BP. Tel: 071-584 7397).
Mining Journal.
Financial Times Mining International Year Book, edited by J. Banfield (Longman).

Missionary work

Mention the word 'missionary', and most people picture a priestly figure striding forth into the jungle, Bible in hand, ready to face up to innumerable hazards in his quest to convert the heathen. The modern reality, however, is very different; a missionary today is just as likely to be a community worker, nurse, engineer or teacher as someone with a qualification in Divinity.

While some missionary societies offer contract posts, missionary work is normally an open-ended commitment. A number of societies invest a good deal of time and effort in preparing their recruits—offering them language tuition as well as professional induction at an institution such as Kingsmead College, Selly Oak. You will have to be adaptable and willing to learn. As Beryl Hulbert of the Methodist Church Overseas Division explains:

> 'We go to serve and to look for opportunities to serve.
> We don't go to dictate. Nowadays we only go to places
> by invitation. Once we are there, we're told what to do.
> We're not given an option. We work alongside our
> colleagues from the country concerned and we're not
> usually expected to take the lead.'

Although people tend to join the society which is most closely linked with their own denomination, mission work these days increasingly involves close collaboration between the different churches. Some missionary societies specialise in a particular region of the world, such as the South American Missionary Society. Others recruit people for virtually everywhere.

One way into a missionary career is to approach your chaplain or parish priest who will put you in touch with the appropriate authorities. For an idea of the enormous range of skills that missionaries are called upon to deploy, look at the twice yearly *Opportunities Abroad*, published by Christians Abroad (1 Stockwell Green, London SW9 9HP. Tel: 071-737 7811; 121 George Street, Edinburgh EH2 4YN. Tel: 031-225 5722). Alternatively, you could approach a society direct. There are some 200 missionary organisations in the UK, so the following list cannot claim to be comprehensive.

African Evangelical Fellowship, 30 Lingfield Road, London SW19 4PU.

African Inland Mission, 2 Vorley Road, Archway, London N19 5HE.

Baptist Missionary Society, 93 Gloucester Place, London W1H 4AA.

Bible and Medical Missionary Fellowship International, Whitefield House, 186 Kennington Park Road, London SE11 4BT. Tel: 071-735 8227.

Bible Churchmen's Missionary Society, 251 Lewisham Way, London SE4 1XF. Tel: 081-691 6111.

Central Asian Mission, 166 Tonbridge Road, Maidstone, Kent ME16 8SR.

Christian Outreach, 34 St Mary's Crescent, Leamington Spa, Warwickshire CV31 1JL. Tel: 0926-315301.

Church Missionary Society, 157 Waterloo Road, London SE1 8UU.

Church of Scotland, 121 George Street, Edinburgh EH2 4YN.

Edinburgh Medical Missionary Society, 12-14 Mayfield Road, Edinburgh EH9 1SA.

International Nepal Fellowship, 69 Wentworth Road, Birmingham B17 9SS.

Interserve, 186 Kennington Park Road, London SE11 4BT.

The Leprosy Mission, Goldhay Way, Orton Goldhay, Peterborough PE2 0GZ.

Medical Missionary Association, 6 Canonbury Place, London N1 2NJ. Tel: 071-359 1313.

Methodist Church Overseas Division, 25 Marylebone Road, London NW1 5JR.

Middle East Christian Outreach, 22 Culverden Park Road, Tunbridge Wells, Kent TN4 9RA.

The Missions to Seamen, St Michael Paternoster Royal, College Hills, London EC4 2RL. Tel: 071-248 5202.

National Council for YMCAs, 640 Forest Road, London E17 3DZ. Tel: 071-520 5599.

Overseas Missionary Fellowship, Belmont, The Vine, Sevenoaks, Kent.

Qua Iboe Fellowship, Room 317, 7 Donegall Square, West, Belfast BT1 6JE.

Quaker Peace and Service, Friends House, Euston Road, London NW1 2BJ.

The Red Sea Team, 33-35 The Grove, Finchley, London N3 1QU.

Regions Beyond Missionary Union, 186 Kennington Park Road, London SE11 4BT.

Salvation Army, 101 Queen Victoria Street, London EC4P 4EP.

South American Missionary Society, Allen Gardiner House, Pembury Road, Tunbridge Wells, Kent TN2 3QU.

SIM International, Joint Mission Centre, Ullswater Cresent, Coulsdon, Surrey CXR3 2HR.

The SUM Fellowship, 75 Granville Road, Sidcup, Kent DA14 4BU.

The Tear Fund, 100 Church Road, Teddington, Middlesex TW11 8QE. Tel: 081-977 9144.

Unevangelised Fields Mission, 47A Fleet Street, Swindon, Wiltshire SN1 1RE.

United Reformed Church, 86 Tavistock Place, Londn WC1H 9RT.

United Society for the Propagation of the Gospel, 157 Waterloo Road, London SE1 8XA.

Viatores Christi, 9 Harcourt Terrace, Dublin 2. Tel: 763050.

Voluntary Missionary Movement, Shenley Lane, London Colney, Herts AL2 8AR. Tel: 0727-248853.

WEC International, Bulstrode, Gerrards Cross, Bucks SL9 8SZ.

Oil and gas

The oil and gas industry is a massive sector comprising such activities as exploration, drilling, production, refining and distribution. In addition to the famous oil companies that are household names, there are hundreds of contractors involved in support activities: transport, maintenance, catering, shipping, pipeline construction, fire and safety, and so on.

A wide range of skills are employed in the industry. In virtually every location there is a need for engineers, geologists, computer personnel, accountants, administrators, medical staff and training personnel. Oil companies operating in the Third World are usually expected to employ as many local staff in their operations as possible, and there is a tendency for only senior and specialist positions to be held by expatriates from the West.

There are still opportunities for tradesmen in certain countries, but increasingly local staff or—in the case of the Arabian Peninsula—Asians get the job. However, there are usually contract jobs available at most levels on offshore oil rigs where staff turn-over is high and the work is demanding; they usually pay well and offer generous and frequent leave. The best prospects of employment seem to be in Algeria, Libya, the Arabian Peninsula, West Africa, Venezuela, Indonesia, the Gulf of Thailand and the North Sea (if you regard this as abroad).

Addresses:
British Petroleum PLC, Britannic House, Moor Lane, London EC2Y 9BU.
Esso, Expro House, 21 Dartmouth Street, London SW1H 9BE.
Occidental Petroleum, 16 Palace Street, London SW1E 5BQ.
Phillips Petroleum, 35 Guildford Road, Woking GU22 7QT.
Shell International PLC, Shell Centre, London SE1 7NA.
Schlumberger Wireline & Testing, 1 Kingsway, London WC2B 6XH.
Texaco, 1 Knightsbridge Green, London SW1X 7QJ.

Recruitment:
Anders Glaser Mills, ARA International, Barnett, BEE Professional, CC&P International, Grange Selection, International Training & Recruitment Link, Christopher Little, Malla, Ian Marshall, Martin Engineering, MDA Computer Group, Network Technical, ORS Exec Recruitment, PER International, Professional Employment Group.

Reference:
Oil and Gas International Yearbook (Longman).

Police
Most countries rely on their own nationals to staff their police forces these days, but opportunities exist for experienced police officers to train local staff either on secondment or through recruitment by an agency such as Crown Agents.

The Hong Kong Police Force continues to recruit officers for senior positions on contract, though this practice may well cease when Hong Kong reverts to China towards the end of the century. The three main ways of getting a job abroad are:

- secondment from your own force to a force in another—usually Commonwealth—country
- through an advertisement in the *Police Review*
- approaching governments that recruit police from the UK on a

fairly regular basis, such as Hong Kong (Hong Kong Government Office, 6 Grafton Street, London W1X 3LB).

Publishing and the media
Book Publishing
Limited opportunities exist for breaking into the publishing world abroad, but they are rare on the editorial or production side. Given that marketing employs more people than these two departments combined and that over one third of the books published in Britain are exported, the main openings are for publishers' representatives, many of whom live abroad. Also remember that educational books are big business these days in most countries, so you are more likely to be promoting these than the latest novel. For these jobs, someone who has worked in education abroad—particularly teaching English as a second language—is often ideal for the job. You could try moving into other branches of publishing at a later date since a number of publishers have overseas branches which publish their own books.

The main advertising medium for these jobs is the *Media Guardian* on Mondays, with the Wednesday issue of *The Times* in second place. Vacancies also appear in *The Independent, The Daily Telegraph* and specialised publications such as *Publishing News*. Among the firms that employ staff abroad are:

Heinemann Educational Books Ltd, 22 Bedford Square, London WC1B 3HH.
Longman Group, Burnt Mill, Harlow, Essex CM20 2JE.
Macmillan Education Ltd, Brunel Road, Houndmills, Basingstoke, Hants RG21 2XS.
Oxford University Press, Walton Street, Oxford OX2 6DP.
Cassell's *Directory of Publishing* or *Writers' and Artists' Yearbook* (A & C Black) can provide further addresses.

Newspapers and journalism
If you work for a newspaper or journal that is part of an international group, such as News International, you could enquire about the possibility of secondment to a sister publication abroad. Otherwise, the best idea might be to get hold of *Benn's International Media Directory* or *Willing's Press Guide* and apply direct to a selection of periodical publishing firms. The *UK Press Gazette* is the main recruitment medium.

To be honest, the likelihood of your landing a foreign reporter's position with a national newspaper are very slim indeed. Such posts are few and far between. A better idea might be to join an agency such as Reuters (85 Fleet Street, London EC4P 4AJ) or United Press International (UK) Ltd (8 Bouverie Street, London EC4Y 8BB), who maintain a network of correspondents worldwide.

Alternatively, there is the possibility of freelancing. This is a particularly attractive idea if you are an accompanying spouse who is not allowed to take up gainful employment in the country to which the family is posted, particularly as a part-time occupation. However, given dedication and plenty of contacts there is no reason why a freelance in the right place should not eventually gain enough commissions to survive.

Broadcasting

You would need to be a seasoned reporter to be offered the chance of a resident post abroad with the BBC or ITN since these opportunities are very few indeed, and they normally have a chosen few who are sent off on short-term assignments. In fact, you may have a better chance for foreign travel if you are an executive in the marketing section of one of the IBA companies or BBC Enterprises, or work for the BBC External Services at Bush House, or the Services Sound and Vision Corporation, Chalfont Grove, Gerrards Cross, Bucks SL9 8TN.

If you want to live abroad a better bet might be to look for radio stations in countries outside the English speaking world, such as the countries of the Arabian Peninsula. Some of these are state-run, while others are commercial or supported by religious foundations. Many of these have an English language service for both internal and external consumption and use British people to produce and broadcast their programmes. *The World Radio and TV Handbook* can provide details.

Finally, do not overlook the TV equivalents of the international news agency. The main companies are Visnews and UPITN.

Writers and Translators

Technical authorship is a growing field and leading hi-tech companies throughout Europe recruit British staff either on a freelance or contract basis. Such companies also recruit translators, who are also needed in international organisations everywhere. Watch out for advertisements in the media and technology sections of journals. The Translators' Guild (26-27 Boswell Street, London WC1N 3JZ) or the Institute of Scientific and Technical

Communicators (17 Bluebridge Avenue, Brookmans Park, Hatfield, Herts AL9 7RY) may be able to help.

Secretarial work

There appears to be an expanding market for secretaries and PAs with good qualifications and foreign language skills, particularly in Europe. Employers tend to be either multinational companies or international organisations. International vacancies are advertised in the columns of *The Times* and *The Guardian*.

Recruitment:
Sheila Burgess, Multilingual Services.

Sport and entertainment

If you are a tennis star you probably enjoy an international career anyway, but you do not have to be one of the top names to work abroad. In the Arabian Peninsula, for instance, there are several football coaches and managers, and on the Continent you may find UK golf and tennis professionals, for example, at sports clubs and leisure complexes.

One area where there is considerable scope is in the field of ski instruction, though this work tends to be seasonal. However, as for most jobs, qualifications are vital, and you really need to take an instructor course with an organisation such as the British Association of Ski Instructors if you are serious about such a career. You could then move on to work either for a holiday firm or on a freelance basis in a ski resort. The best source of information on coaching jobs and other opportunities is the professional magazine devoted to your particular sport; the relevant sports association or its sister association in your target country may also be able to suggest openings.

Most professionals in the entertainment business rely on the services of an agent who will usually have foreign contacts. *The White Book* (Birdhurst Ltd, (PO Box 55), Staines TW18 4UG. Tel: 0784-64441) is a directory dealing with the entertainment and leisure industries, and has a useful international section. Most issues of *The Stage* carry advertisements for vacancies in foreign countries.

Opportunities also occur for English speaking disc jockeys in ski resorts and summer resorts. Advertisements for such posts occur from time to time in *Record Mirror*. (See also **Hotels & Catering** in this section).

Technical co-operation

Most countries of the developed world are in the business of giving aid to the Third World either by channelling it through international aid agencies or running their own bi-lateral programmes. Some of this aid takes the form of professional and skilled personnel who advise and assist governments and governmental organisations within these countries—and who are salaried or employed on volunteer terms. Virtually all these posts are contract posts.

Recruitment:
Overseas Development Administration, Crown Agents, the UN and its various agencies, Commonwealth Development Corporation (33 Hill Street, London W1A 3AR), The European Association for Cooperation (Europe Centre, rue Archimède 17A, B-1040 Brussels), see also Chapter 9.

Reference:
British Overseas Development. A periodical which you can get from the Information Department, Overseas Development Administration, Eland House, Stag Place, London SW1E 5DH.

Tourism and travel

Many of the jobs in the tourist industry are seasonal. The work usually involves acting as a resort representative or courier for a package holiday firm based in Britain. Some knowledge of foreign languages is often useful for sorting out problems with the local populace, though many of the people you will be dealing with (including the tourists in your charge) will speak reasonable English.

There are permanent jobs, too, but most are British based with off-season visits to resorts to negotiate terms with hotels and local travel agencies. One of the best ways to land such a job is to approach a package holiday firm direct. Here is a selection of the ones you might try:

Thomson Holidays, Greater London House, Hampstead Road, London NW1 7SD.
Intasun Ltd, Intasun House, 2 Cromwell Avenue, Bromley, Kent BR2 9AQ.
Club Méditerranée, 106-108 Brompton Road, London SW3 1JJ.
Ski Europe, 6 Kew Green, Richmond, Surrey.
Club Cantabrica Holidays Ltd, 146-148 London Road, St Albans AL1 1PQ.

However, virtually every travel organisation takes on extra staff during the holiday season, and for addresses you have only to look at travel advertisements in newspapers and magazines. The Association of British Travel Agents (55 Newman Street, London W1) or the Association of Independent Tour Operators (The Knoll House, Purser's Lane, Peaslake, Guildford, Surrey GU5 9SJ. Tel: 0733-558588) should be able to provide a list of their members.

If you are in search of adventure as well as work, you could join an overland tour operator as a driver/guide. In many cases you will need to have a HGV or PSV licence, and since you could find yourself in remote areas the ability to communicate and cope with mechnical breakdowns is generally demanded. Among the companies currently operating in this field are:

Encounter Overland Ltd, 267 Old Brompton Road, London SW5.
Exodus Expeditions, 100 Wandsworth High Street, London SW18 4LE.
Tentrek Expeditions Ltd, Tentrek House, 152 Maidstone Road, Ruxley Corner, Sidcup, Kent DA14 5HS.
Top Deck Travel, 133 Earls Court Road, London SW5 9RH.

If you are fond of the sea, there are opportunities aboard passenger cruise liners and ferries. A list of these appears in *The Traveller's Handbook*.

Recruitment:
Travel Trade Employment Bureau, Halton House, 20-23 Holborn, London EC1N 2JD.

Reference:
Travel Trade Directory (Morgan Grampian Books, 30 Calderwood Street, London SE18 4QH).
Working in Ski Resorts—Europe, V. Pybus and C. James (Vacation Work Publications 1989).
Careers in the Travel Industry, C. Chester (Kogan Page 1989).

Airlines offer a number of opportunities for people wishing to spend part of their lives overseas. However, most British aircrew members working for British airlines are based in Britain and only have stopovers in foreign locations if they are involved with long-haul flights. If you would like to be based abroad, try applying to a foreign airline. A number of Middle Eastern and African airlines, for example, still employ British personnel.

The British Merchant Navy is, alas, a shadow of its former self, and there are only limited opportunities here. But you could try foreign shipping companies; cruise lines, in particular, sometimes have vacancies for English speaking staff to look after passengers.

United Nations work

The United Nations and its agencies have offices throughout the world, and employ over 25,000. There are two kinds of permanent positions available:

- **Professional posts:** Specialists in economics, science, data processing, statistics, social affairs, finance, and so on. This also includes translators, precis writers, interpreters and technical assistance experts (mainly high level personnel).
- **General Service posts:** Secretarial, administrative, information, clerical and accounting (much of the promotion is done internally).

There are in addition contract positions, for which the International Recruitment Department of the Overseas Development Administration sometimes acts as a recruitment agency (See Chapter 4).

The UN and its agencies recruit from all UN member states and try to maintain a balance of nationalities amongst their staff. To this end priority in recruitment is given to nationals of countries that are underrepresented on the staff. Unfortunately for British applicants, the UK is heavily overrepresented, so the selection process may be weighted against you. However, applicants for the secretarial and linguistic branches are not affected by this proviso.

United Nations Secretariat
Headquarters (New York)
UN Geneva Office
UN Vienna Office
UNCTAD—United Nations Conference on Trade and Development (Geneva)
UNDRO—United Nations Disaster Relief Co-ordinator (Geneva)
HABITAT—United Nations Centre for Human Settlements (Nairobi)
ECE—Economic Commission for Europe (Geneva)
ESCAP—Economic Commission for Asia and the Pacific (Bangkok)
ECA—Economic Commission for Africa

ECLAC—Economic Commission for Latin America and the Caribbean (Santiago)
ESCWA—Economic and Social Commission for Western Asia (Baghdad)

Applications for posts in any of these departments of the UN Secretariat should be sent to The Professional Recruitment Service, Room 2465, UN Secretariat, New York, NY 10017, USA. The Recruitment Programmes Section at the same address can evaluate a candidate's credentials and hold a person's details on file. Other departments of the United Nations Secretariat are responsible for their own recruitment:

ICJ—International Court of Justice, Peace Palace, 2517 KJ The Hague, Netherlands.
UNICEF—United Nations Children's Fund, 866 UN Plaza, 6th Floor, New York, NY 10017.
UNDP—United Nations Development Programme, 1 UN Plaza, New York, NY 10017.
UNPFA—United Nations Fund for Population Activities (as UNDP).
UNEP—United Nations Environment Programme, (PO Box 30552), Nairobi, Kenya.
UNRWA—United Nations Relief and Works Agency for Palestinian refugees, Vienna International Centre, (PO Box 700), A-1400, Vienna, Austria.
UNHCR—United Nations High Commissioner for Refugees, Palais de Nations, CH-1211 Geneva 10, Switzerland.
UNITAR—United Nations Institute for Training and Research, 801 UN Plaza, New York, NY 10017.
UNU—United Nations University, Toho Seimei Building, 29th Floor, 15-1 Shibuya 2-chome, Shibuya-ku, Tokyo 150, Japan.

Specialised UN agencies and other international organisations
FAO—Food and Agricultural Organisation, Via delle Terme di Caracalla, 00100 Rome, Italy.
ILO—International Labour Organisation, 4 route des Morillons, CH-1211 Geneva 22, Switzerland.
UNESCO—United Nations Educational, Scientific and Cultural Organisation, 7 Place de Fontenoy, 75700 Paris, France.
ICAO—International Civil Aviation Organisation, 1000 Sherbrooke Street West, Suite 400, Montreal, Quebec, Canada H3A 2R2.

WHO—World Health Organisation, 20 avenue Appia, CH-1211 Geneva 27, Switzerland.

IMF—International Monetary Fund, 700 19th Street NW, Washington, DC 20006, USA.

UPU—Universal Postal Union, Casa Postale, CH-300 Berne 15, Switzerland.

ITU—International Telecommunication Union, Palais de Nations, CH-1211 Geneva 10, Switzerland.

WMO—World Meteorological Organisation, Casa postale No. 5, CH-1211 Geneva 20, Switzerland.

WIPO—World Intellectual Property Organisation, 34 Chemin des Colombettes, CH-1211 Geneva 20, Switzerland.

IFAD—International Fund for Agricultural Development, Via del Serafico 107, 00142 Rome, Italy.

UNIDO—United Nations Industrial Development Organisation, Vienna International Centre, (PO Box 300), A-1400, Vienna, Austria.

IAEA—International Atomic Energy Agency, Vienna International Centre, (PO Box 100), A-1400 Vienna, Austria.

GATT—General Agreement on Tarriffs and Trade, Centre William Rappard, 154 Rue de Lausanne, CH-1211 Geneva 21, Switzerland.

World Bank (including International Bank for Reconstruction and Development, International Development Association, International Finance Corporation), 1818 'H' Street, NW, Washington, DC 20433, USA.

There are other international organisations and foundations which are not linked to the UN. Many of the most important are listed at the beginning of *The Europa Year Book*.

18
Recruitment Consultants And Agencies

On page 246 you will find a quick reference table of recruitment firms (agencies, executive search consultants, etc) that conduct recruitment for positions abroad. Their addresses and requirements are listed in greater detail after the table. It does not include government or voluntary agencies.

Please note that this information is based on the information supplied by the firms in question. However, recruitment requirements can change and information of this nature quickly goes out of date. The list does not claim to be comprehensive and inclusion in this section does not imply recommendation by the author or publisher.

KEY TO TABLE

Region:
A = Africa; C = Caribbean; E = Europe; F = Far East; L = Latin America; M = Middle East; N = North America; O = Australasia; P = Pacific; S = South and South East Asia.

Client:
B = British company; F = Foreign company; M = Multinational company; G = British Government; O = Other governments; I = International organisation.

Sector:
A = Agriculture; B = Banking & Finance; C = Computing/IT; D = Construction; E = Education & Training; F = Manufacturing; G = Pharmaceuticals; H = Hotels & Catering; I = Engineering; L = Military; M = Medical/Hospitals; N = Mining; O = Oil; P = Nannies and Au Pairs; Q = Aeronautics; R = Transport; S = Science; T = Telecommunications; U = Utilities (water, power generation, etc.); V = Tourism; X = Electronics.

244

Method of recruitment:
A = Advertising; D = Candidate Register/Database; E = Executive Search; R = Recommendation.

Journals used for advertising:
1 = *Telegraph/Sunday Telegraph*; 2 = *Times/Sunday Times*; 3 = *Guardian*; 4 = *Independent*; 5 = *Financial Times*; 6 = *Express*; 7 = Specialist journals; 8 = Other tabloids; 9 = All sections of the national press.

Contract length:
$\frac{1}{2}$ = less than 1 year; 1 = 1 year; 2 = 2 years; 3 = 3 or more years; U = Unlimited contract/Permanent position.

ADDRESSES AND REQUIREMENTS OF RECRUITMENT FIRMS LISTED OVERLEAF

Note:
FRES denotes that the consultancy is a member of the Federation of Recruitment and Employment Services, 36-38 Mortimer Street, London W1N 7RB. Tel: 071-323 4300.

Advanced Technology Recruiters, Regency House, Dedmere Road, Marlow, Bucks SL7 1PB. Tel: 0628-890575.

Recruits a small number of graduates annually for the IT, manufacturing, medical and telecommunications sectors in Australia.

Adler Recruitment, 8 Falstaff Drive, Droitwich, Worcs WR9 7SN.

Recruits graduate civil engineers with several years' experience for Europe and Africa.

AMC Recruitment Ltd, 381 Wanstead Park Road, Ilford Essex IG1 3TT. Tel: 081-554 6566.

Recruits up to 300 experienced people annually for Europe, Middle East and Far East. Construction, manufacturing, petrochemicals, power generation, telecommunications, training, etc.

Anchor Language Services, 30 Brick Row Cottages, Babraham, Cambridge, CB2 4AJ. Tel: 0223-836017.

Recruits English teachers for Europe, especially Turkey.

Anders Glaser Wills, International Personnel Consultants, 134 High Street, Southampton S01 0BR. Tel: 0703-223511 (with offices in London, Bristol and Birmingham).

AGENCY	Regions	Client	Sector	Method	Contract
Advanced Technology Recr.	0	BFM	CEFT	ADE	U
AMC Recruitment	EFM	BFM	CDEFI OTV	A(1267) DR	2
Anchor Language Services	E	F	E	AD	1
Anders Glaser Wills	AMN	BMF	DFOT	A(16)D	1
Angel International Recr.	Most	All	All	DRA	1
Aplin Phillimore	AEM	BFM	R	A(79)DE	1
ARA International	AM	FMI	DEMO	A(167)D	2U
Arabian Careers	M	O	BCEM	A(17)R	1
James Baker Associates	EMN	BFMI	CT	DA(27)	123U
Barnett Consulting Group	EMN	BFMOI	BCDEF MOTV	AED	U
BEE Professional	ACFM	BMFI	CDFMO T	ADR	½ 2
Beechwood Recruitment	EN	All	CDEFI	A(7)D	2U
Benney Electronics	E	I	S	D	U
British Mining Consultants	ALNOS	FI	N	DR	2
British Nursing Assoc	EMN	FO	M	A(7)	½ 1
Sheila Burgess	E	BFMI	BEFT	RDA(2)	½ U
CC&P International	AELMN	BFMOI	ABCDE FMNO RTV	A(79)ED	U
William Channing	EN	BFMI	BFRV	E	U
Clark Rich Associates	EO	M	CT	EA(2)	U
Cliveden Technical	EF	All	E	AD	-
Computer Consultants Australia	O	All	BCF	A(7)R	12
Computer Search & Selection	E	BMFI	C	AR	½
Consultancy Int'l	EN	BFM	BFI	DE	3U
Dalroth & Partners	EMNFL	MF	C	AE	2U
Daulton	ECMO	BFM	DO	A(7) DER	2U
Delton Personnel	I	MS	O	A(17)D	½ 12
Electronics Recruitment Co	E	BFM	CFT	DA(7) RE	U
English Worldwide	EFLM	FMOI	E	A(37)DR	12U
Expatriate Resources Co	Most	BFMI	BCET	A(7)E	3U
FIS Associates	FM	ASI	CFMOT	A(7)DR	12U
Flexcareer	N	F	M	A(7)R	1
F M Recruitment	E	BFMI	CH	DARE	2
Forsyth Executive	E	M	C	EA(27) DR	U
Gabbitas Truman & Thring	Most	F	E	AD	123
Grange Selection	EMN	BMI	CDFOT	AE	123
Dorothy J Hopkins	MN	FO	M	A(79)DR	12
Heston (Middle East)	MS	BFMG OI	CDEM NOT	A(267) DR	1

AGENCY	Regions	Client	Sector	Method	Contract
Hospital Locum Service	AM	BFM	M	A(7)D	½
ILC Recruitment	EMSF	BF	E	AD	½ 123
Ingineur Ltd	E	BFM	K	A(7)D	U
Inlingua	ES	F	E	AD	1
INS International Recr't	MN	-	M	DA(7)R	1
Intereurope Recruitment	AM	B	D	DA	1
International House	Most	BF	E	AD	½ 123U
Int'l Training & Recr Link	AEFM NS	BFMOI	BCDEF LMOT	A(27) DER	2
Intertech Computer Consult.	E	FM	BC	DA(247) RE	1U
Jenrick CPI	E	BFMI	C	A(7)R	12
Jones Agricultural Services	AM	FI	A	-	U
Christopher Little	EFmas	BMF	BDFM OR	AE	U
Malla Exec Selection	AEFMS	BFMI	ABDF MO	A(1) DRE	1
Ian Marshall Staff Recr't	M	FMOI	DELMO RT	A(79)DR	2
Martin Engineering	EM	FM	DO	AD	½ 1
MDA Computer Group	EFNO	BFMI	ABCFL NORT	DA(7) RE	12
Medic International	EAMNO	FO	M	AD	½ 12
Mediservice	FMN	FOI	M	A(7)D	1
Merton Associates	All	All	BCDFM E	U	
Modus International	E	BFM	C	A(7)DR	½
Morgan & Day	EFM	BF	CDEOT	A(167) DRE	1
Anthony Moss	AEFM	BFMI	ABDEI NOW	A(12)D ER	1
Multilingual Services	E	BFM	All	A(2)DR	123
Network Technical	CM	BFI	ADEF MOT	ADRE	1
Network Overseas	M	BFM	ADEFL OQT	A(167) DRE	1
Anthony Nevile Int'l	SFMO	MI	BDFMN TV	E	2
Norfolk Care Search	EN	F	P	A	½ 1
Offshore Specialist Appts	ECF	FI	B	A(7) DRE	2
ORS Exec Recruitment	MS	BFMI	DMOQ	A(1678) DR	2
ORT Int'l Cooperation	AL	OI	ABCDE MR	ADR	2
Overseas Technical Service	AMS	BFM	O	A(1)D	½ 12
PER International	EACM	BFMI	ADFM OT	A(12)D	12

AGENCY	Regions	Client	Sector	Method	Contract
Prescot Computers	AENO	All	C	A(7)DR	-
Professional Employment Gp	EMS	BM	DFNOT	RA(167)	½ 1
Professional Management Resources	AFM	BFM	BCDEF MORT	A(7) DRE	1
Recruitment International	EFMNO	BFMOI	BCDEF MNOT R	2	
RIBA Appointments Bureau	M	BFMO	C	D	12
Sabre International Search	AEFMN OP	BFM	BCDFN OT	E	-
F J Selleck	MF	BFM	CDO	A	1
Specialist Language Services	EMA	F	E	ADR	½
Team-Sel International Ltd	M	FI	CO	A(9)D	1
VIP International	All	All	HV	A(7) DER	2U
Vision Appointments	EO	BFMI	CT	A(27)E	3
Weltec	EFM	FM	OT	A(167)	1
Wickland Westcott & Ptnrs	E	BFM	BF	A(79)ED	U
Wrightson Wood	EN	BM	BFT	E	U

Recruits more than 300 annually for Kenya, Nigeria, Saudi Arabia, UAE, USA. Construction manufacturing, oil industry, telecommunications (FRES).

Angel International Recruitment, Angel House, 50 Fleet Street, London EC4Y 1BE. Tel: 071-583 1661.

Recruits some 500 people annually for Europe, the Middle East and USA. Most sectors but particularly medical staff. Minimum of 3 years' post qualification experience required.

Aplin Phillimore, Circle House North, 29-71 Wembley Hill Road, Wembley, Middx HA9 8BL.

Recruits a small number of people annually for Europe, the Middle East, Africa. Motor industry, distributive trades and personnel staff.

ARA International, 6th Floor, Carolyn House, Dingswall Road, Croydon, Surrey CR0 9XF.

Recruits some 800 annually for Africa and the Middle East (especially Saudi Arabia). Construction, oil industry, education and training, medical sector. Type of staff needed: doctors and nurses with 2 years' post qualification experience; technicians with City & Guilds and 5 years' experience; engineers with 10 years' experience and BSc.

Arabian Careers Ltd, 115 Shaftesbury Avenue, Cambridge Circus, London WC2H 8AD. Tel: 071-379 7877.

Recruits some 300 qualified people annually for Saudi Arabia, notably for the financial, medical, computer and education sectors.

James Baker Associates, 32 Savile Row, London W1X 1AG. Tel: 071-439 9311.

Recruits graduate computer specialists for USA, Holland, France, Germany, Scandinavia. Contract and permanent vacancies.

Barnett Consulting Group Ltd, Providence House, River Street, Windsor, Berks SL4 1QT. Tel: 0753-856723.

Recruits for middle and top management posts in most sectors, especially information technology, based in Europe, the Middle East and North America.

BEE Professional, 51 Queen's Road, Brighton BN1 3XB.

Recruits up to 200 qualified, part-qualified and experienced staff for Africa, the Middle East, Far East and Caribbean. Main areas of specialisation: IT, construction, manufacturing, medical services, oil and telecommunication. Short assignments and 2 year contracts.

Beechwood Recruitment Ltd, 221 High Street, London W3 9BY.

Recruits specialists with a degree/HND and at least 3 years' experience for the USA, Germany, France and Holland. Main fields: IT, construction, electronics, manufacturing, mechanical engineering, telecommunications (FRES).

British Mining Consultants, (PO Box 18), Mill Lane, Huthwaite, Sutton in Ashfield, Notts NG17 2NS. Tel: 0623-441444.

Recruits experienced mining engineers and geologists—age range 30-50—as well as managers and specialists for Africa, Asia, Australasia, and the Americas.

British Nursing Association, 443 Oxford Street, London W1R 2NA. Tel: 071-629 9030.

Recruits qualified nurses for hospitals and clinics particularly in Saudi Arabia, United Arab Emirates, Holland, Switzerland, USA, Canada and Australia. It has 100 branches throughout the UK and has 35,000 nurses on its register (FRES).

Sheila Burgess, The Power House, Alpha Place, Flood Street, London SW3 5SZ. Tel: 071-351 6931.

Recruits around 100 bi-lingual secretaries annually (mainly graduates with secretarial training) for France and Belgium. Age range 20-45. Adaptability and foreign experience important.

CC&P International Ltd, 26-28 Bedford Row, London WC1R 4HF. Tel: 071-242 8998.

Recruits around 30 people annually from a variety of disciplines for permanent positions mainly in the EC, Saudi Arabia and Africa. Age range: 25-50.

William Channing, Clarendon House, 11-12 Clifford Street, London W1X 1RB. Tel: 071-491 1338.

Recruits senior management for permanent positions in banking, finance, manufacturing, tourism and transport in France, Switzerland, Belgium, Holland, USA and Canada.

Clark Rich Associates Ltd, 31 Peascod Street, Windsor, Berks SL4 1EA.

Recruits senior professionals with experience for permanent posts in IT and telecommunications, particularly in Holland and Australia.

Cliveden Technical Recruitment, 92 The Broadway, Bracknell, Berks RG12 1AR.

Recruits personnel for IT, construction, manufacturing, electronics and telecommunications in Hong Kong and Europe (FRES).

Computer Consultants Australia Pty Ltd, 2 Bedford Square, London WC1B 3RA.

Recruits IT staff (mainly at the analyst/programmer level and with a minimum of 3 years' experience) for 1-2 year contracts in Australia and USA.

Computer Search & Selection PLC, Hamilton House, Marlowes, Hemel Hempstead HP1 1BR.

Recruits IT staff (from operations staff to senior consultants), preferably graduates, and with at least 3 years' data processing experience. Mainly short term assignments in Holland, Belgium and Germany (FRES).

Consultancy International Ltd, 40-41 Pall Mall, London SW1Y 5JG.

Recruits 50-75 staff annually on banking, finance, manufacturing and engineering for long-term and permanent vacancies mainly in France and the USA.

Dalroth & Partners Ltd, Dalroth House, 12 Gloucester Place, London W1H 3AW. Tel: 071-935 2983.

Specialises in the Computing/MIS/Communications and Data Processing areas from shift leader up to project director level. Vacancies mainly in US, Middle East and Europe.

Daulton Construction Personnel, Premier House, 10 Greycoat Place, London SW1P 1SB. Tel: 071-222 0817/8.

Recruits skilled construction staff in most disciplines for the construction and oil industry worldwide with an increasing emphasis on Europe. Knowledge of a European language a definite bonus.

Delton Personnel Ltd, Carrington Business Park, Urmston, Manchester M31 4DD.

Recruits over 100 senior engineers annually aged 40 plus for the oil industry in the Middle East and S E Asia.

Electronics Recruitment Company, ERC House, 32-33 North Street, Lewes, East Sussex BN7 2PQ. Tel: 0273-480088.

Specialises in the recruitment of electronics and computer graduates with a minimum of 2-3 years' experience for permanent appointments with companies in Germany, Holland, France, Belgium, Switzerland, Italy and USA. Adaptability and linguistic skills (for Europe) are important.

English Worldwide, 17 New Concordia Wharf, Mill Street, London SE1 2BB. Tel: 071-252 1402.

Recruits annually some 120 teachers of all subjects for schools and colleges in Europe, Middle East, Far East and South America.

Expatriate Resources Co. Ltd, 16 Dumaresq Street, St Helier, Jersey. Tel: 0534-68881.

Recruits banking executives, finance directors, fund managers, IT specialists, trust managers especially for the Caribbean, Southern Europe and the Far East, Long-term engagements. Over 600 placements annually.

FIS Associates, Avenue House, 6 Victoria Avenue, Harrogate, N Yorks HG1 1ED. Tel: 0423-576662.

Recruits well qualified professionals and people with 'hands-on' experience for the Middle East and Hong Kong. Sectors: IT, manufacturing, medical, oil/gas and telecommunications.

Flexcareer Ltd, 59 The Vale, London W3 7RR. Tel: 071-749 3013.

Recruits registered general nurses with a minimum of 2 years' post registration experience for hospitals in the north-east of the USA. In some cases Flexcareer is the employer.

FM Recruitment, 6 Conduit Street, London W1R 9TQ. Tel: 071-491 2277.

Recruits financial and systems management graduates or equivalent for the hotel and leisure industry, particularly in Europe (FRES).

Forsyth Executive, 87 Jermyn Street, London SW1Y 6JD.

Recruits a small number of bi-lingual graduates up to MBA level with experience in sales, marketing, support and management for international IT companies in France, Germany, Italy and Spain.

Gabbitas, Truman & Thring, Broughton House, 6-8 Sackville Street, London W1X 2BR. Tel: 071-439 2071.

Recruits teaching and administrative staff for schools and colleges worldwide.

Grange Selection, 1 Jubilee Road, Chelsfield, Orpington, Kent BR6 7QZ.

Recruits staff at all levels for the IT, construction, manufacturing, oil and telecommunications sectors in Europe and the Middle East, especially Saudi Arabia (FRES).

Heston (Middle East) Ltd, 4 The Promenade, Castletown, Isle of Man. Tel: 0624-824595.

Recruits over 200 staff annually at all levels for a wide range of sectors in southern and S E Asia as well as the Middle East.

Dorothy J Hopkins, Claridge House, 29 Barnes High Street, London SW13 9LW. Tel: 081-876 8666.

Recruits all grades of medical, nursing, administrative and ancillary staff for hospitals in Saudi Arabia, United Arab Emirates and the USA. 1-2 year contracts plus locum contracts of up to 3 months.

Hospital Doctor Locum Service Ltd, 17 Hope Street, Liverpool L1 9BQ.

Recruits experienced British qualified hospital doctors willing to undertake locum work for short periods in the Middle East and Africa (FRES).

ILC Recruitment, International Language Centres Ltd, White Rock, Hastings, East Sussex TN34 1JY. Tel: 0424-720109.

Recruits teachers for language schools in Europe, the Middle East and Asia.

Ingineur Ltd, Pendicke Street, Southam, Warwickshire CV33 0PN. Tel: 0926-817612.

Recruits electronics graduates with at least 2 years' industrial experience in R & D for European Community countries (FRES).

Inlingua Teacher Service, 10 Rotton Park Road, Egbaston, Birmingham B16 9JJ. Tel: 021-455 6465.

Recruits teachers for language schools in Europe and Singapore.

INS International Recruitment, 10 Artillery Passage, Bishopsgate, London E1.

Recruits nurses and paramedics for hospitals in the USA and the Middle East.

Intereurope Recruitment Ltd, 19-21 Denmark Street, Wokingham, Berks RG11 2QX.

Recruits a very limited number of civil and structural engineers (preferably with chartered status) for construction companies in the Middle East and Africa. One year contracts.

International House, 106 Piccadilly, London W1V 9FL. Tel: 071-499 2598.

Recruits around 200 teachers annually for language schools around the world.

International Training & Recruitment Link, 51A Bryanston Street, London W1H 7DN. Tel: 071-706 3646.

Recruits fire and safety specialists with oilfield and airfield experience; operations and maintenance technicians and engineers for the oil industry; doctors and nurses. Main countries are Saudi Arabia, the Gulf States and Libya.

Intertech Computer Consultants Ltd, British National House, Harland Road, Haywards Heath, W Sussex RH16 1TD.

Recruits computer professionals with at least 3 years' experience for 1 year contracts, and business analysts for permanent placements. Main countries are Germany, Switzerland and Austria (FRES).

Jenrick-CPI Ltd, CPI House, 140 High Street, Egham, Surrey TW20 9HL. Tel: 0784-31411.

Recruits around 100 computer consultants at all levels for 1½-2year contracts in Holland, Germany, France and Belgium. Dutch or German speakers are in great demand (FRES).

Jones Agricultural Services, 108 Trinity Street, Gainsborough, Lincs DN21 1HS.

Not a recruitment agency as such but assists other agencies in the recruitment of agricultural professionals, especially for Saudi Arabia and East Africa.

Christopher Little Consultants Ltd, 49 Queen Victoria Street, London EC4N 4SA. Tel: 071-236 5881.

Recruits a small number of managers annually for the banking, insurance, construction, manufacturing, medical, oil and transport sectors particularly in Europe and the Far East. Speculative applications are accepted but cannot be acknowledged (FRES).

Malla Exec Selection, 173-175 Drummond Street, London NW1 3JD. Tel: 071-388 2284.

Recruits middle and senior managers for contracts in the oil and gas industries, and with agricultural and construction firms in Europe, Africa, Middle East and Asia. Also maintains an International Experts Register and seconds specialist personnel for short-term assignments (FRES).

Ian Marshall Staff Recruitment Ltd, 11 Great Russell Street, London WC1B 3NH. Tel: 071-255 1696.

Recruits personnel for the construction, training, medical, military, oil, telecommunications, transport and O & M support service sectors notably in Saudi Arabia, Oman and the Yemen.

Martin Engineering Co, Southward House, Beaulieu Road, Dibden Purlieu, Southampton SO4 5PT. Tel: 0703-845543.

Recruits mainly experienced chartered and graduate engineers (process, instrument, civil, etc.) for contracts of one year or less. Main destinations: Holland, Norway, UAE and Saudi Arabia (FRES).

MDA Computer Group, Sceptre House, 169-173 Regent Street, London W1R 7FB. Tel: 071-439 7871.

Recruits up to 100 graduates with experience annually for most sectors, particularly in Benelux and the USA.

Medic International, 4 Thameside Centre, Kew Bridge Road, Brentford, Middlesex TW8 0HB. Tel: 081-568 4300.

Recruits nurses and paramedics for hospitals and clinics in Europe, North America, the Middle East, Australia, South Africa and Bermuda. Normally a minimum of one year's post qualification experience is required. Medic Int'l publishes a regularly updated vacancy list (FRES).

Mediservice, Bournemouth International Airport, Christchurch, Dorset BH23 6EB. Tel: 0202-572271.

A division of Airwork Ltd that recruits over 125 nursing staff (mainly RGN) annually for USA, Middle East and Far East.

Merton Associates (Consultants) Ltd, Merton House, 70 Grafton Way, London W1P 5LN.

Recruits senior managers and technical specialists for firms throughout the world. Merton is also the co-ordinating office for Transearch, an association of consultancies based in Australia, Belgium, Canada, France, West Germany, Holland, Italy, Japan, Spain, Sweden, the USA, Hong Kong and Singapore.

Modus International, Kingswood House, Heath & Reach, Leighton Buzzard, Beds LU7 0AP. Tel: 0525-222222.

Recruits up to 200 experienced computer personnel yearly for the IT, training and telecommunications sectors in the Benelux countries (FRES).

Morgan & Day (Overseas) Ltd, The Old Coach House, 5A Holywell Hill, St Albans, Herts A11 1ET. Tel: 0727-836266.

Recruits mainly engineering, training and maintenance personnel at all levels for Europe, Middle East and Far East.

Anthony Moss & Associates Ltd

Recruits up to 150 people a year for supervisory, middle and senior management posts in Europe, Middle East, Far East and Africa. Sectors include agriculture, construction, mining, telecommunications and the water industry.

Multilingual Services, 22 Charing Cross Road, London WC2H 0HR. Tel: 071-836 3794.

Recruits bi-lingual secretaries, translators and other support staff for the countries of the European Community. No speculative applications (FRES).

Network Overseas, 35/37 Grosvenor Gardens, London SW1W 0BS.

Recruits 200 professionals annually for Saudi Arabia and the UAE. Sectors include agriculture, aviation, education, manufacturing, military, oil, sport and telecommunications.

Network Technical Recruitment Ltd, Queen Anne House, High Street, Coleshill, Warwicks B46 3BT.

Recruits qualified engineers and other professionals for the agriculture, construction, training, manufacturing, medical, oil and telecommunications sectors particularly in Saudi Arabia and the Caribbean (FRES).

Anthony Nevile International Ltd, 31 Castle Street, Farnham, Surrey GU9 7JB.

Recruits professionally qualified people aged 35 plus with a UK salary of at least £25,000 for the banking, finance, construction, manufacturing, medical, mining, telecommunications and tourism sectors particularly, in South East Asia.

Norfolk Care Search Agency, 19 London Road, Downham Market, Norfolk PE38 9BJ.

Recruits trained or experienced children's nannies aged 18 plus for 1 year contracts in Canada, and au pairs aged 18-27 for France and Spain (FRES).

Offshore Specialist Appointments, Tower Hill Steps, 16 Le Brodage, St Peter Port, Guernsey.

Recruits newly qualified accountants, lawyers, chartered secretaries up to age 30 to work in auditing, accountancy, and company/trust administration in tax havens/off-shore centres— Luxembourg, Monaco, Hong Kong, Bermuda, Bahamas, etc.

ORS Executive Recruitment International Ltd, 9 Leicester Street, Northwich, Cheshire CW9 5LA.

Recruits some 500 people per year from technician/supervisors for aircraft equipment maintenace to senior consulting engineers in all disciplines on 2 year contracts. Main sectors: construction, medical, oil and airport operations. Main countries: Saudi Arabia, Indonesia, Malaysia (FRES).

ORT International Cooperation, Sumpter Close, Finchley Road, London NW3 5HR. Tel: 071-435 4784.

An organisation which recruits experts for foreign governments and international organisations operating in the Third World, notably Africa and South America. Main sectors: agriculture, finance, construction, IT, education, mining and transport.

Overseas Technical Service (Harrow) Ltd, 100 College Road, Harrow, Middlesex HA1 1BQ.

Recruits mainly technical personnel with a minimum of 5 years' experience for the oil and gas industry in West Africa, Middle East and South East Asia.

PER International, 4th Floor, Rex House, 4-11 Regent Street, London SW1Y 4PP. Tel: 071-930 6573/4/5/6/7.

Recruits up to 75 professionals annually for a wide range of sectors in Europe, the Middle East, Africa and the Caribbean.

Prescot Computers Ltd, 11-13 Broad Street, London WC2 5QN.

Recruits computer professionals with a minimum of 3 years' experience for Australia, New Zealand, South Africa, Benelux and Italy in particular.

Professional Employment Group, The Hermitage, 45 Church Street, Epsom, Surrey KT17 4PW.

Recruits professionals in design, installation or management for the construction, manufacturing, mining, oil and telecommunications sectors especially in Saudi Arabia and Belgium. Minimum qualifications: HNC, 5 years' experience and 25 years old (FRES).

Professional Management Resources Ltd, Oxford House, 15-17 Mount Ephraim Road, Tunbridge Wells TN1 1EN. Tel: 0892-513664.

Together with its sister company Medical Resources PMR recruits for the Middle East, Far East and Africa. Main sectors: finance, computers, construction, training, manufacturing, medical, oil, telecommunications and transport.

Recruitment International, 2nd Floor, Copthall Tower House, Station Parade, Harrogate HG1 1IS. Tel: 0423-530533.

Recruits 300 personnel annually (including TEFL teachers) for most parts of the world including Eastern Europe.

RIBA Appointments Bureau, 66 Portland Place, London W1N 4AD.

The official recruitment consultancy of the Royal Institute of British Architects handles vacancies for architects mainly in Saudi Arabia and the Gulf states. 1 and 2 year contracts (FRES).

Sabre International Search, Seymour House, 17 Shouldham Street, London W1.

Recruits middle and senior management for several sectors of industry and commerce particularly in the European Community.

F J Selleck Associates, Prospect House, 17 North Hill, Colchester CO1 1DZ. Tel: 0206 65252.

Recruits engineers, project managers and other experienced graduates for the oil and gas industry and civil engineering projects in the Middle East and Asia, normally on 1 year renewable contracts.

Specialist Language Services, Cromwell House, 13 Ogleforth, York YO1 2JG.

Recruits English language teachers for short assignments with companies in Europe, the Middle East and Africa.

Team-Sel International, 147 King Street, Great Yarmouth NR30 2NT. Tel: 0273 480088.

Recruits some 50 people annually with good technical qualifications and experience for the construction and oil sectors in Libya, Saudi Arabia, Kuwait and Qatar (FRES).

VIP International, 17 Charing Cross Road, London WC2H 0EP. Tel: 071-930 0541.

Recruits qualified catering personnel with at least 4 years' experience in 4/5 star establishments for the tourism and hospitality industry world-wide (FRES).

Vision Appointments, Eastgate House, 16-19 Eastcastle Street, London W1N 7PA. Tel: 071-631 4146.

Recruits a small number of sales and marketing professionals for the computer and telecommunications sectors in France, Germany, New Zealand and Australia.

WELTEC Ltd, Romney House, Romney Place, Maidstone, Kent ME15 6LG. Tel: 0622-678031.

Recruits 200 designers, engineers and supervisors a year for the oil and petrochemical sectors in the Middle East, Far East and Europe.

Wickland Westcott & Partners, Springfield House, Water Lane, Wilmslow, Cheshire SK9 5QS. Tel: 0625 532446.

Recruits senior managers and directors in the manufacturing and service industries in Europe.

Wrightson Wood Ltd, 11 Grosvenor Place, London SW1X 7HH.

Headhunts senior management earning £50,000 plus for the financial, manufacturing, telecommunications and property sectors in European Community countries and the USA.

19
Further Reading

PERIODICALS

Benefits and Compensation International (monthly). 11 Tufton Street, London SW1P 3QB.

Careers International (bi-weekly). PS Publishing, Speer House, 40-44 The Parade, Claygate, Surrey KT10 9QE. Tel: 0372-68833. An international publication specialising in executive vacancies.

The Expatriate (monthly). First Market Intelligence Ltd, 56A Rochester Row, London SW1P 1JU. Tel: 081-670 8304. A monthly newsletter with subscribers in 70 countries which does not accept advertising. It deals with all matters of concern to people working abroad, including country briefings and advice on health, finance and legal matters. It also includes regular listings of jobs abroad and a guide to comparative costs of living and housing around the world.

Expat World (monthly). PO Box 1341, Raffles City, Singapore 9117.

EXPATXTRA! (monthly). (PO Box 300), Jersey, Channel Islands. Tel: 0534-36241. A monthly newspaper with readers in 160 countries with particular emphasis on financial and legal matters.

Home and Away (monthly). Expats International Ltd, 62 Tritton Road, London SE21 8DE. Tel: 081-670 8304. The monthly magazine of Expats International—an organisation with 8,000 members—which deals with all matters of concern to expatriates, including finance, family matters, overseas jobs markets. Subscribers, many of whom are on overseas contracts, also receive an extensive list of vacancies in the UK and abroad, and can have their details circulated to employers registered with the organisation.

Inside Tracks, 10 Hartswood Road, London W12 9NQ.

The International, Modbury Marketing, Sealarm House, Back Street, Modbury, Devon PL21 0RF.

Investment International, Boundary House, 91-93 Charterhouse Street, London EC1M 6HR. Tel: 071-250 0646.

Jobs in Europe, Workforce Publications, 52 Queens Gardens, London W2 3AA. Tel: 071-402 3236.

Middle East Expatriate and *Far East Expatriate*, Hilal International, Regal House, London Road, Twickenham TW1 3QS. Tel: 081-891 3362.

Nexus (monthly). Expat Network, 56 Knights Hill, London SE27 0DJ. Tel: 081-761 2575. A new publication (started September 1989) containing jobs information for expatriates of all disciplines. Includes advertisements and editorial.

Resident Abroad (monthly). Editorial: Financial Times Business Information, 102-108 Clerkenwell Road, London EC1M 5SA. Tel: 071-251 9321; Subscriptions: Central House, 17 Park Street, Croydon CR0 1YD. Tel: 081-680 3786. A glossy magazine which tends to concentrate on expatriate financial matters. It carries extensive financial advertising and analysis.

GENERAL READING

Series and publishers

The British Expatriates Handbook Series, Directory Profiles Ltd, 51A George Street, Richmond, Surrey TW9 1HJ. Tel: 071-938 5692.

The Economist Business Travel Guides. These include insights into the cultural, political and economic background of a given country or region and cover the Arabian Peninsula; China; France; Germany; Japan; SE Asia; United States.

Expat World, PO Box 1341, Raffles City, Singapore 9117. A general life-style newsletter for expatriates.

The International, Modbury Marketing, Sealarm House, Back Street, Modbury, Devon PL21 0RF.

Inside Tracks, 10 Hartswood Road, London W12 9NQ.

Jobs in Europe, Workforce Publications, 52 Queens Gardens, London W2 3AA. Tel: 071-402 3236.

The World Today Series, Sky Corp/Stryker Post Publications, 888 Seventeenth St, Washington DC 20006. Africa, Canada, East Asia & West Pacific, Latin America, Middle East & South Asia, Soviet Union & Eastern Europe, Western Europe.

The World of Information Reviews, World of Information, 21 Gold

Street, Saffron Walden, Essex CB10 1EJ. Latin America and the Caribbean; Middle East; Europe; Africa; Asia & the Pacific.

Books

Accepting a Job Abroad: A Practical Guide, M. Tideswell (British Institute of Management, 1980).

Allied Dunbar Expatriate Tax Guide (Longman). Annual.

Asian Living Costs (Confederation of British Industry, Centre Point, 103 New Oxford Street, London WC1A 1DV).

Brits Abroad: A Guide to Living and Working in Developing Countries, H. Brown and R. Thomas (Express Books, 1981).

Culture & Interpersonal Communication, William D. Gudykunst & Stella Ting-Toomey (Sage Publications 1988).

Culture Shock series (Times Editions, Singapore). Includes Sri Lanka, Thailand, Malaysia & Singapore, Philippines, Indonesia, Borneo, Burma, Korea, France, USA, China, Japan, Britain, India (UK distributors Pandemic, 71 Gt Russell St, London WC1B 3BN. Tel: 071-242 3298; and Millbank Books, 20 Richmond Rd, E Finchley, London N2 8JT. Tel: 081-346 2338).

Employee Benefits in Europe, Howard Foster (Longman).

Employment Benefits in Europe, H. Foster (Longman).

Evaluating an Overseas Job Opportunity, John Williams (Pilot Books, 103 Cooper Street, Babylon, New York 11702).

Executive Compensation Reports (Business International—Human Resources Division, 12-14 Chemin Rieu, 1211 Geneva 17, Switzerland and 40 Duke Street, London W1A 1DW).

Executive Cost of Living Survey (Business International, see above).

Executive Resources International: ERI Salary and Living Cost Survey. These annual surveys on the Middle East and Nigeria are in abeyance at the time of writing, but there is a possibility that this series will be restarted.

Expatriate Salary Survey (Inbucon Management Consultants Ltd). Salary and benefit details in 47 countries.

Handbook for Development Workers Overseas, G. Roberts (Returned Volunteer Action, 1 Amwell Street, London EC1R 1UL. Tel: 071-278 0804).

Handbook for Women Travellers (Piaktus, 5 Windmill Street, London W1P 1HF).

How to Get the Job you Really Want, Roger Jones (Allborough Press, Cambridge 1990).

How to Get the Job You Want Overseas, A. Liebers (Pilot Books).

How to Teach Abroad, Roger Jones (Northcote House Publishers Ltd, Harper & Row House, Estover Road, Plymouth PL6 7PZ).

International Benefits Guidelines (William J Mercer International, 4 Southampton Place, London WC1A 2DA). Deals with such matters as retirement benefits, death benefits, sickness and disability benefits, medical benefits, social security contributions, and taxation. The 1989 edition covers 60 countries in Europe, North America, Latin America, South and South East Asia, the Far East and the Middle East plus parts of Africa.

International Dimensions of Organisational Behaviour, Nancy J. Adler (Kent Publishing Co, Boston 1986).

International Pay and Benefits Survey (PA Personnel Services, Hyde Park House, 60a Knightsbridge, London SW1X 7LE).

Living Abroad, Ingmar Tobiörn (John Wiley 1982).

The Management of Expatriates, C. Brewster (Cranfield Business School; obtainable from Cranfield Bookshop, Wharley End, College Bookshop Road, Cranfield MK4 0ST. Tel: 0234-751122).

Management Remuneration in Europe (Monks Publications, Debden Green, Saffron Walden, Essex CB11 3LX. Tel: 0371-830939).

Managing Cultural Differences, Philip R. Harris & Robert T. Moran (Gulf Publishing Co, Houston, Texas, 1987).

Middle East Living Costs (Confederation of British Industry, Centre Point, 103 New Oxford Street, London WC1A 1DV).

Overseas Assignments: The Treatment of Expatriate Staff (Institute of Personnel Management, 1971).

Rural Development and the Developing Countries, I. Poustchi (PO Box 1256, Guelph, Ontario, Canada; distributed by 3rd World Publications, 151 Stratford Road, Birmingham B11 1RD. Tel: 021-773 6572).

Strategies for Getting an Overseas Job, K.O. Parsons (Pilot Books).

The Traveller's Handbook, edited by M. Shales (WEXAS). A mine of information for anyone who is likely to be visiting several countries either for business or pleasure. Included in its extensive reference section is information on visa requirements, duty free allowances, airport departure taxes, currency restriction, hospitals with English speaking staff, weather information, business hours, foreign diplomatic representations in Australia, Canada, New Zealand, USA and UK.

Travelling Alone—A Guide for Working Women, R. Balley (Macdonald Optima 1988).

West European Living Costs (Confederation of British Industry, Centre Point, 103 New Oxford Street, London WC1A 1DV).

Wives Abroad, C. L. Salobir (published by author, Mayenfischstr 19, D7750 Konstanz, W Germany, 1988).

Women Overseas: A Practical Guide, N. Piet-Pelon and B. Hornby (Institute of Personnel Management, 1986).

Working Abroad?, H. Brown (Northcote House Publishers Ltd, Harper & Row House, Estover Road, Plymouth PL6 7PZ).

Working Abroad, D. Young (Financial Times Business Information).

Working Abroad: The Daily Telegraph Guide to Working Overseas (Kogan Page, 1987).

Worldwide Total Renumeration (Towers, Perrin, Foster and Crosby, 77-91 New Oxford Street, London WC1A 1PX).

Directories

The Au pair and Nanny's Guide to Working Abroad, S. Griffith and S. Legg (Vacation Work Publications, 1989).

Australia and New Zealand Employment Guide (Overseas Consultants (PO Box 152), Douglas, Isle of Man).

Australia and New Zealand Employment Guide (Overseas Employment Services (PO Box 460), Town of Mount Royal, Quebec, Canada H3P 2C7).

Directory of American Companies Overseas (Overseas Consultants (PO Box 152), Douglas, Isle of Man).

Directory of American Companies Overseas, (Overseas Employment Services (PO Box 460), Town of Mount Royal, Quebec, Canada H3P 2C7).

Directory of Canadian Companies Overseas (Overseas Employment Services, see above for address).

Directory of Canadian Employment Agencies (Overseas Consultants (PO Box 152), Douglas, Isle of Man).

Directory of Canadian Firms Overseas (Overseas Consultants (PO Box 152), Douglas, Isle of Man).

Directory of English Employment Agencies and Recruitment Firms (Overseas Consultants, see above).

The Directory of Jobs and Careers Abroad, A. Lipinski (Vacation Work Publications, 1989).

Directory of Organisations for Long-Term Voluntary Service (UNESCO, 1 rue Miollis, 75015 Paris).
Directory of Summer Jobs Abroad, D. Woodworth (Vacation Work Publications, annual).
The Directory of Work and Study in Developing Countries, D. Leppard (Vacation Work Publications, 1986).
Employment Agencies All Over the World (Europa Bokvörlag AB, Stockholm, 1989).
Executive Grapevine, J.S. Baird and J.M. Hickson (79 Manor Way, London SE3 9XG). A handbook of executive recruitment consultants operating in the UK and abroad.
International Directory of Employment Agencies (Overseas Consultants (PO Box 152), Douglas, Isle of Man).
International Directory of Employment Agencies (Overseas Employment Services (PO Box 460), Town of Mount Royal, Quebec, Canada H3P 2C7).
The International Directory of Voluntary Work, D. Woodworth (Vacation Work Publications, 1989).
Jobs in Japan, J. Wharton (Global Press, USA, distributed by Vacation Work, 1989).
Middle East Employment Guide (Overseas Consultants (PO Box 152), Douglas, Isle of Man).
Middle East Employment Guide (Overseas Employment Services (PO Box 460), Town of Mount Royal, Quebec, Canada H3P 2C7).
Summer Employment Directory of the United States (Writer's Digest, USA, distributed by Vacation Work). Annual.
Work Your Way Round the World, S. Griffiths (Vacation Work Publications, 1989).
Working Holidays (Central Bureau, Seymour Mews, London W1H 9PE). Annual.
Working in Ski Resorts—Europe, V. Pybus and C. James (Vacation Work Publications, 1989).

Overseas vacancy bulletins

Connaught Executive Bulletin (Connaught Publishing Co, 32 Savile Row, London W1X 1AG. Tel: 071-439 0076).
The Intel Job Abstract (Intel, Duke House, 33 Waterloo Street, Hove BN3 1AN. Tel: 0273-27508). A weekly abstract of job vacancies occurring in European and North American newspapers plus a selection of unadvertised positions.
Job Finder (Overseas Consultants, (PO Box 152), Douglas, Isle of Man). Fortnightly.

News & Jobs (Bureau for Overseas Medical Service, Africa Centre, 38 King Street, London WC2E 8JT. Tel: 071-836 5833). Opportunities for health professionals with voluntary agencies in the Third World.

Opportunities Abroad (Christians Abroad). Current openings with missionary bodies and volunteer agencies.

Overseas Employment Newsletter (Overseas Employment Services (PO Box 460), Town of Mount Royal, Quebec, Canada H3P 3C7. Tel: 514-739-1108). Fortnightly.

See also under entries for *Careers International, The Expatriate, Home & Away* and *Nexus*.

Many of the books mentioned are available for reference in public and academic libraries. In the case of some titles it will be necessary to approach a specialised business library, such as the City of London Business Library (Fenchurch Street, London EC3) or the City of Westminster Reference Library (St Martins Street, London WC2). Many provincial cities and towns also have libraries with substantial business reference sections and are also able to obtain particular books for readers.

20
Useful Addresses

Audio Forum, 31 Kensington Church Street, London W8 4LL. Tel: 071-937 1647.

Blair Consular Services Ltd, 10 Fairfield Avenue, Staines, Middx TW18 4AB. Tel: 0784-462831. Visa service.

Braham Masters Ltd, Staplehurst Road, Sittingbourne, Kent ME10 2BQ. International mail order shopping service.

British Airways Travel Clinic, 75 Regent Street, London W1. Tel: 071-439 9584. Also at a number of other locations.

British Association of Removers, 279 Grays Inn Road, London WC1. Tel: 071-594 7790.

BBC World Service, (PO Box 76), Bush House, Strand, London WC2B 4PH. Tel: 071-240 3456.

Career Development Centre for Women, 97 Mallard Place, Twickenham, Middlesex TW1 4SW. Tel: 071-892 3806.

CBI Employee Relocation Council, Centre Point, 103 New Oxford Street, London WC1A 1DV. Tel: 071-379 7400 (offers advice to companies relocating staff; publishes *Relocation News*).

Centre for Information on Language Teaching and Research, Regent's College, Inner Circle, Regent's Park, London NW1 4NS. Tel: 071-468 8221.

Centre for International Briefing, Farnham Castle, Surrey GU9 0AG. Tel: 0252-721194.

Christians Abroad, 1 Stockwell Green, London SW9 9HP. Tel: 071-737 7811.

Commonwealth Information Centre, Commonwealth Institute, Kensington High Street, London W8 6NQ.

Council for the Accreditation of Correspondence Colleges, 27 Marylebone Road, London NW1 5JS. Tel: 071-935 5391.

Department of Health Leaflets Unit, (PO Box 21), Honeypot Lane, Stanmore, Middx HA7 1AY. Tel: 0800-555777.

Department of Social Security, Overseas Branch, Benton Park Road, Newcastle upon Tyne, NE98 1YX.

Department of Trade and Industry, 1 Victoria Street, London SW1H 0ET.

ECIS (European Council for International Schools), 21B Lavant Street, Petersfield, Hants GU32 3EW. Tel: 0230-68244.

Employment Conditions Abroad, Anchor House, 15 Britten Street, London SW3 3TY. Tel: 071-351 7151.

Expat Network, 56 Knights Hill, London SE27 0JD. Tel: 081-761 2575 (operates Joblink register and offers various benefits to subscribers).

Expatriate Advisory Services PLC, 14 Gordon Road, West Bridgeford, Nottingham, NG2 5LN. Tel: 0602-816572. Expatriate financial advisors.

Expatriates Association, (PO Box 24), Warminster, Wilts BA12 9YL. Tel: 0985-212236.

Expat Tax Consultants Ltd, Churchfield House, North Drive, Hebburn, Tyne & Wear NE31 1ES. Tel: 091-483 7805.

Expats International, 62 Tritton Road, London SE21 8DE. Tel: 081-670 8304.

FOCUS Information Services, 47-49 Gower Street, London WC1E 6HR. Tel: 071-631 4367.

Gabbitas Truman & Thring, Broughton House, 6-8 Sackville Street, London W1X 2BR.

Golden Arrow Shippers, Horsford Kennels, Lydbury North, Shropshire SY7 8AY. Tel: 05888-240 (Pet transportation experts).

Good Book Guide, 91 Great Russell Street, London WC1B 3PS. Mail order book service.

Hall-Godwins (Overseas) Consulting Co., Briarcliff House, Kingsmead, Farnborough, Hants GU14 7TE. Tel: 0252-521701. Expatriate financial advisers.

Harley Medical Services, 117A Harley Street, London W1N 1DH. Tel: 071-935 1536. Visa service, medicals.

Inland Revenue Claims Branch, Foreign Division, Merton Road, Bootle L69 9BL.

ISIS (Independent Schools Information Service), 56 Buckingham Gate, London SW1E 6AG. Tel: 071-630 8793.

ISPA (International Society for the Protection of Animals), 106 Jermyn Street, London SW1Y 6EE. Tel: 071-839 3066.

Institute of Freight Forwarders, Redfern House, Browells Lane, Feltham, Middlesex. Tel: 081-844 2266.

International Baccalaureate European Office, 18 Woburn Square, London WC1H 0NS. Tel: 071-637 1682.

Kings Barn Export Ltd, Unit 29, Station Road, Southwater Industrial Estate, West Sussex RH13 7HQ. Tel: 0403-732020. International mail order shopping service.

Linguaphone, 124-126 Brompton Road, Knightsbridge, London SW3.

Management Games Ltd, Methwold House, Northwold Road, Methwold, Thetford, Norfolk IP26 4PT. Tel: 0366-728215.

Manor Car Storage, PO Box 28, Clavering, Saffron Walden, Essex CB11 4RA. Tel: 0799-550021.

MASTA (Medical Advisory Services for Travellers Abroad Ltd), Bureau of Hygiene and Tropical Medicine, Keppel Street, London WC1E 7HT. Tel: 071-636 8636.

Mercers College, Ware, Herts SG12 9BU. Tel: 0920-5926.

Moran Stahl and Boyer, Merrill Lynch Relocation, 136 Bond Street, London W1. Tel: 071-629 8222.

National Institute of Adult Continuing Education, 19B De Montford Street, Leicester LE1 7GE. Tel: 0533-551451.

NatWest Expatriates' Service, PO Box 12, 2nd Floor, National Westminster House, 6 High Street, Chelmsford, Essex CM1 1BL. Tel: 0245-261891, ext 304 (Complete banking and financial service for expatriates).

Outbound Newspapers Ltd, 1 Commercial Road, Eastbourne BN21 3XQ. Tel: 0323-412001 (Publishers of *Australasian News, Canada News* and *South Africa News*).

Par Air Services, Warren Lane, Colchester, Essex CO3 5LN. Tel: 0206-330332 (Pet shipping agents).

Royal Commonwealth Society, 18 Northumberland Avenue, London WC2N 5BJ. Tel: 071-930 6733.

SATCO, Linda Jones, 69 Kilravock Street, London W10 4HY. Tel: 081-968 8543. Visa service.

Spratt's Animal Travel Service, 756 High Road, Goodmayes, Ilford, Essex IG3 8SY. Tel: 081-597 2415.

Women's Corona Society, Commonwealth House, 18 Northumberland Avenue, London WC2N 5BJ. Tel: 071-839 7908.

Worldwide Education Service, Strode House, 44-50 Osnaburgh Street, London NW1 3NN. Tel: 071-387 9228.

21
Help with European Application Forms

English	French	German	Spanish
Surname	Nom de famille	Name	Apellido
Forenames	Prénom	Vorname	Nombre
Address	Adresse	Anschrift	Dirección
Street	Rue	Strasse	Calle
Town	Ville	Stadt	Ciudad
Country	Pays	Staat	Pais
Date of Birth	Date de naissance	Geburtsdatum	Fecha de naciamento
Place of Birth	Lieu de naissance	Geburtsort	Lugar de naciamento
Sex	Sexe	Geschlecht	Sexo
Male	Masculin	Männlich	Masculino
Female	Féminin	Weiblich	Feminino
Marital Status	Situation de famille	Familienstand	Estado Civil
Nationality	Nationalité	Staatsange-hörigkeit	Nacionalidad
Language ability	Connaissance de langues	Sprach-kenntnisse	Habilidad para hablar idiomas

Education	Formation	Ausbildung	Estudios
Skills	Capacités	Leistungs- fähigkeit	Conocimiento prático
Career	Expérience profes- sionelle	Berufser- fahrung	Experiencia
Position	Emploi	Stelle	Puesto
Employer	Entreprise	Firma	Compañía
From...to	De...jusqu'à	Von...bis	De...a
Salary	Salaire	Gehalt	Salario
Reference(s)	Références	Zeugnis	Referencias
Applicant	Candidat	Bewerber	Solicitate
Interview	Entrevue	Interview	Entrevista
Employment Certificate	Certificate de travail	Arbeitszeugnis	Certificado de trabajo

APPLICATION LETTER IN FRENCH

Londres
le 18 septembre 1990

Direction de Personnel
Société Bloggs International
Paris

Monsieur le Directeur

Suite à l'annonce parue le 10 septembre dans The Times
je me permets de poser ma candidature au poste de
technicien principal.

Agé de 30 ans je suis originaire de Portsmouth
(Angleterre). Actuellement je suis employé comme
technicien supérieur aux établissements Plessey à John
O'Groats, et je désire trouver une situation qui soit plus
en rapport avec mes capacités.

Vous trouverez ci-joint mon curriculum vitae
mentionnant les études effectuées et les postes occupés.

Si ma proposition pouvait retenir votre attention je vous
serais très reconnaissant de bien vouloir me convoquer à
vos bureaux afin que je puisse vous soumettre mes
certificats, diplômes et références.

Dans l'attente d'une réponse favorable, je vous prie
d'agréer, Monsieur, l'expression de mes sentiments les
plus distingués.

George Stephenson

APPLICATION LETTER IN GERMAN

London
den 18 September 1990

Firma
Bloggs International A G.

Ried im Innkreis
Goethestr. 18.

Sehr geehrte Herren.

Auf Ihr Stellenangebot in der Londoner Times vom
10.09.90 bewerbe ich mich um die Stelle als Technischer
Leiter und ich sende Ihnen die erforderlichen
Unterlagen—Lebenslauf, Zeugnisabschriften usw.

Wie Sie aus den Unterlagen sehen, bin ich 30 Jahre alt,
stamme aus Portsmouth, und habe eine gute technische
Ausbildung am Lands End Technical College genossen.

Seit 1986 bin ich als Techniker bei der Firma Plessey in
John o'Groats angestellt. Jetzt aber möchte ich eine neue
Stelle aussuchen, die meinen Fähigkeiten besser
entspricht.

Ich würde mich freuen, wenn Sie meine Bewerbung in
die engere Wahl ziehen könnten, und bin
selbstverständlich gerne bereit, mich persönlich
vorzustellen.

Mit vorzüglicher Hochachtung
George Stephenson

APPLICATION LETTER IN SPANISH

Londres, 18 de Septiembre 1990

Bloggs International SA
Calle Costa del Sol, 80
Madrid

Muy Sres mios

En respuesta a su anuncio en el Times de 10.09.90 me apresuro a ofrecerme para el puesto de director tecnico en la sede de su empresa.

Tengo 30 años y soy natural de Portsmouth. Asistí al Instituto Tecnico de Lands End y en 1981 aprobé el examen de Higher National Diploma. He trabajado durante los últimos tres años en la compañía Plessey en John O'Groats.

La unica razón por la que quiero dejar mi puesto es que deseo conseguir otro de más responsabilidad.

Acompaña la presente mi curriculum vitae y fotocopias de certificados de estudios y de trabajo junto con una foto reciente.

En espera de recibir una contestación favorable, les saluda muy atentamente.

George Stephenson

A SAMPLE CV IN FRENCH

Anita LYONS
14 Edinburgh Close,
Berwick on Tweed
Grand Bretagne
Tél: (0111) 99 99 99

Née le 30 janvier 1965, à Dundee (Écosse); 25 ans
Nationalité britannique
Célibataire

Formation
Juillet 1983:   'A' Level (diplôme de fin d'études
                secondaires, équivalent du baccalauréat) en
                français, physique, économie

Juin 1987:   BSc (licence en quatre ans) d'économie,
                Université d'Aberdeen

Langues:
Anglais   — langue maternelle
Français   — parlé et écrit couramment
Chinois   — notions

Expérience professionelle
1987 à 1989 Enquêtrice pour une société de marketing à
             Belfast
Depuis 1989 Interprète pour une société de tourisme à
            Penzance

Divers
Voyages: Séjours fréquents à l'étranger, en France, en
         Espagne et en Suisse.
Sports: Natation, tennis, ski

Autres Renseignements
Permis de conduire
Prête à voyager et à travailler à l'étranger

A SAMPLE CV IN GERMAN

Anita LYONS
14 Edinburgh Close,
Berwick on Tweed
Grossbritannien
Tel: 0111/99 99 99

Am 30 Januar 1965 in Dundee, Schottland geboren;
25 Jahre alt
Britisch
Ledig

Beruf des Vaters	Ingenieur
Konfession	r. kath
Bildungsweg	Grundschule von 1970 vis 1975
	Gymnasium von 1975 bis 1983

Leistungskurse

Juli 1983	'A' Level (Äquivalent des Abiturs) in Deutsch, Wirtschaftskunde und Mathematik
Juni 1987	BSc (vierjähriger Kurs) in Wirtschaftskunde, Aberdeen Universität

Sprachkenntnisse

Englisch	— Muttersprache
Deutsch	— sehr gut
Japanisch	— Grundkenntnisse

Berufstätigkeit

1987 bis 1989	Interviewerin für eine Marktforschungsfirma
Seit 1989	Dolmetscherin für eine Reisefirma

Ausserberufliche Interessen

Reisen:	Häufige Auslandreisen, nach Deutschland, Österreich und Amerika
Sport:	Schwimmen, Tennis, Skifahren

Andere relevante Informationen
Führerschein
Bereit im Ausland zu arbeiten

A SAMPLE CV IN SPANISH

Anita LYONS
14 Edinburgh Close,
Berwick on Tweed
El Reino Unido
Tfo. (0111) 99 99 99

Fecha de nacimiento	30 de noviembre de 1965
Nacionalidad	Británica
Estado Civil	Soltera

Educación

Julio 1983	Obtuve el certificado 'A level', en 3 asignaturas, español, francés y ciencias económicas (Este es equivalente al bachillerator y COU)
Junio 1987	Estudié 4 años para obtener el grado de BSc en las asignaturas de ciencias económicas en la universidad de Aberdeen. (El BSc es equivalente a la licenciatura)
Idiomas	El inglés como lengua materna El español en forma adecuada El francés que lo hablo y escribo correctamente Tambien tengo conocimiento del alemán

Experiencia de trabajo

1987 a 1989	Tuve un trabajo con una compañía de estudios de mercado en Londres

Intereses extra-profesionales
Natación, tenis, esquiaje

Otros
Poseo permiso de conducir válido obtenido en 1985

SAMPLE EUROPEAN COMMISSION APPLICATION FORM

The terminology is taken from the different language versions of the application form used by the European Commission, whose assistance with this section is gratefully acknowledged.

APPLICATION FORM / ACTE DE CANDIDATURE *(French)* / BEWERBUNGSFRAGEBOGEN *(German)* / IMPRESO DE CANDIDATURA *(Spanish)* / SOL-LICITATIE FORMULIER *(Dutch)* / FORMULARIO DI CANDIDATURA *(Italian)*.

Surname / Nom / Familienname / Apellidos / Naam / Cognome:

Forenames / Prénoms / Vornamen / Nombre / Voornamen / Nome:

Address / Adresse / Anschrift / Dirección / Adres / Indirizzo:

Telephone number / N° tél / Telefonnummer / N° de teléfono / Telefoonnummer / N. di telefono:

Date and place of birth / Date et lieu de naissance / Geburtsdatum und Geburtsort / Fecha y lugar de naciemento / Plaats en datum van geboorte / Luogo e data di nascita:

Sex: male—female / Sexe: masculin—féminin / Geschlecht: männlich—weiblich / Sexo: masculino—femenino / Geslacht: mannelijk—vrouwelijk / Sesso: maschile—femminile.

Present nationality / Nationalité actuelle / Derzeitige Staatsangehörigkeit / Nacionalidad actual / Huidige nationaliteit / Cittadinanza attuale:

Knowledge of languages / Connaissances linguistiques / Sprachkenntnisse / Conocimientos lingüísticos / Talenkennis / Conoscenze linguistiche:

Education / Études / Ausbildungsgang / Estudios / Genoten onderwijs / Studi: \

Certificates and/or diplomas obtained / Certificats ou diplômes obtenus / Erlangte Zeugnisse und Diplome / Certificados o títulos obtenidos / Verworven getuigschriften of diploma's / Certificati o diplomi conseguiti:

Primary, secondary, advanced secondary or technical education / Études primaires, secondaires, moyennes ou techniques / Primarschule, Sekundarschule, Mittlere Schulbildung oder Lehrlingsausbildung / Enseñanza primaria, secundaria, media o técnica / Lager, middelbaar of technisch onderwijs / Studi elementari, medi o tecnici:

Higher education / Études supérieures / Hochschulstudium / Enseñanza superior / Tertiair onderwijs / Studi superiori:

Postgraduate education / Études post-universitaires / Aufbaustudium / Estudios postuniversitarios / Postuniversitair onderwijs / Studi postuniversitari:

Published works / Ouvrages publiés / Veröffentlichungen / Publicaciones / Gepubliceerde werken / Pubblicazioni:

Office skills: typing—wordprocessing / Connaissances des techniques de bureau: dactylographie—traitement de texte / Bürotechnische Kenntnisse: Maschinenschreiben—Textverarbeitung / Conocimiento de técnicas de oficina: mecanografia—tratamiento de textos / Kennis van typen en tekstverwerking: typen—tekstverwerking / Conoscenze delle tecniche d'ufficio: dattilografia—trattamento testi:

Career to date / Expérience professionnelle / Berufser-
fahrung / Experiencia profesional / Beroepservaring /
Esperienza professionale:

Present or most recent post / Emploi actuellement occupé
ou emploi le plus récent / Derzeitige oder letzte Stelle /
Puesto de trabajo actual o más reciente / Huidige of
laatste betrekking / Posto attuale o ultimo posto occupato:

Previous post / Emploi précédent / Vorherige Stelle /
Puesto de trabajo precedente / Vorige betrekkingen /
Posto precedente:

Dates—length in months—gross monthly salary /
Dates—durée en mois—traitement ou revenu mensuel
brut / Dauer—Dauer in Monaten—Bruttomonatsgehalt /
Fechas—duración en meses—sueldo o ingresos men-
suales brutos / Data—duur in maanden—bruto-
maandsalaris / Date—durata in mese—stipendio mensile
lordo:

Exact designation of post / Titre exact de vos fonctions /
Genaue Berufsbezeichnung / Denominación exacta de sus
funciones / Nauwkeurige aanduiding van uw functie / Def-
inizione esatta delle mansioni esplicate:

Employer / Employeur / Arbeitgeber / Empresa /
Werkgever / Datore di lavoro:

Nature of Work / Nature de votre travail / Beschreibung
der Tätigkeit / Descripción del trabajo / Aard van de
functie / Descrizione del lavoro svolto:

Reasons for leaving / Raisons pour quitter / Kün-
digungsgründe / Motivos del cese / Redenen voor het
vertrek / Motivi dell'abbandono dell'impiego:

Period of notice required to leave your present post /
Délai de préavis de votre emploi actuel / Kündigungsfrist
bei Ihrer derzeitigen Stelle / Plazo de preaviso en su
puesto de trabajo actual / Opzegtermijn van uw huidige
betrekking / Termine di preavviso per l'impiego attual-
mente occupato:

Long periods spent abroad / Séjours importants à
l'étranger / Längere Auslandsaufenthalte / Estancias
importantes en el extranjero / Perioden van verblijf van
langere duur en het buitenland / Soggiorni importanti
all'estero:

Interests and skills not connected with work / Activités ou
aptitudes extra-professionelles, sociales, sportives, etc. /
Ausserberufliche soziale und sportliche Tätigkeiten und
Fähigkeiten / Actividades o intereses extra-profesionales,
sociales, deportivos, etc. / Aktiviteiten of bekwaamheden
buiten de beroepssfeer, bezigheden op sociaal gebied, op
sportgebied, enz. / Attività o attitudini extraprofessionali:
sociali, sportive, ecc.:

Have you a physical handicap? / Avez-vous un handicap
physique? / Haben Sie eine körperliche Behinderung? /
Tiene usted algún impedimento físico? / Heebt u een
lichamelijke handicap? / Ha una minorazione fisica?

Have you ever been convicted or found guilty of any
offence by any court? If so give details. / Condamnations
pénales, sanctions administratives / Vorstrafen und Dis-
ziplinarstrafen / Condenas penales, sanciones adminis-
trativas / Gerechtelijke veroordelingen en disciplinaire
straffen / Eventuali condanne penali e sanzioni
amministrative:

I, the undersigned, declare on my word of honour that the information provided above is true and complete.

Je soussigné(e) déclare sur l'honneur que les indications portées au présent acte de candidature sont véridiques et complètes.

Ich, der (die) Unterzeichnete, erkläre ehrenwörtlich, dass die Angaben in diesem Bewerbungsfragebogen wahrheitsgetreu und vollständig sind.

El (la) abajo firmante declara por su honor que la información suministrada en el presente impreso de candidatura es verdica y completa.

Ik verklaar op erewoord dat de in dit sollicitatieformulier verstrekte gegevens waarheidsgetrouw en volledig zijn.

Io sottocritto/a dichiaro sul mio onore che le informazioni fornite nel presente formulario sono veridiche e complete.

I am willing to undergo the compulsory medical examination to ensure that I am physically fit to perform the duties involved.

J'accepte de me soumettre à la visite médicale réglementaire destinée a vérifier que je dispose bien des aptitudes physiques requises pour l'exercice des fonctions envisagées.

Ich bin bereit, mich der vorgeschriebenen ärztlichen Untersuchung zum Nachweis meiner körperlichen Eignung für die Ausübung der angestrebten Tätigkeit zu unterziehen.

Acepta someterse al reconocimiento médico reglamentario que tiene por finalidad verificar que reúne las condiciones físicas exigidas para el ejercicio de las funciones contempladas.

Ik ben bereid mij te onderwerpen aan het voorgeschreven medische onderzoek naar de lichamelijke geschiktheid voor het vervullen van de desbetreffende functie.

Accetto di sottopormi alla visita medica regolamentare per l'accertamento della mia idoneità fisica all'esercizio delle funzioni oggetto del presente bando.

General Index